THE
GOLDEN BOOK
OF
HAND & NEEDLE ARTS

THE GOLDEN BOOK OF HAND & NEEDLE ARTS

selected from **THE FAMILY CREATIVE WORKSHOP**
created by Plenary Publications International, Inc.

 GOLDEN PRESS · NEW YORK

Western Publishing Company, Inc.
Racine, Wisconsin

A FAMILY CREATIVE WORK SHOP BOOK

ELLEN FOLEY
PEGGY ANNE STREEP
Project Editors

ALLEN DAVENPORT BRAGDON
Originating Editor of THE FAMILY CREATIVE WORKSHOP.

AFGHAN STITCH: technical assistance and
materials courtesy of Reynolds Yarns.
APPLIQUE: quilt designs, page 16, courtesy
of The Stearns and Foster Company.
EMBROIDERY: embroidered coif and matching
forehead cloth, page 68, courtesy of The Metropolitan
Museum of Art, gift of Irwin Untermyer, 1964.
HOOKED RUGS: Shaker hooked rug, page 119, courtesy of Index
of American Design, National Gallery of Art, Washington, D.C.
LACE: *Woman Making Lace*, page 146, by Nicolas Maes,
courtesy of The Metropolitan Museum of Art,
The Michael Friedsam Collection, 1931.
REVERSE APPLIQUE: *Molas*, pages 27, 29, and 32, courtesy of
Laurice Keyloun Boutique, White Plains, New York;
contributing consultant: Pauline Antaki.
SAMPLERS: perforated paper for sampler, page 102,
courtesy Sewmakers, Inc.; embroidery cotton for sampler,
page 102, by DMC; antique samplers, pages 92 through 95,
from the private collection of Glee Krueger.

The text and illustrations in this book originally appeared in
THE FAMILY CREATIVE WORKSHOP published by Plenary Publications
International, Inc., 300 East 40 Street, New York, New York 10016,
for the Blue Mountain Crafts Council

Printed in the U.S.A.

Library of Congress Catalog Card Number: 76-28677

Contents

A Word from the Editors

Discovering your own abilities is an exciting experience, and the satisfaction gained by creating something with your own hands is not easily equaled. When you make something unique, something handmade which will endure, something which no one else has made, you not only feel pride in your accomplishment, but you also help to preserve the great tradition of individual craftsmanship. The many needlecraft projects contained in these pages have been especially prepared by expert craftspeople—artisans who believe in this tradition, and who also believe that the channeling of our energies into creative endeavors enriches the quality of life for us all.

The Golden Book of Hand and Needle Arts is a virtual treasure trove of information, ideas, and projects in a broad spectrum of textile crafts: lace making, quilting, hand and machine sewing, rug hooking, embroidery, needlepoint, inkle weaving, crochet, appliqué, macramé, and decorative stitching. There are more than 50 projects here, selected from THE FAMILY CREATIVE WORKSHOP, a multi-volume encyclopedia of crafts. Chosen for their appeal to beginning as well as advanced needleworkers, they range from fashion accessories to home furnishings, from quick-and-easy projects to more ambitious ones. There are practical items for you to make—and some you'll want to try just for the pleasure of expressing yourself creatively. There are things to make for children, and things to make for yourself and for your family and friends. Among them are projects as varied as a woven watchband, embroidered placemats and napkins, an appliquéd jacket, wall or window hangings of lace and other materials, a quilted vest, a needlepoint rug, even a sculpture made with macramé.

These projects have all been developed by experienced, practicing craftspeople (introduced at the beginning of every chapter) who are adept at describing the important first steps to learning a new craft. Because they know these first steps are always the trickiest, they introduce each hand and needle art with a simple, basic project. The projects which follow use more advanced techniques and offer more challenging designs. This enables you to master the fundamental skills first, and then learn how to go about using them to create your own variations and adaptations.

Special symbols at the beginning of every project (see the box below) give an advance indication of the approximate cost, time, tools, and skill required. Then, like a recipe, each project lists and describes the necessary tools and materials. Many chapters have special "Craftnotes" sections which offer useful background information and practical hints for working in the craft area being discussed.

As you will discover, the art of textile crafts can become a tremendously expressive form with the aid of just three simple tools: the material, the needle, and, perhaps the most reliable and versatile tool of all, the human hand.

We hope you will enjoy countless hours creating needlecraft treasures for yourself and your loved ones, to give as gifts or perhaps even develop into an extra source of income. Whether your interest is in just relaxing with a satisfying hobby, making practical, budget stretching items, or learning new techniques of already familiar needlecrafts, **The Golden Book of Hand and Needle Arts** will provide you with a multitude of ideas.

Editor-in-Chief

The Project-Evaluation Symbols appearing in the title heading at the beginning of each project have these meanings:

Range of approximate cost:
¢ Low: under $5 or free and found natural materials

$ Medium: about $10

$$ High: above $15

Estimated time to completion for an unskilled adult:
Hours

Days

Weeks

Suggested level of experience:
Supervised child or family project

Unskilled adult

Specialized prior training

Tools and equipment:
Small hand tools

Specialized equipment

AFGHAN STITCH
A Crochet Favorite

Sandra Vogt, who made the granny afghan, vest, and child's skirt shown in this feature, came to crafts via the related paths of art and photography. Like many mothers, she has found that a variety of crafts can provide a creative outlet. In addition to crochet, Sandy does macrame, knitting, and sewing. The afghan on the opposite page was designed for The Family Creative Workshop by the staff of Reynolds Yarns.

The afghan stitch is a variation of crocheting based on the chain stitch. Just why it is called afghan stitch, nobody seems to know. It is sometimes called Tunisian crochet. Crochet in general is thought to have originated among the nomad tribes of Africa and Asia, which these names would seem to bear out. How the afghan (the throw or coverlet) and the stitch are related is also not clear. The Oxford English Dictionary assures us the term is not derived from Afghanistan. Perhaps it can be assumed the stitch came first and the coverlets made with the stitch got their names that way. Certainly it is a nice, thick, warm stitch ideal for a cozy throw. The even firmness of the finished stitch has, in recent years, made it popular as a background for colorful cross-stitch embroidery.

Vest and child's skirt

The Vest

A handsome, first venture to test your skill with afghan stitch is the vest shown on page 10. For key to abbreviations, see page 14.

Sizes: Directions are for misses' size 8. Changes for sizes 10 and 12 are in parentheses.

Materials: 2 (3-3) 4-oz. skeins Yellow Knitting Worsted. A few strands of Blue Worsted. Afghan hook size G. Aluminum crochet hook size E. Yarn needle with large eye.

Gauge: 9 stitches = 2 inches; 3 rows = 1 inch.

Back: With afghan hook and yellow, ch 73 (77-81). Work in afghan st for 10 inches, or desired length to underarm. *Shape Armhole:* Dec by sl st across next 4 sts. Work across row in pattern to last 4 sts, and sl st these. Fasten and cut yarn. Rejoin yarn to continue return row. Dec 2 sts at each end of next 3 (3-4) rows. Work in pattern until armhole is 7½ inches (7½ inches-8 inches). *Shape Shoulder:* Ch 1, sc across. Turn, ch 1, sl st across 8 sts, sc across to last 8 sts, sl st. Fasten.

Left Front: Ch 37 (39-41). Work in pattern until same length as back to underarm. *Shape Armhole:* Work as Back. At same time, dec 2 sts at neck edge every 4th row until 16 sts remain. Work until armhole measures same as Back, ending at neck edge. *Shape Shoulder:* Work same as shoulder on Back.

Right Front: Work same as Left Front, reversing all shaping.

Finishing: Weave shoulder and side seams. Block or steam-press. With size E hook and yellow, work 1 row sc around entire vest and armholes. Work 1 row of cross-stitch around front and neck edges with blue.

These old-fashioned patchwork squares, worked in simple crochet stitches, are often referred to as afghan stitch. This type of patchwork is correctly called Granny Squares. The throw on the opposite page has been worked in true afghan stitch, which produces a firm, warm, evenly textured surface.

This afghan looks like a traditional Aran knit, but actually it is crocheted in panels of afghan stitch. Directions for making it are on page 13.

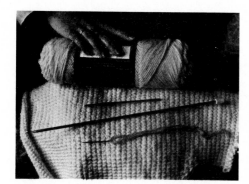

1: The basic materials you will need to do the afghan-stitch project: yarn, a crochet hook, an afghan hook, and sometimes a yarn needle.

2: The differences between a conventional crochet hook and an afghan hook shown here. The crochet hook is much shorter and has a flattened area so it can be grasped comfortably. The afghan hook is longer and smooth. This is because, in afghan stitch, an entire row is held on the hook. In crochet, only a few loops are kept on.

3: Close-up of the detail of the edging on the vest, showing the cross-stitch embroidery on both right and wrong sides.

Afghan stitch is ideal for making warm outerwear with a tailored look. Sandra designed and made this vest to wear during the chill of early spring planting season.

Child's skirt

This charming little-girl's skirt has a tweedy pink-and-white texture because the rows were worked in alternating colors.

Sizes: Directions are for size 4. Changes for sizes 6 and 8 are in parentheses.

Materials: One 4-oz. skein White Knitting Worsted; 1 4-oz. skein Pink. Afghan hook size F. Steel crochet hook size 5. One yard 1-inch elastic.

Gauge: 5 stitches=1 inch; 3 rows=1 inch.

Pattern Stitch: Row 1: Work 1st half in Pink; work return half in White. Row 2: Work 1st half in White; work return half in Pink.

Skirt Back: Begin at lower edge with Pink, and chain 65 (69-73). Work in afghan stitch and color pattern for 2 inches (3-4 inches) from start, or 9 inches less than desired skirt length. Dec 1 st at each end of new row. Repeat dec every 2 inches 3 times

Tweedy effect is given to skirt executed in plain afghan stitch by using a combination of wool colors. Sandra designed skirt for her young neighbor, Darlene.

4: Detail of waistband casing that holds the elastic in place inside the skirt. Instructions for casing and inserting elastic are in directions at left.

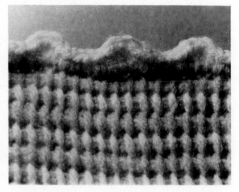

5: Close-up of the skirt edging, showing scalloped trim that is crocheted around skirt bottom. Instructions for edging are given under Finishing, at left.

6: Afghan stitch in the making. Note how the afghan hook passes under the vertical bar of the previous row to pull up a loop.

more. Work even until piece measures 11 inches (12-13 inches), or ½ inch shorter than desired skirt length. Sc across top. Fasten and cut yarn. Pick up White, and sc across previous sc row. Fasten and cut yarn.

Front: Work same as for Back.

Finishing: Steam-press pieces, or block. Backstitch or weave side seams. With White, work bottom edging: 2 sc, * (1 hdc, 2 dc, 1 hdc) in next st, 4 sc. * Repeat from * to * all around bottom. Fasten and cut yarn.

Casing: With White, join yarn to inside top edge, * make a chain 1 inch long, sl st in stitch ½ inch to left in row 1 inch below, make a ch 1 inch long, sl st at top of skirt ½ inch to left of last st. Repeat from * around top of skirt. Cut elastic to waist measurement. Weave elastic through casing; sew ends together. See photograph 4.

Afghan stitch, with its smooth surface and stable edges, makes this trim game-room pillow that doubles as a tic-tac-toe board. X and O markers are movable.

Tic-tac-toe pillow

Directions to make pillow and markers:
Size: Approximately 14 inches square.

Materials: 4-ply acrylic-and-nylon Knitting Worsted, 1 skein each of White, Black, and Red. Afghan hook size H, 14 inches long. Crochet hook size F for markers. Yarn needle. Pillow form. Coffee-stirrer sticks cut into ten 2¼-inch lengths.

Gauge: Afghan stitch: 17 stitches = 4 inches; 7 rows = 2 inches. Finished square = 3¾ inches. Markers: 5 sc = 1 inch.

Board Squares: Make 10 White and 10 Black. Ch 14. Pull up a loop in 2nd ch from hook and in each ch across (14 loops on hook). Yo, and draw yarn through first loop on hook. *Yo, and pull through 2 loops. Repeat from * across row until 1 loop remains. Work 9 more rows in afghan pattern. **Border Row:** Insert hook into center of next bar between front and back strands; yo, draw up a loop, and sc. Repeat in every bar. Work 2 sc in ch at end of row. Work 1 row of sc on side edge, inserting hook under both sides of sts. Work

3 sc in corner st, work 1 row sc on back side of bottom ch, 3 sc in corner and 1 row up side edge. End with 1 sc in top st, sl st. Fasten.

Red-Stripe Panels (2¼ inches wide finished): Make 2 panels 14 inches long and 2 panels 11 inches. Ch 8, and work in afghan pattern until correct length. There will be approximately 50 rows in the longer panels and 36 in the shorter. Work border row as in squares.

Finishing: Sl st pieces together from wrong side, inserting hook through top loops only on each side. After squares are assembled, join shorter panels to opposite sides, then longer ones. With right sides together, sl st around 3 sides. Turn to right side; insert pillow form, and whipstitch open side closed.

Markers, X: Make 10 halves. With Red and size-F crochet hook, ch 10. **Rnd 1:** Sc in 3rd ch from hook, sc in each of next 6 ch, 2 sc in last ch; working on opposite of starting-ch, 2 sc in first ch, sc in 6 ch, 2 sc in last ch. Join with sl st in ch at

beg of round. **Rnd 2:** Ch 1. Sc in first sc, sc in each of 7 sc, 2 sc in each of next 2 sc, sc in next 8 sc, 2 sc in last sc. Join in first ch-1. Break yarn, leaving 10-inch end for sewing. Fold strip in half lengthwise; insert stick; sew edges together through both loops of sc. Sew 2 together to form X shape.

Markers, O: Make 5. With Red and size-F crochet hook, ch 10. Join with sl st in first ch, to form ring. Ch 1. **Rnd 1:** 12 sc in ring. **Rnd 2:** Ch 1. Work 16 hdc in ring, covering sc of last rnd. Join in first sc. End off.

Tassels: Make 4. For each tassel, wind yarn loosely around a piece of cardboard 7 inches wide. Wind 7 times. Cut one end. Fold strands, and tie tightly about ½ inch from fold. With a yarn needle, thread yarn through tassel top, and sew loops to pillow corners. Trim evenly.

If you'd like to make a chess afghan to match the pillow, write for Kit No. 24, International Creations, Box 55, Great Neck, N.Y. 11023.

Popcorn-and-leaf afghan

The afghan shown in the color photograph on page 8 is an unusual combination of popcorns and raised leaves worked against the even, basketlike weave of plain afghan stitch. It is made in strips.

Size: Approximately 47 by 60 inches, including borders. Afghan consists of 9 Leaf Strips and 4 Popcorn Strips.

Materials: 16 4-ounce skeins Knitting Worsted, or acrylic and nylon (4-ply cream). Afghan hook size G, or use size to obtain specified gauge. Steel crochet hook size 0, for joining and borders.

Gauge: Afghan stitch: 11 stitches = 2 inches; 8 rows = 2 inches.

Note: Each Leaf Strip is 1⅝ inches wide, approximately 58¾ inches long. Each Popcorn Strip is 6 inches wide, approximately 58 inches long.

Leaf-Pattern Strip: Make 9. With afghan hook, ch 9 and work 6 rows in plain afghan st (see page 15).

Start Leaf Pattern: Row 7: Draw up a loop in 2nd, 3rd, 4th, and 5th vertical bars (5 loops on hook), make leaf as follows: Yo and draw up a loop in 3rd vertical bar from right end of strip but 3 rows below, (which is plain row 4), * yo and draw through 1 loop, yo and draw through 2 loops, yo and draw up a loop in 4th vertical bar from right end of strip, but 4 rows below, (which is plain row 3), and repeat from * to * (7 loops on hook), yo hook twice, draw up a loop in 5th vertical bar (center) from right end of strip but 5 rows below, (which is plain row 2), yo and through 1 loop, yo and through 2 loops twice, yo and through 1 loop (8 loops on hook); yo and draw up a loop in 6th vertical bar from right end of strip but 4 rows below, (which is plain row 3), and repeat from * to * (9 loops on hook); yo and draw up a loop in 7th vertical bar from right end of strip but 3 rows below, (which is plain row 4), and repeat from * to * (10 loops on hook); yo and draw through 6 loops on hook and ch 1 to close leaf; draw up a loop in each of the last 4 vertical bars in plain Row 6 (9 loops on hook). Work off as for plain afghan st. *Rows 8 through 13:* Work in plain afghan st. Repeat Rows 7 through 13 for Leaf Pattern, or until there are 34 patterns from start, ending with pattern Row 7—238 rows worked. Bind off. (To bind off, see Craftnotes, page 14).

Popcorn Strip: Make 4. With afghan hook ch 33 and work Row 1 and first half of Row 2 in plain afghan st. Yo and through first loop, * yo and through 2 loops twice, ch 3 (for popcorn) *, repeat from * to * 6 times more (7 popcorns); yo and through 2 loops 3 times, ch 3, repeat from * to * 6 times more, ending with yo and through 2 loops 3 times. *Row 3 and all Odd Rows:* Work plain afghan st, keep popcorns on right side. (33 loops). *Row 4:* Repeat first half of Row 2 in plain afghan st. Yo and through first loop, * yo and through 2 loops twice, ch 3 *, repeat from * to * 5 times more (6 popcorns), yo and through 2 loops 7 times, ch 3 and repeat from * to * 5 times, ending yo and through 2 loops 3 times. *Row 6:* Work first half of row 2 in plain afghan st. Yo and through first loop, * yo and through 2 loops twice *, ch 3, repeat from * to * 4 times more, yo and through 2 loops 11 times, ch 3, repeat from * to * 4 times, ending yo and through 2 loops 3 times. Continue to work 1 popcorn st fewer at each side of center plain sts. and work 4 more plain afghan sts in center on second half of every even row until there is 1 popcorn at each side and there are 27 plain sts in center (14 rows). This is the center of one diamond. Continue as before, working one more popcorn st at each side of center plain sts and 4 sts fewer in plain afghan st at center on second half of every even row until there are 14 popcorns across row. Work 1 row of plain afghan st. Work a second row of 14 popcorns for start of second diamond. Continue as before, working 1 popcorn fewer at each side, as in first diamond, until there is 1 popcorn at each side. Continue in this manner until there are 9 diamond patterns from start—235 rows worked. Bind off.

To Join Panels: Attach yarn in first row of a diamond strip at right-hand edge. With steel crochet hook, work a sc in first row, * ch 5, skip 1 row, sc in next row at side, repeat from * to top of strip, ending 1 sc in last row. Ch 5, pick up Leaf-Pattern Strip, and work a sc in the last row of this strip. ** Ch 2, work a sl st in 3rd ch of last "loop" of Popcorn Strip, ch 2, skip 1 row of Leaf Strip, sc in next row of Leaf Strip, repeat from ** down, easing in the extra 3 rows on Leaf Strip to fit Popcorn Strip ending sc in first row of Leaf Strip. Cut yarn, and fasten. Continue to join strips in this manner, joining 2 more Leaf Strips, then 1 Popcorn Strip, 3 Leaf Strips, 1 Popcorn Strip, 3 Leaf Strips, and 1 Popcorn Strip. With steel crochet hook work 1 row of sc at each long side edge of afghan.

Borders for Each End of Afghan: Attach yarn in first row at lower edge of afghan. Ch 5, * skip 1 st, ch 5, repeat from * across lower edge of afghan, working a sc at each side of joinings with a ch 5 between. *Row 2:* Ch 3, turn * sl st in center of ch 5, ch 5, repeat from * across, ending sl st in center of ch 5. Repeat Row 2 for 2 more rows. Cut yarn and fasten.

Fringe: Cut yarn into 20-inch lengths. Attach fringe as follows: Fold 6 strands in half, and knot in first ch-5 loop. Then knot in every other ch-5 loop across lower edge. *Row 1:* Divide "tassels" in half. Skip first half of outside tassel; * knot next 2 adjoining halves together about 1½ inches from border. Repeat from * across, skipping last half-tassel. *Row 2:* Starting with free half of first tassel, knot this half together with half of second tassel, about 1½ inches down from last knot; * knot next 2 adjoining halves. Repeat from * across. Trim ends evenly.

Abbreviations

ch	chain	rnd	round
dec	decrease	sc	single crochet
dc	double crochet	sl st	slip stitch
hdc	half double crochet	st(s)	stitch(es)
inc	increase	tr	treble crochet
*	repeat from	yo	yarn over

To Increase with Afghan Stitch: At the beginning of a row, pull up a loop in the 2nd vertical bar; then insert hook under stitch between vertical bar just worked and next one. One extra loop has been added. At end of row, make the increase loop between 2nd and 3rd vertical bars from the end.

To Decrease with Afghan Stitch: At the beginning of a row, slip hook under 2nd and 3rd upright bars, and draw up one loop. At the end of row, decrease in same manner on 2nd and 3rd bars from end.

To Bind Off: Work a single crochet in each stitch.

Chain stitch
Make a slipknot, and slide on a crochet hook.

Hold crochet hook with right index finger and thumb (left if you're left-handed). Wrap yarn through fingers of other hand to provide tension, and guide with index finger.
Bring yarn over and around crochet hook.

Catch yarn on hook, and pull through existing loop. Original loop slips off. Repeat for a foundation chain.

Slip stitch
Working on a foundation chain, skip one stitch, and insert hook in top strand of the second chain. Yarn over, and draw through both loops on hook.

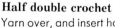

Single crochet
On a foundation chain, insert the hook into the second chain from the hook.

Yarn over, and draw through stitch (2 loops on hook).

Yarn over, and draw yarn through both loops.

Half double crochet
Yarn over, and insert hook into third chain from hook.

Pull up a loop (3 loops on hook).

Yarn over, and draw through all 3 loops.

CRAFTNOTES

Double crochet

Yarn over, and insert hook in fourth chain from hook.

Draw up loop (3 loops on hook). Yarn over; pull through 2 loops.

Two loops remaining on hook.

Yarn over, and pull through last 2 loops.

Treble crochet

Yarn over twice; insert hook in fifth chain from hook.

Draw up a loop (4 loops on hook).

Yarn over; draw through 2 loops (3 loops on hook).

Yarn over; draw through 2 loops (2 loops on hook).

Yarn over; pull through last 2 loops (1 loop on hook).

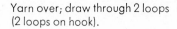

Fastening Yarn: Bring end through loop of last stitch, and cut yarn 3 or 4 inches long. Thread end on yarn needle, and weave along a row of stitches on the wrong side for a few inches. Clip excess yarn.

Blocking: On an ironing board, pin each piece of work wrong side up and to accurate measurements. Use rustproof pins. Set iron for wool, and cover work with damp cloth. Do not rest weight of iron on crocheted article, but pass iron slowly over it. Let article dry before unpinning.

Afghan stitch

Make a chain the desired length, not including loop on hook, which counts as first stitch of next row. Insert hook in second chain, and draw up a loop.

Pull up a loop in each chain, keeping all loops on hook. (This is first half of row.)

Yarn over hook, and draw through first loop.

Yarn over hook, and draw through 2 loops. Repeat with all loops on hook. (This is second half of row.)

Remaining loop is first stitch of next row.

Insert hook in second vertical bar, and draw up a loop. Proceed across row, drawing up a loop in each vertical bar and retaining them all on hook. In last stitch, insert hook through double loop, and pull up a loop.

Return as in steps 3 and 4 above.

APPLIQUE
Fabric Collage

Pauline Fischer is widely known as an artist and craftswoman, and has needlework in the collections of Colonial Williamsburg and the Metropolitan Museum of Art, among others. Author of the authoritative Bargello Magic, *she teaches in New York City, both privately and at the Embroiderer's Guild. She learned applique from her Belgian mother and grandmother. Her home is a delightful gallery of museum-quality needleworks of art.*

Applique is the art of fabric collage. The process is to stitch pieces of fabric—by hand or by machine—to a base material. The art is the picture or motif created by the appliqued scraps, and this design traditionally originates in the mind of the needleworker. Applique dates back to Europe and the Middle Ages. In Colonial America, where fabrics were precious, it flowered as nowhere else and stood as a symbol of neighborliness because so often the work was done in groups and as a gift.

Materials

Materials are the base fabric and the scraps from which the picture is created. Natural-fiber fabrics are the easiest to work with—cotton, linen, wool, and silk. Synthetics don't crease well and tend to crawl instead of staying in place while you are sewing on the pattern pieces.

Use natural or synthetic threads; I find six-strand embroidery cotton is best. Beads, ribbons, lace, and other trimmings can be added.

The tools include: Sewing scissors, embroidery needles suited to the thread selected, pincushion, thimble, tracing and carbon paper, ruler, a steam iron, and a ballpoint pen with a fine nib. For machine applique you will need a zigzag sewing machine with a special applique foot to replace the presser foot, and a can of spray glue.

Hand applique

Because handmade appliques take time and require painstaking stitches, they often become family heirlooms. To me, the work is most appealing when I have designed the motif for the applique myself. To design an applique:
□ Choose a base fabric suited to the project and select harmonizing fabric scraps from which to make the applique pieces.
□ Rough out a design on paper—your own or a copy—and cut it out.
□ Pin this pattern into place on the base fabric and adjust it, adding or subtracting elements and colors. From it make the final pattern.

These basic moves in designing an applique can vary. When I designed the tablecloth pictured on page 25, I spread an old sheet on the dining table. On it I marked the hemline, and from it worked out the dimensions of the fabric I needed. To see where an applique would show to best advantage, I set the table as for a formal dinner. Then I drew on the sheet a rough outline for the pattern free-hand with a ballpoint pen. I perfected the design. From it I made a pattern with carbon paper, then traced the pattern on cardboard.

Hand appliqued quilt blocks are for expert needlecraft artists to make. Patterns for appliqued quilts are available from supply houses such as Stearns and Foster.

Pauline Fischer made this doll for her daughter 25 years ago. Applique pattern for the apron is on page 19.

Stitching is the last step in the long process that begins with the creation of the applique design.

Applique is sewn to the base fabric with dainty little stitches of point de Paris.

In the tradition of applique, this table cloth designed and made by Pauline Fischer will remain in her family. The fabric is linen; the applique is bronze silk satin.

The directions, given below, for making this tablecloth applique illustrate the basic steps in making a hand applique. The fabrics used are fine white linen, appliqued with bronze silk satin.

After you have determined the size of your cloth, following the steps described on the preceding page, enlarge pattern, figure A, (see page 117) and, on tracing paper, make a paper pattern of the design motifs.

Trace pattern pieces of the individual motifs on thin cardboard, leaving no seam allowance. Cut out the pieces of the cardboard pattern. Then trace as many motifs as needed for your cloth on the applique fabric, allowing ½-inch seam around each piece. Space the motifs on the applique fabric ½-inch apart. Cut out the motifs.

To ready a piece for appliqueing, wrap it around its cardboard pattern so that the seam allowance folds to the back. Fasten fabric at the back

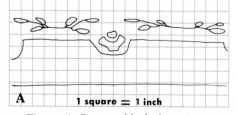

1 square = 1 inch

Figure A: Party tablecloth pattern.

and catch the turned-back allowance with hand stitching so the thread goes from top to bottom and side to side. Pull fabric taut. With a moderately hot iron, press the underside. Cut free from cardboard. The seam is now pressed flat and the piece ready to applique. Snip into curved edges so they will lie flat and trim off excess allowance to ¼ inch.

Pin the motif into place on the design outlined on the base material. Baste firmly with big stitches in thread of contrasting color.

With a single strand of embroidery thread, stitch all around the applique with point de Paris, page 20. Prepare and sew on each applique until the design is complete. Hem the cloth with point turc, page 20.

Working with Small Applique Motifs

It isn't necessary to prepare a cardboard pattern for very small applique motifs. Trace each design element directly onto the wrong side of the scrap from which it will be cut, using the paper pattern.

Designs for the doll's apron, page 17, and the bib and holder shown here, are given in figures B and C. When making the pattern pieces, add a ¼-inch seam allowance to each grid. Remember that each element of a picture must have its own pattern—the horse, the saddle, the rider. The rider's nose and mouth are executed in satin stitch, page 20.

The applique for the trains shown on the doll's apron can be made of fine cotton or linen, appliqued to a child's blouse or a doll's dress, using the basic applique procedures described above.

The bib and holder are of fine linen, appliqued with linen. To attach the seam side of the pink scallop to the bib, machine stitch the wrong side of the bib and the right side of the scallop, edges together; then press scallop to the right side.

When you applique the picture pieces to the base cloth, be sure to follow a sequence that starts with the larger bottom pieces first. For the bib, for instance, sew the horse onto the bib, and outline his jaw in point de Paris. Then sew the saddle to the horse, stitching through the base fabric; the rider is appliqued next; flowers and leaves are sewn last. Ground lines, and rider's nose and mouth, are done in satin stitch.

A generous-size appliqued bib with its own case is a perfect gift for the baby who travels. The fine details of the design will intrigue a seamstress-grandmother.

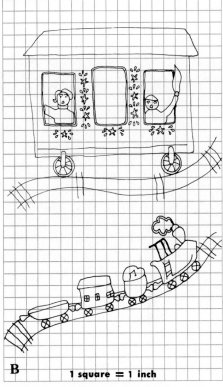

B   1 square = 1 inch

Figure B: Applique design on the apron pictured on page 17.

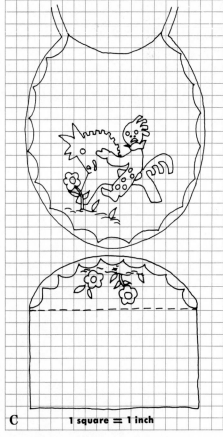

C   1 square = 1 inch

Figure C: Bib and holder design.

EMBROIDERY CRAFTNOTES

Satin stitch

Bring needle up from the wrong side at A and insert it at B. Bring needle up again next to A and reinsert it at B. Continue making smooth stitches.

Point de Paris

1: Use a blunt needle and fine, strong thread for this stitch. Come up from the underside at A, and with the needle horizontal, stitch back from B to point A.

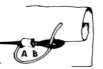

2: Return to B, and with the needle at an angle, come up through C, just above A. Process is the same, whether hemming, as here, or sewing.

3: Return to point A, go through at A again, and come up through point D. Point D is level with point A. This is important to note: If you go above or below A as you move forward, the openwork line will become ragged.

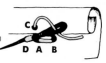

4: Repeat the three steps above, pulling each stitch firmly to create openwork holes.

5: The finished effect is a row of openwork holes laced by a raised ridge of fabric and thread. Fine, even stitches are essential for a neat point de Paris hem.

Point turc

1: Use a blunt needle and fine, strong thread for this stitch, too. As you work, pull each stitch firmly to open holes in fabric. From the underside, come up through A, go in at B to the right of A and above it. Come up through A.

2: Go in at B with the needle level, and come up in C. Note C is straight across from B, but left of A. Distance between these three points is equal; they form a triangle.

3: Repeat the step above, stitching from B through C again, with the needle horizontal.

4: Stitch from B through C again, with the needle still in horizontal position. You have formed a double stitch.

5: Now close the triangle by stitching through point A and coming up through the stitches at point C. The needle is slanted.

6: Return to point A and with the needle horizontal, come up at point D, level with A. D is as far from A as C is from point B.

7: Repeat the stitch from A through point D, with the needle in horizontal position.

8: Repeat the stitch from A through D, as before, with the needle set horizontally, so that a double stitch is made from A through D. Be sure to keep the needle straight. Return to step one and repeat through step eight.

9: This diagram shows the outline of the stitches. Actually the final stitching is not so spread out but looks like the drawing below.

10: Dark spaces here depict holes opened in the fabric by pulling firmly on the thread as you complete each stitch. The stitches should be so tight that they almost disappear. Developing firm, even stitches and symmetrical rows requires time and a lot of practice to achieve.

Machine applique ¢ ⌛ 👤 🔬

Machine applique is faster than hand applique because the pattern pieces are glued, not basted, and machine stitched instead of hand stitched. It's a method particularly suited to bold designs. To learn the basic techniques of machine applique, study the step-by-step instructions below.

The first step in making the Charlie Chaplin applique for the denim jacket (pictured on page 23) is to draw the pattern pieces, figure D, page 22, on tracing or transfer paper. Tips that make this easier are pictured in photographs 1 through 4.

□ Select the fabrics. I used fake fur for the eyebrows and the mustache, crepe-backed satin for the hat, and the whitest possible cotton for the face. The shirt is a textured, off-white cotton.

□ Wash and dry the denim jacket, if new, and all the fabrics chosen for the applique pieces to make sure there won't be any shrinkage later. Starch and iron each piece of the applique fabric, except fake fur.

□ Transfer the pattern pieces from the tracing paper onto the fabrics and cut out the parts in silhouette, nose, eyes, and all.

□ Compose Charlie on the jacket back, playing with the pieces until you find just the look you want. This is the time to evaluate your design. Mark the positions of the smaller pattern pieces on the silhouette.

□ Decide which piece is to be stitched on in what order so you can avoid doubling or crossing stitch lines.

Margaret Cusack, a graduate of Pratt Institute in New York, designs applique that is machine-stitched for magazine covers and advertisements. The projects pictured here show her handiwork with fabric collage–and a sewing machine.

1: Keep the lines uncomplicated as you draw or enlarge the design to its final size with a fine-tipped felt pen.

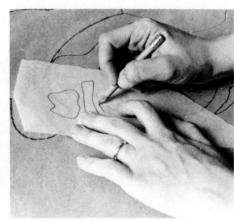

2: With tracing paper (use white on black fabric) and a pencil on a sunny window, trace overall outline on base piece.

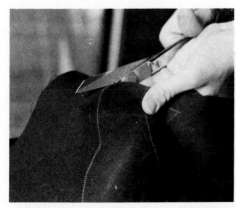

3: After applying spray glue to hold tracing paper to fabric, cut out very small shapes; peel off paper, position on base.

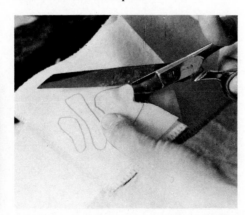

4: Using one sheet of tracing paper for all pieces to be cut from the same fabric makes transfer and cutting easy.

5: Assembling Charlie to see how he looks before pieces are glued and then sewed onto the silhouette. This is the time to fix his facial expression.

Figure D: Pattern for Charlie Chaplin.

D   1 square = 1 inch

6: Smaller pattern components are sprayed lightly with glue, face down on newspapers.

7: Glue-sprayed pieces are assembled on the cutout for the Charlie Chaplin face.

□ Place newspapers on the floor, set the small pattern pieces face down on the papers and spray lightly with glue. Do not spray the large, background parts of the applique.

□ Position small pieces on base fabric, face up now, and iron on.

□ Using a satin stitch on a zigzag sewing machine with a special applique foot, sew everything to Charlie's silhouette. Iron. Spray glue on the back of the silhouette and position it on the jacket. Iron again and zigzag the silhouette edges to the jacket with satin stitch.

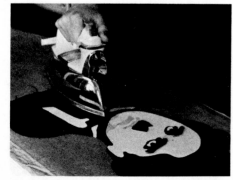
8: Iron at each stage of the applique to give finished work a professional look.

9: Use matching thread and satin stitch to sew down the components. Note eye whites.

10: Last step is to stitch the assembled design to the denim jacket back.

The machine-stitched Charlie Chaplin. The machine technique, a different approach to applique, is fast and easy.

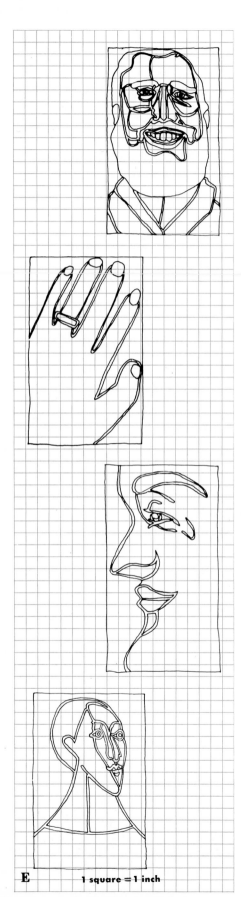

E   1 square = 1 inch

Figure E: Pillow patterns.

Machine-appliqued people pillows, by Margaret Cusack. Patterns for the appliqued profile pillows can be made from photostatic enlargements of snapshots.

People pillows

The machine applique techniques used to make the Charlie Chaplin jacket can be applied to make the people pillows pictured here.

The first step is to prepare a pattern. The pattern of the hand, shown in figure E, is the easiest. Enlarge the pattern on a scale of one square equals one inch and transfer the design, as described on page 117. Next, from a sturdy fabric such as closely woven cotton, cut front and back pillow casing pieces of equal size. Including seams, these will be about 11 by 14 inches and 14 by 20 inches. The dimensions aren't critical.

Machine applique the pieces to the pillow front, as explained in the Charlie Chaplin design instructions; then, with the pieces inside out, sew the casings together across the top and down two sides with 1-inch seam allowances. Turn to right side, slip over a pillow, tuck in rough open ends and hand sew.

Make a pillow applique of a friend's profile from a photograph enlarged by a photostat shop to 9 by 12 inches. Trace the profile onto tracing paper and proceed as above. Use polished cotton for flesh areas, fake fur or shiny fabrics for hair and beard, discarded clothing for garment pieces.

Applique a centerpiece

My own design of flowers and leaves allows center space for candlesticks in this machine-stitched-applique cloth. Copy this design exactly (figure F), or plan your own color scheme to complement your china. Follow the basics of the Chaplin machine-stitched applique to make your tablecloth.

More Applique Tablecloth Ideas

For the way to approach tablecloth design, see Pauline Fischer's suggestions on page 16. Unless you are appliqueing a tablecloth that will be cherished for generations and taken out for only the most formal or festive occasions in your home, use materials that can be machine-washed. Silk, for example, is suitable only for careful hand-laundering. Linen on linen, stitched with cotton or linen embroidery thread, is quite durable when machine-laundered at a moderate temperature. Organdy, another suitable material, works into an exquisite cloth. Because of organdy's transparent quality, you can applique it on the underside, so the applique shows through in a shadow effect. Synthetics are difficult to use.

F 1 square = 1 inch

Figure F: Tablecloth centerpiece pattern.

▼ This tablecloth by Margaret Cusack is machine-appliqued. Glue or pin parts in place, then machine-sew to the cloth.

REVERSE APPLIQUE
Spectacular Cutaways

Reverse appliqué differs from traditional appliqué in that rather than adding small pieces of fabric on top of a larger background fabric to form a design, you begin by basting together a sandwich of several layers of fabrics of different colors. Then you form the design by slitting or cutting away selected areas of the top layers of fabric, exposing different colors in the desired shapes. The cut edges are turned under and sewn by hand using tiny stitches. While this technique is somewhat more complicated than traditional appliqué, reverse appliqué is really quite simple to do. The extra planning and imagination it requires make it more challenging, and therefore a more exciting needlecraft.

Reverse appliqué is a technique favored by Loretta Holz, a crafts writer and designer. She is the author of Teach Yourself Stitchery, *a book for children;* Mobiles You Can Make; *and* Many Ways to Sell What You Make: A Marketing Guide for Artists and Craftspeople. *She has designed for many magazines, including* Creative Crafts, McCall's Needlework and Crafts, Woman's Day, Lady's Circle, *and* Golden Hands Monthly.

Cuna Indian women wear *mola* blouses, and not just for special occasions. Some have more than two dozen, each representing hours of hand-stitching on two to seven layers of colorful cotton cloth.

Molas

Reverse appliqué plays an important part in the culture of the Cuna Indians, who live on the San Blas islands off the coast of Panama. According to Cuna tradition, there is a special place in heaven reserved for artists, and the women of this proud, independent society are world famous for their striking reverse appliqué panels, called *molas* (opposite).

The Cunas have no written language, so there is no record of the development of the *mola*. However, it is assumed that the influence of nineteenth-century missionaries and the new availability of brightly colored cotton fabrics brought by traders were a combination volatile enough to cause the women, who used to paint their bodies, to give up their paint and paintbrushes in favor of needles, thread, and cloth. The word *mola* originally meant clothing but has come to mean a woman's blouse, with a front and back decorated with panels of reverse appliqué (above). In response to tourist demand, the Cunas now produce the panels separately. Such *mola* panels (one is featured here as a project) can be incorporated into utilitarian objects—lampshades, pillows, cushions, skirts, jackets, dresses, or tote bags—as well as blouses. Or they can simply be appreciated for their own beauty and hung on the wall as works of art.

Cuna Indians of the San Blas islands produce the world's most spectacular reverse-appliqué panels, which they call *molas*. The *mola* opposite is a fine example of the Cunas' remarkable talent for transforming any scene or object—in this case, flowers—into a dramatic and stylized pattern. The balanced design, sophisticated colors, and meticulous workmanship (note the hand-stitched rickrack) are qualities that the best *mola* makers strive to incorporate in their work.

Materials

Most of the materials required for reverse appliqué are those used for any sewing project: fabric; thread; needles; scissors; straight pins; and tailor's chalk. Lightweight cotton fabric is traditionally used for reverse appliqué and is the best for this type of work. You may use any crisp, tightly woven, lightweight fabric (such as a cotton-and-polyester blend), but pure polyester is a poor choice. The coarser the weave, the more difficult it becomes to keep the turned-under edges from popping out and raveling. The thread you use should match the color of each fabric layer except the bottom one. In addition, you will need: paper, ruler, and pencil (to make the patterns); and a pair of small, sharp-pointed scissors such as embroidery scissors.

1: To start a reverse appliqué, baste the layers of fabric together all around the edges. This practice swatch consists of three layers.

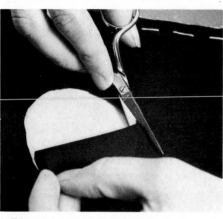

2: To cut out a shape, first pierce the top layer of fabric with the scissors. Then make short, controlled snips to avoid cutting the underlayer.

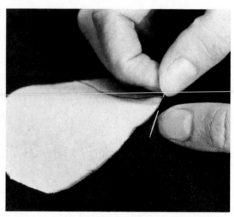

3: Turn under and sew all around the edge, making tiny stitches that are perpendicular to the edge on the right side but diagonal underneath.

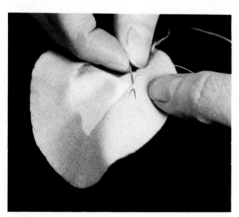

4: The procedure for turning under and sewing the cut edge of lower layers is the same as for sewing the top layer.

Procedure

The technique, once mastered, is a simple one, but you should practice cutting and stitching an experimental swatch before you begin any project. Cut three pieces of pressed fabric, each approximately 7 inches square. Place the squares together, raw edges even. Baste through all three layers to keep them from shifting as you cut and stitch (photograph 1). In the center of the swatch, pick up the top layer of fabric. Pierce the fabric with the sharp points of the scissors; cut out a shape and remove it (photograph 2). When you work from a pattern, cut ⅛ inch inside the marked outline to provide a turn-under allowance. Thread a needle with thread that matches the top layer of fabric; knot the end. With the point of the needle, poke the cut edge under ⅛ inch; hold it down with the thumb of your free hand. To begin sewing, bring the needle up from the back to the front through all layers of fabric, catching a few threads of the turned-under edge. Then insert the needle from front to back through the under layers, making a tiny stitch that is perpendicular to the fold. Bring the needle up diagonally through all three layers, again catching the folded edge (photograph 3). Continue stitching in this fashion until the entire cut edge of the top layer has been folded under and stitched down. To end a thread, take a few small stitches through the bottom layer where they will not show. To cut shapes from subsequent layers, follow the same procedure, again choosing thread that matches the layer being sewn down (photograph 4).

Helpful Hints

When you fold and stitch tight curves, you will find it easier to fold the edge under if you make tiny clips in the turn-under allowance. You may find that you prefer to turn under the entire edge of a cut-out section and secure it with pins before you begin to stitch, rather than turning it under bit by bit as you sew. When you work with larger pieces of fabric, add lines of basting stitches diagonally across the layers to keep them from shifting. You can easily snip away these large stitches if they get in your way while you work. Since keeping the fabric flat and unpuckered is important, press the fabric before you begin, and again each time you complete a step. Sewing around tiny cut-out circles is the most difficult of all reverse appliqué steps. If the design calls for small circles, cut them out of a scrap of fabric and appliqué them on top, turning the edge under and using the same stitching technique.

Designing Your Own

There are many sources of reverse appliqué designs. The photographs below will give you some ideas, but keep your eyes open for others. Fabrics, flowers, book jackets, and designs worked in other techniques such as embroidery, mosaics, stained glass, and patchwork suggest patterns that can be adapted for reverse appliqué.

A quick way to try out a design is to experiment with construction paper. Arrange layers of paper that correspond to the colors of the fabrics you intend to use. Staple the layers together at one side; then cut the planned design one layer at a time, holding the other layers aside as you cut.

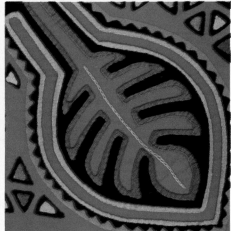

Some Cuna Indians draw a design on the fabric, but most work without a pattern. They plunge right in, and cut and stitch with an assurance born of years of experience. You may eventually do the same, but at the beginning cut a paper pattern for each section of your design. Pin the pattern in place on the fabric, and trace around the edge with tailor's chalk. Then cut the fabric ⅛ inch inside the chalk line, and turn the fabric under along the line.

When you baste the fabric layers together, place the color that you want to appear most often directly below the top layer. This way you avoid cutting through more than one layer unnecessarily. Occasionally you may want to go directly to the third or fourth layer, bypassing intermediate layers so they do not show at all. To do this, cut the design from the top layer as usual. Then reach through the opening, and cut away the second layer (and the third and fourth if necessary) until you reveal the desired layer. Cut the intermediate layers farther back than the top opening; then stitch the top layer to the layer you want to show.

Experiment with small-patterned fabrics as well as solid colors. Heavy fabric is hard to turn under neatly, but you might use one for the bottom layer, which is not cut. And try using felt—the cut edges need not be turned under since they do not ravel, so they can be glued down instead of sewn.

The Cuna Indians believe that bathing the hands of a woman in a potion made from the leaves of a special tree will inspire her to create wonderful *mola* designs. These details were all taken from authentic Cuna *molas;* they might serve as your inspiration when you design your own.

29

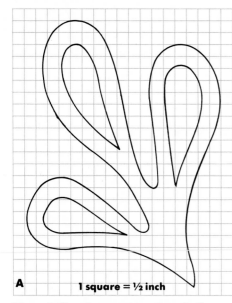

A **1 square = ½ inch**

Figure A: To make a quarter-pattern for the splash design, copy this pattern onto paper that you have ruled in ½-inch squares. Transfer the lines, one square at a time, onto the larger grid.

Splashes

Although there are six colors in the reverse appliqué design of the pillow top pictured below, only three layers of fabric were used. The multihued middle layer is made by sewing four pieces of fabric together, patchwork fashion.

Materials
For the top and bottom layers of the pillow top, and for the back of the pillow, you will need: three 22-by-26-inch pieces of fabric (two black and one red); for the middle layer you will need: four 13½-by-11½-inch pieces of fabric (pink, green, yellow, and blue). You will also need: thread to match each fabric except the bottom layer; an 11-by-13-inch piece of paper for the pattern; ruler; pencil; tailor's chalk; straight pins; sewing needle; iron and ironing board; small and large scissors. The pillow form requires two 22-by-26-inch pieces of muslin or other inexpensive, lightweight fabric, and polyester fiber filling for stuffing.

Making the Pillow
To begin, enlarge the quarter-pattern (Figure A), and cut along the outer edge of the splash. Put aside the pattern. Stitch the four small fabric rectangles together to form one larger piece. To do this, place two rectangles together, right sides facing; sew along one shorter side, making a ½-inch seam and forming a strip. Press the seam to one side. Sew the two remaining rectangles together the same way. Then sew the two strips together, forming a 22-by-26-inch rectangle, and press the seam to one side. Place this middle layer between the black layer and the red layer (Figure B). Baste the layers together around the edges and diagonally across.

With tailor's chalk, divide the pillow top into quarter sections. Pin the pattern to it, centering the pattern within one of the quarters. Trace around the edge of the pattern with tailor's chalk, and remove the pattern. Referring to the directions and photographs on page 28, cut the top layer of fabric ⅛ inch inside the chalk line, exposing the patchwork fabric underneath. Using black thread to match the top layer, turn under the cut edge and stitch all around. Cut the top layer a little at a

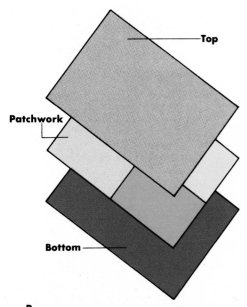

B

Figure B: You will need only three layers if you make a four-color patchwork layer for the center of your sandwich, placing it between the black top layer and the red bottom layer.

Top

Patchwork

Bottom

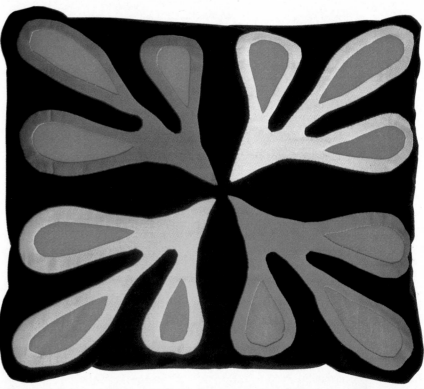

This pillow, with its large, bold splashes of color, demonstrates how dramatic reverse appliqué can be. But the cutting and sewing are easy enough to make this a good first project in this technique.

time, and make sure your stitches penetrate all three layers. Next, cut out the tear-drop-shaped inner sections of the pattern. Pin these patterns in place on the pillow top, and trace around their edges with tailor's chalk. Cut through the middle fabric layer, exposing the red bottom layer of the fabric. Using thread to match the middle layer, turn under the cut edges and stitch them to the bottom layer. Repeat this procedure for each of the four quarters of the pillow top, revealing each color in turn.

To finish the pillow cover, place the pillow top and the pillow back together, right sides facing. Sew all around, making ½-inch seams. Round the corners as you sew, and leave a 10-inch opening on one short side. Clip the raw edges in to the seam at the rounded corners; then turn the pillow cover right side out. To make the inner pillow, sew the two muslin pieces together as you did the outer pillow. Turn the inner pillow cover right side out and stuff it with polyester fiber filling. Fold the raw edges of the opening ½ inch to the inside; sew the opening closed by hand with tiny stitches. Insert this pillow in the pillow cover; stitch the cover opening closed by hand.

Cat tote bag

This design adds several advanced techniques to the basic procedure of sewing reverse appliqué (page 28). The narrow stripes on the cat's back are just slits with the edges turned under and stitched down. A small piece of yellow fabric was added only for the face. Finally, embroidery was used to represent the cat's whiskers, a detail that could not be defined successfully in reverse appliqué.

Materials
To make the tote you will need fabric in the following colors and amounts: ½ yard each of solid red (for the outside layer of the tote) and red print (for the lining); one black and one blue piece measuring 12 inches square (for the second and third layers); and one 3-inch square of yellow (for the face). You will also need: red and black sewing thread; a small amount of yellow embroidery thread; paper for the pattern; pencil; ruler; a single-edged razor blade; tailor's chalk; small and large scissors; straight pins; and a needle.

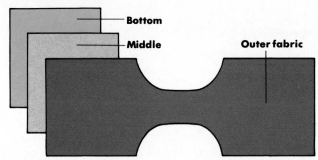

D

Figure D: To assemble the fabrics for cutting, pin and baste the blue bottom layer, the black middle layer, and the top red layer together, keeping bottom (left) and side edges even.

Making the Tote
Enlarge the pattern (Figure C) for the tote and the reverse appliqué design. To cut out the tote, place the outer fabric and the lining fabric together; fold in half crosswise, forming four layers. Pin the pattern to the four layers with the top of the pattern on the folded edge of the fabric. Cut out the outer tote and lining, following the outer line of the pattern. Set aside the lining.

Pin the blue bottom layer, the black middle layer, and the red top layer together (Figure D). Baste around the edges. Cut out the cat design from the pattern, using the razor blade to slit the stripes on the cat's back, and eyes, nose, and mouth. Pin the cat pattern to the tote in the position shown in Figure C. With tailor's chalk, trace around the pattern; unpin the pattern. Following the photographs and directions on page 28, cut the cat shape from the red fabric only, revealing the black fabric underneath. Cut ⅛ inch inside the marked outline, a little at a time, and use

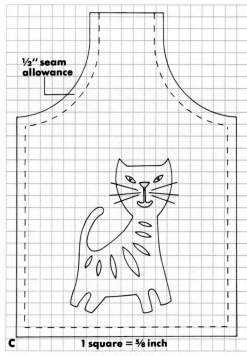

½" seam allowance

C   **1 square = ⅝ inch**

Figure C: Enlarge this pattern for a tote bag by copying it onto paper that you have ruled into ⅝-inch squares. Transfer both the outline of the tote and the cat design to the larger grid, copying the lines one square at a time.

If you are a cat fancier, you will especially appreciate this reverse appliqué tote, a handy size for either women or girls.

31

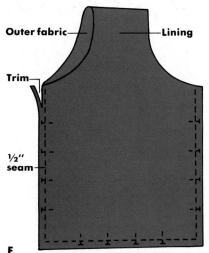

E

Figure E: Stitch the lining and outer fabric pieces together, right sides facing, along the curved edges, making ½-inch seams. Clip into the seam allowance as necessary to ease the curves. Then turn the tote bag right side out by pulling one end through the sewn middle section as indicated by the arrow.

F

Figure F: With the lining facing the outside, pin, then stitch the front and back sections of the tote together from curve to curve. Make a ½-inch seam, and round the corners. Before turning the tote right side out, trim the seam.

red thread to stitch down the folded-under edge. When the cat design has been entirely stitched, pin the cat pattern back on the tote. With tailor's chalk, trace the cut-out shapes on the back and face. Remove the pattern, and slit the black fabric along the center of the marked areas. Clip into the seam allowance around the back slits, and turn the edge under along the chalk lines, exposing the blue fabric underneath. Sew the edges down, forming stripes. Insert the piece of yellow fabric between the second and third layers by slipping it through the nose-and-mouth slit. Pin or baste it in place. Clip into the seam allowance around small curves, fold the cut edges under along the marked lines, and stitch down with black thread. To finish the cat, make two long stitches with black sewing thread for the pupil of each eye; add the whiskers by making six longer stitches with yellow embroidery thread.

Place the outer tote and the lining together, right sides facing, with edges even. Following Figure E, stitch along the curved edges, making ½-inch seams. Then turn the tote right side out. Press well, especially along the seams. Then pin the front and back sections together with the lining on the outside. Stitch together as shown in Figure F. Trim the seam, and finish with a zigzag stitch or cover the edge with bias tape. Turn the tote right side out and press well.

This *mola* panel with a stylized bird as the motif was worked by a Cuna Indian woman. Such bright effects are achieved by inserting small fabric swatches of various colors between the top and bottom layers and exposing them in limited areas.

San Blas bird

The Cuna Indian woman seeks a fresh approach with each *mola* she undertakes. Even though she may use a traditional design, no two *molas* are exactly alike. Native flowers, animals, and birds are often stylized almost into abstractions. But the Cunas have a subtle sense of humor that is often reflected in *molas* that tell a story. Panels may depict a medicine man's incantations gone awry; or lobster and fish brandishing knives and forks in anticipation of a dinner consisting of a man sitting in a casserole. There are even *molas* showing women making *molas*. Although the directions that follow allow you to duplicate the *mola* above, in the true spirit of *mola* making you may prefer to choose and arrange your own color inserts.

Materials

To make the reverse appliqué bird panel in the colors shown, you will need two 15-by-20-inch pieces of fabric, one red (top layer) and one white (bottom layer); 17 small pieces of fabric (about 3 by 4 inches) in assorted colors such as light and dark blue, black, pink, yellow, orange, light and dark green, and brown; red sewing thread; paper for the pattern; pencil; ruler; small and large scissors; straight pins; and a sewing needle. If you wish to use the panel as a hanging, you will also need two 5-inch squares (for the hanging tabs), one 15-by-20-inch piece of red fabric (for the backing), and a 19-inch wooden dowel.

Making the Hanging

With raw edges even, place the top red layer and the bottom white layer of fabric together; baste all around the edges and diagonally from corner to corner. Enlarge the pattern for the bird (Figure G). Cut out the bird shape, including the eye, and pin it, centered, on top of the red fabric. Trace around the pattern edges with tailor's chalk, and remove the pattern. Then draw straight lines to indicate the slits, using a ruler and tailor's chalk (refer to the photograph opposite as a guide).

To do the reverse appliqué, begin with the outline of the bird and the slits in the wings, tail, and feet that radiate from the outline. Working on one small area at a

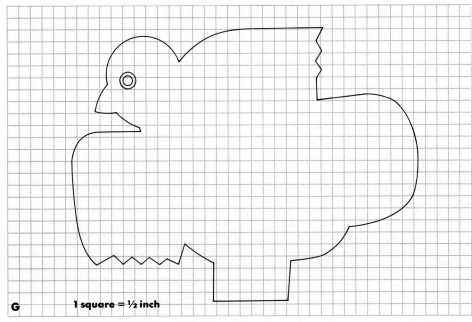

G **1 square = ½ inch**

Figure G: To enlarge this bird pattern, draw a grid whose squares measure ½-inch; then copy the pattern one square at a time.

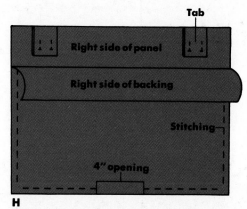

H

Figure H: To turn the panel into a wall hanging, pin the tabs to the right side of the top edge of the panel, raw edges even, 2 inches in from either side. Pin the backing fabric on top, raw edges matching. Stitch together, making ½-inch seams, but leave a 4-inch opening so you can turn the panel right side out. The tabs will be held in the seam.

time, slit along the marked line through the top layer only. Then turn the edges under ⅛ inch, revealing the white fabric underneath, and stitch them down with red thread (see page 28 for basic directions). Next, cut and stitch the eye, and appliqué a small black circle within it. Make small scattered cuts in the head area; fold edges under and stitch down to form dots. Then cut and stitch the slits that will be white. Finally, cut and stitch the slits that are various colors. For each group, slip a piece of colored fabric through the first slit you cut before you stitch it down. Position each insert so it shows through as in the photograph. Some inserts must be irregularly shaped to fit, such as the brown piece to the left of the beak.

To finish the panel as a hanging, fold each of the two 5-inch squares in half, and stitch them together along the long edge, forming two tubes. Turn each tube right side out, and fold in half, making tabs. Pin the red backing and the finished panel together, right sides facing, with the tabs between (Figure H). Stitch together, leaving an opening so you can turn the panel right side out. Press well, turning the raw edges of the opening in ½ inch. Sew the opening closed by hand using tiny stitches. Insert the dowel in the loops, and hang on the wall.

QUILTING
From Rags to Riches

Potholders and sleeping bags may seem an unlikely pair, but they are related—and the word quilted tells you how.

Quilting is the process used to hold together layers of fabric by sewing a series of small stitches through the layers. Usually there are three such layers: a top, a bottom (the backing), and a filling. Today, the middle layer usually is a soft, fluffy, thick substance called batting that provides efficient insulation from heat (as in potholders) and cold (as in sleeping bags). It is also useful where extra thickness, body, and padding are needed; long ago quilted garments were worn under, and sometimes substituted for, military armor.

Quilting has long been popular in China, India, Iran, Egypt, and some areas of Africa. The Crusaders took quilting to Europe when they returned from Asia wearing quilted undergarments. Quilting (particularly of bedcovers, which have come to be called quilts because of a long association with this technique) reached the status of a minor art in Europe in the fourteenth century, which had the coldest winters in the modern history of that continent. Portions of one of the oldest surviving quilts, made in Sicily around 1400, are preserved in the Victoria and Albert Museum, London, and in the Bargello in Florence. By the seventeenth century, quilted bedcovers and clothing reached a high level of popularity that lasted for two centuries. Many fine examples date from this period.

From Europe, quilting and quilt designs traveled to North America. The first American quilts were patchwork—patches of fabric sewn together to form one large piece. Many of these quilts were crazy quilts, patchwork with no particular pattern or design, made with fabric scraps of random size, shape, and color. Eventually, individualistic pioneers added design characteristics that reflected their own tastes, needs, and materials. Although patchwork and appliqué (stitching small fabric pieces to a larger piece of background fabric) probably did not originate in America, most of the designs embellishing today's handmade quilts stem from the creativity and ingenuity of American women. American pioneers treasured these techniques because they provided a way of reusing imported printed and colored fabrics that were too expensive (and too pretty) to be used only once. The striking patterns that were devised become even more impressive when you realize that such works arose from piles of rags. American quilters introduced another unique feature by making rows of quilting stitches that followed the contours of the patches or appliqués. Often the contours were repeated in ever-widening waves. This type of quilting is favored in Hawaii, where women have developed a style that is unique (photograph, page 38).

Quilting Today

Quilting with a filling sandwiched between two layers of fabric originally served only a utilitarian purpose—to provide warmth. Despite today's central heating and electric blankets, few experiences are more comforting than snuggling under a cozy, handmade quilt. Two very different quilts, both suitable for snuggling, are described here (pages 46 and 51). An increasing number of contemporary quilters are also using old and new quilting techniques simply for the visual effects they produce. The wall hanging, opposite, and the shoulder bag, page 38 do not need a layer of batting for insulation, but the batting puffs up around the lines of quilting, adding an interesting sculptured effect.

Modern materials allow design freedom never before possible. When quilts were frugally and painstakingly pieced together from recycled fabrics, creating a thing of beauty was a great challenge. Today, the fabric palette is almost limitless. Fabrics made of natural and synthetic fibers are available in a dazzling array of

Barbara Barrick McKie lives in Ledyard, Connecticut with her husband, James, who provides some of the designs that Barbara's flashing needle turns into bed quilts and quilted hangings. Both are scientists whose interest in crafts and design was aroused by a visit to the Guggenheim Museum in New York. After brief forays into batiking and ceramics, Barbara took up quilting in 1971. Intrigued by quilts as decorations, she has been quilting ever since.

In pioneer days, quilting was a social craft. When a woman completed a quilt top, she would stretch it on a quilting frame and invite her neighbors to help make the quilting stitches. Conversation, dancing, eating, and games often accompanied these quilting bees.

Barbara McKie's quilted wall hanging is an example of artistic collaboration. Her husband, James, contributed the design, and Barbara provided the needlework skills needed to turn the design into a finished work. Directions for the quilted and appliquéd hanging begin on page 41.

In this detail of the album quilt, pictured at right, you can clearly read the year in which the quilt was made—1846. For such quilts, a different person made each block and then embroidered her name or signed it in indelible ink. The quilt was then assembled and quilted by one person or by all during a quilting party.

In nineteenth-century America, friends would often gather to make an album quilt such as this one for a bride-to-be, an honored member of the community, or a westward-moving neighbor.

textures and color. Synthetic batting requires less quilting to keep it from bunching up than the fillings used in the past; so it takes less time to make quilting stitches. With a sewing machine (which even hand-quilters use to seam fabric patches together) and polyester batting, making quilted items can be a joy rather than the time-consuming drudgery of yore.

Tools and Materials

Of the three layers in a quilt, it is the decorative top layer that reflects the taste and personality of the quilter. It can be made in a number of ways. Unless you are sewing a plain quilt with a single piece of fabric as a top layer (as the shoulder bag on page 38), or you plan to do a lot of decorative quilting stitches, creating the quilt top will take the most work. Most tops are done in patchwork or appliqué, or a combination of these two. In the heyday of handmade quilts, the women making them considered their time and effort to be the least expensive ingredients. For modern quilters, these are proportionately worth much more. Using ill-suited materials wastes time and effort, since they can ruin the effect you are seeking.

Fabrics

There is nothing wrong with using scraps of fabric from previous sewing projects, if you like them and the way they look together. One way to multiply your scrap pile is to acquire scraps from friends, neighbors, and relatives. But don't use scraps salvaged from worn-out clothing if you want a long-lasting quilt. The type of fabric you choose will depend on the use to be made of the quilted object and whether you intend to launder it or have it dry-cleaned. If you combine fabrics, make sure their laundering requirements, weight, and textures are compatible. Satin does not mix well with corduroy, for example. Calico, broadcloth, chintz, gingham, percale, batiste, and cotton-and-polyester blends (the higher the percentage of cotton to polyester, the better) are usually used for quilting. But you can also use corduroy, wool, chambray, satin, velvet, duck and sailcloth if you quilt by machine or make large quilting stitches by hand. Avoid loosely woven fabrics, polyester fabrics, knits, and acrylics. Since color is not important for the quilt backing, usually an inexpensive fabric such as muslin is used. (Muslin may be used for parts of the top, too.) If you are making a bed quilt by machine, a sheet may be used for the backing. This can be a time-saver, since for most quilts you would otherwise need to piece several lengths of fabric together for the backing. If you are planning to wash your finished quilt, prewash all fabrics as a safety precaution. This will preshrink them to prevent later puckering; it will also release any dye that might run. Press the fabrics before you cut them to remove wrinkles and thus ensure accuracy.

Filler or Interlining

The filler sandwiched between the quilt top and the backing serves two purposes. It adds to the warmth of a bed quilt or quilted garment, and it imparts thickness and body, heightening the sculptural effect of the quilting stitches. In leaner times, rags, yarns, feathers, wool, grasses, even corn husks were used as fillers. When cotton batting became available, it was a great improvement, but nevertheless, it required a large amount of quilting to keep it from lumping. Many intricately designed quilting patterns were born of this necessity. Today's improved cotton batting, which comes in smooth, preshrunk blanket-sized sheets, still tends to lose its resiliency after many washings; so quilting stitches through it should leave no loose pockets larger than 3 by 3 inches. Most quilters now use polyester batting, which comes in large, seamless sheets in sizes that approximate those of blankets. This synthetic batting is light, machine-washable, and quickly dried. A good-quality polyester batt is covered on both sides with a light finish called sizing. This lets you handle the batting like fabric because its fibers will not loosen while you are working with it. Polyester batting allows greater design flexibility, since it doesn't require as much quilting as cotton batting—you can leave unquilted pockets as large as 8 by 8 inches. There are two other types of filler that are not quite substitutes for batting since they are not fluffy. Lightweight cotton blankets come in convenient sizes and are available in retail stores. They must be preshrunk before being used in a quilt that will be washed. Their main advantage is price, but since they are thin and flat, the quilt won't look as luxurious. Cotton flannel, a cotton fabric with a nap, is good to use in baby quilts, since it is very sturdy and can be washed often. It is sold in yard goods stores in widths of 36 to 45 inches.

Barbara McKie is shown at one of her favorite pastimes, sitting with her quilting hoop. The quilt she is working on is done in appliqué, with quilting stitches that follow the contours of the appliqués.

Needles

The lengths of hand-sewing needles are designated by the words *sharps* (1½ inches) and *betweens* (1¼ inches). Both sharps and betweens (No. 7, 8, 9 or 10) can be used for any quilt-making operation. Experiment to see which works better for you. Beginners usually use betweens for quilting and some manufacturers call their betweens quilting needles. Experienced quilters tend to prefer sharps for quilting. For sewing or quilting by machine, the size of the needle should be related to the weight of the fabric being sewn; in most instances, a No. 14 needle will be right.

Thread

Making a quilted item involves two stitching operations—sewing and quilting. For sewing patches together or sewing appliqués to a background fabric, use No. 50 mercerized cotton sewing thread or cotton-wrapped polyester sewing thread; the latter comes in only one weight. To quilt by hand, it is best to use special quilting thread that is silicone-treated to prevent knotting, a common occurrence in hand-stitching. It comes in white and colors. You can also use mercerized cotton or cotton-wrapped polyester sewing thread for quilting by hand or machine. But if you quilt by hand with one of these threads, draw it over a cake of beeswax to make it smoother and stiffer, thus counteracting the tendency to knot and tangle.

Frames and Hoops

If you want to hand-quilt the layers, you can put them on a quilting frame or in a quilting hoop to keep the fabric flat and wrinkle free. A quilting hoop (top, right) is available through large department stores and mail-order companies; it works on the same principle as the embroidery hoop. It consists of two concentric circles or ovals, one fitting inside the other. Both are mounted on a floor stand or a table clamp. You put the quilt, one section at a time, between the rings, and quilt from the center toward the edges. A hoop is especially handy for small articles. A quilting frame, available from mail-order companies, is more efficient for large bed quilts. This advantage can be a disadvantage, however, for a frame is uncomfortably large for the rooms in today's homes. A quilting frame is a large rectangular frame of wood, sometimes with legs. To use the frame, you cover the top and bottom crossbars with heavy fabric, stapled or thumbtacked in place. Opposite ends of the quilt are pinned to each of the crossbar fabric pieces; a turn of the clamps tightens the quilt slightly.

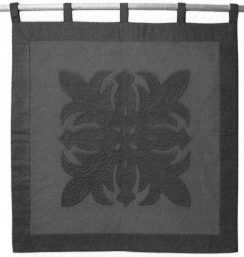

Hawaiian quilt designs, such as this one executed by Barbara McKie, usually suggest the luxurious plant life of the islands. The symmetrical designs are large appliqués, all cut from a single piece of fabric. The technique for cutting an appliqué resembles that used by children to make paper snowflakes; the fabric is folded into eighths, then cut into along the folds to form an eight-pointed design. The quilt is then contour-quilted with lines of stitches around each appliqué.

This large shoulder bag, 12 by 12 by 3 inches, sturdy but lightweight, was designed and made by Barbara McKie. The quilting stitches, done with thread of a color that contrasts with the fabric, produce a sharply delineated design with the three-dimensional effect characteristic of quilted work.

Hoops and frames are optional equipment. Today's quilter is more likely to want something portable to work on. The bed quilts described here accommodate this need. The quilting is done in convenient lap-sized pieces, rather than in one large unit. None of the three quilters represented here uses a quilting frame, and only one, Barbara McKie (page 37) uses a hoop.

Miscellaneous

Dressmaker's shears, especially bent trimmers, are most efficient for cutting out many pieces of fabric from patterns. When you buy a pair, try it on for size and comfort (and if you need a left-handed pair, by all means buy it). A good pair of scissors should cut the fabric without leaving frayed edges, and blades should open and close smoothly. Reserve your best scissors for cutting only fabrics; use another pair for cutting paper and cardboard that will dull the blades. It is not necessary to own a sewing machine to make most quilted articles. However, machine sewing is faster and stronger than hand sewing. A simple straight-stitch machine can be used for all the projects in this entry except the vest (page 50), which is appliquéd with a satin stitch obtainable only with a zigzag machine. For making and transferring patterns to fabric, you will need: pencils; a ruler or yardstick (never use a tape measure which tends to stretch and cause inaccuracies that can be disastrous in quilt making); paper; cardboard; straight pins; masking tape; a thimble (optional); and a stitch ripper for removing mistakes. For patterns, use thin, stiff poster board or cardboard, or thin plastic cut from the flat parts of containers. For marking light-colored fabrics, use a soft lead pencil; for dark fabrics, use a light-colored drawing pencil. The use of a thimble is optional; some people find one indispensable and others a nuisance.

Snow-star shoulder bag   ¢ ⊠ ♣ 🖐

The simple shoulder bag pictured at the left is an example of how effective quilting can be when used on a solid-color fabric. The same star design is quilted three times—on the flap, the front, and the back of the bag; the gussets, bottom, and strap have straight rows of quilting.

Materials

To make the shoulder bag you will need: ⅞ yard of 45-inch-wide cotton duck or other heavy-weight solid-color fabric (for the outside or top layer); ½ yard of 45-inch-wide unbleached muslin or other inexpensive medium-weight fabric (for the backing); ½ yard of 45-inch-wide light-weight or medium-weight solid or printed cotton or cotton-polyester fabric (for the lining); polyester quilt batting (a baby quilt size is more than enough, or use pieces left over from previous projects); a piece of tracing paper at least 6 by 6 inches; 12-by-12-inch square of crisp, heavy paper (for the perforated pattern); masking tape; pencil; yardstick or ruler; painter's powdered chalk; sandpaper; a cotton wad; scissors; sewing and quilting needles; sewing machine (optional); thread for sewing and quilting to contrast with or match the outer fabric.

Making the Pattern

By using powdered chalk with a perforated pattern, you can clearly mark a dark fabric; the chalk rubs off easily when you finish quilting. The quilting pattern, an eight-pointed star with a border, is first transferred to pattern paper. Figure A shows the entire pattern in a reduced size (opposite, top left) and a full-sized drawing of one-eighth of the pattern, which is repeated to obtain the entire design. Trace the full-sized drawing onto tracing paper, making the lines very dark. Fold the pattern paper into eighths as diagramed in Figure B; then open it and tape it to a window or a light box. Slip the one-eighth pattern section between the pattern paper and the glass, matching the dashed lines of the wedge with folds of the pattern paper. Trace over the solid pattern lines with a pencil. Remove the wedge and turn it over, pivoting along line a-b. Moving clockwise, insert it under the next section, again matching dashed lines with folds. Trace the pattern and

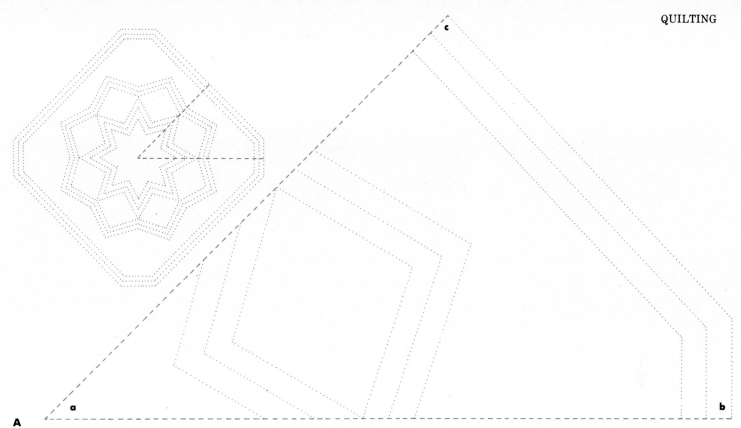

A

Figure A: The entire quilting pattern for the snow-star design is shown in reduced size (top left); the dashed line indicates the one-eighth wedge-shaped section that is drawn full size (above). Place tracing paper over the full-sized drawing and trace all the dashed and dotted lines. Mark the points a, b, and c.

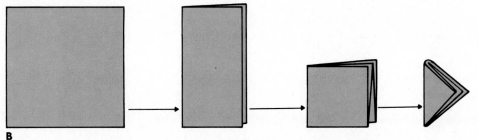

B

Figure B: Fold a 12-inch square of pattern paper into quarters, then diagonally into eighths, forming a wedge shape that corresponds to that of the one-eighth pattern section in Figure B.

remove the wedge. Turn the wedge over and repeat the procedure. Continue until the pattern is complete. Remove the pattern and run it through an unthreaded sewing machine, perforating the solid lines. This may also be done by hand; put the pattern on a folded towel, and use a needle or straight pin to pierce holes about ⅛ inch apart along the lines. Turn the perforated pattern over, and rub the rough side gently with fine sandpaper so the holes will not close while you are using the pattern.

Making the Bag

Use a pencil and ruler to measure, mark, and cut the fabrics and batting into the pieces required. All measurements given include a ½-inch seam allowance. The layers of the front, bottom, back, and flap (the main purse section) are each cut in one piece (Figure C). From the outer fabric, cut one 13-by-40-inch main section, one 12-by-32-inch strap, and two 4-by-13-inch gusset pieces. From both the lining and backing fabrics, cut one 13-by-40-inch main section and two 4-by-13-inch gusset pieces. Since batting is harder to mark than fabric, pin the cut backing pieces to the batting and use them as patterns as you cut one main section and two gusset pieces. Also mark and cut one 3-by-32-inch piece of batting for the strap. With pencil and ruler, mark the dashed lines and dots of Figure C on the backing fabric and on the wrong side of the lining fabric.

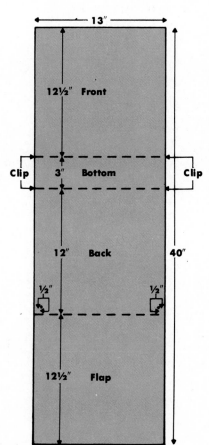

C

Figure C: Follow this diagram of the main purse section when you mark the backing and lining fabrics. The dashed lines indicate folds; the dots mark where the seams will end.

39

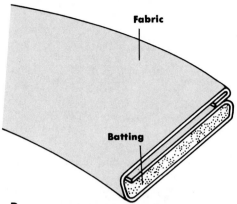

D

Figure D: To make the shoulder-bag strap, wrap the outer fabric around the batting strip, as shown in this cross-section diagram. What will be the underside of the strap has two layers of the outer fabric, one with an edge turned under ¼ inch. Quilting stitches will hold the sandwich together.

1: To transfer the perforated pattern to fabric, rub powdered chalk gently through the perforations, using a wad of cotton.

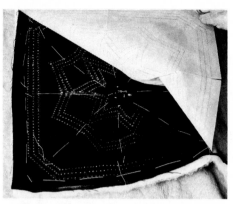

2: If you handle the fabric carefully, the chalk should not dust off accidentally during quilting. But if it does, you can always repeat the process.

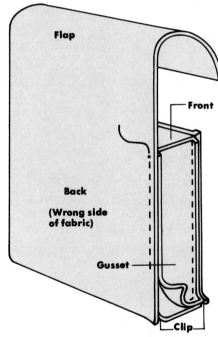

E

Figure E: Right sides facing (the bag is inside out), sew the side gussets to the main purse section, making ½-inch-wide seams. Before stitching, clip ⅜ inch into the seam allowance for the main section. (See also Figure C, page 39).

Basting: When all the pieces have been cut and marked, baste the corresponding backing, batting, and outer fabric pieces together. (The lining is attached after the quilting is done.) To baste the main section together, place the outer fabric, face down, on a flat surface, place the batting on it; then place the backing (marked side up) on top of the batting. Pin the three layers together, making sure edges are even. Then baste them together along the dashed lines, diagonally from corner to corner across each section, and around the outside edges. Pin each of the two sets of three gusset pieces together; baste around the outside edges. To assemble the shoulder strap, encase the batting in the outer fabric piece as shown in Figure D. Pin the layers together, and baste around the outside edges.

Transferring the quilting pattern: Pin the perforated pattern to the outside-fabric flap section, leaving a ½-inch seam allowance at the sides and ends of the flap. Transfer the pattern to the fabric (photograph 1), using powdered chalk and a wad of cotton. This will make lines of dots (photograph 2). After you quilt the flap, you will repeat the pattern transfer process on the front and quilt it, then on the back and quilt it.

Quilting the shoulder bag: The Craftnotes on page 45 tell how to quilt by hand or by machine. Quilt the star design and borders on the flap, front, and back, following the chalked lines in sequence. To quilt the gusset pieces, make 11 parallel rows of stitches along the longest dimension. Place the first row ¼ inch in from the seam line, and space subsequent rows ¼ inch apart. Quilt the bottom as you did the gussets, placing the first row on the marked fold line. Quilt the shoulder strap the same way, but omit the three center rows.

Assembling the bag: To assemble the quilted fabric pieces, first pin the gussets to the main section, right sides facing so the bag is inside out, as shown in Figure E. While you are pinning, clip into the seam allowance of the main section about ⅜ inch at the points indicated in both Figures E and C (page 39). This clipping should match points ½ inch from the corners of the gusset pieces; it allows the fabric to turn and lie properly. Sew the gussets to the front, bottom, and back of the main section; make ½-inch seams, pivoting at the bottom just inside the clip. End the stitching at the dot marked in Figure E and Figure C. This leaves the top ½ inch of the gusset free. Turn the bag right side out and set it aside.

Assemble the lining pieces in the same manner as you assembled the quilted bag, again with right sides facing. However, gradually increase the seam allowance to ¾ inch when you reach the bottom and make the clips (indicated by the dots) ⅝ inch deep. This is to make sure that the lining will fit inside the bag without bunching. Leave the assembled lining inside out.

Press the raw edges of the outer bag ½ inch to the inside; press the raw edges of the lining to the outside. Wrong sides facing, place the lining inside the outer bag. Pin together all around; leave the flap for last, and adjust any excess lining there. Insert the strap ends ½ inch deep between the lining and the outer bag gussets. Then stitch the lining to the outer bag, sewing ⅛ inch in from the turned-under edges. Double- or triple-stitch along the top edges of the gussets to reinforce the joining points.

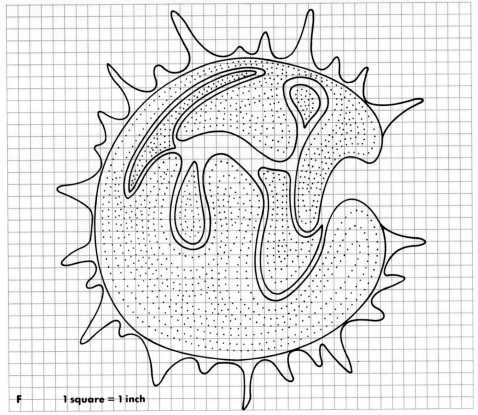

Figure F: To make a full-sized pattern for the quilted hanging, draw a 1-inch grid on plain paper. Square by square, copy the pattern onto the larger grid. The solid lines of the pattern are the cutting lines; include the dotted lines as a quilting guide if you wish to mark them rather than quilting freehand.

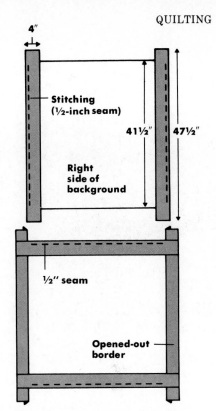

Figure G: Pin the lengthwise borders to the background fabric, right sides facing, with raw edges even and centers matched. Stitch together with ½-inch seams, beginning and ending ½ inch in from the side edges of the background fabric (top). Open out the lengthwise border strips and pin the crosswise borders to the background fabric, right sides facing, again matching the centers and raw edges. Sew the crosswise borders only to the background fabric (not to the lengthwise borders), making ½-inch seams (bottom). Open out the crosswise borders.

Organic wall hanging $ ⌛ 🧍 🧵

The unusual design of the 42-by-45½-inch wall hanging pictured on page 34 was inspired by the microscopic studies of cells. This type of quilting, called contour quilting, was done by hand in concentric rows that parallel the outlines of the green and turquoise appliqués.

Materials
The fabrics used for this hanging are medium-weight cotton or cotton-and-polyester blends. You will need the following amounts of 45-inch-wide fabric: 2⅜ yards of purple; 2½ yards of ivory; ¾ yard of green; and ⅜ yard of turquoise. In addition, you will need: one piece of polyester batting measuring at least 42 by 46½ inches; a 36-by-36-inch square of thin, stiff paper (for enlarging the pattern); pencil; ruler or yardstick; scissors; sewing and quilting needles; sewing machine (optional); straight pins; sewing thread; and quilting thread in black and white. The quilting may be done freehand, without marking any guidelines on the fabric. If you prefer to follow marked lines when quilting, you will need the following materials to transfer the pattern: light-colored painter's chalk, fine sandpaper, and a wad of cotton. To hang the finished piece, you will need a wooden dowel 1 inch in diameter and at least 42 inches long.

First Steps
Prepare the patterns: Enlarge the pattern for the appliqué pieces (Figure F). If you would like to have quilting lines on the fabric rather than quilting freehand, add them to the enlarged pattern, using a pencil of a different color to distinguish them from the cutting lines. Cut the pattern into pieces along the cutting lines so you have one pattern piece for the purple fabric, one for the green, and four for the turquoise. If you have transferred the quilting lines, perforate the pattern by machine-stitching along these lines with an unthreaded machine or pierce holes ⅛ inch apart with a straight pin or needle. Turn the perforated pattern over and smooth the perforations lightly with sandpaper to keep them from closing later.

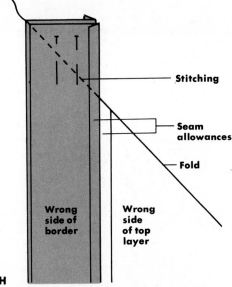

Figure H: To miter a corner, place the adjacent border edges together, right sides facing. (This will make a diagonal fold in the background fabric.) Secure the strips with pins; then stitch them together, as shown, at a 45-degree angle.

41

3: To make a temporary guideline to follow when you do freehand contour quilting, make an indentation in the fabric with the needle point.

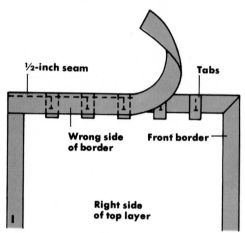

Figure I: Pin the folded tabs to the top front border, spacing them evenly, with the middle tab at the center. Pin the back border strips to the corresponding front border strips, right sides facing, sandwiching the tabs between along the top. Sew together on all outer edges, making ½-inch seams and catching the tabs in the top seam.

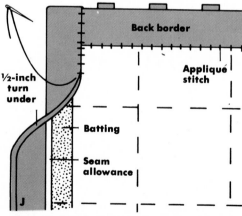

Figure J: Fold the back borders to the back, turn the unstitched raw edges under ½ inch, and press. Then sew the folded edges to the backing fabric.

Cut the fabric: Pin the individual pattern pieces to fabric of the right color, with grid lines parallel to the grain (lengthwise and crosswise threads) of the fabric. Cut out the appliqués ¼ inch outside the edge of the patterns to provide a turn-under allowance. In addition to the appliqués, cut the following: from the ivory fabric, cut two 37-by-41½-inch pieces (for the background and the backing); from the purple fabric, cut four 4-by-47½-inch strips, four 4-by-43-inch strips (for the borders), and one 3-by-45-inch strip (for the hanging tabs).

Appliquéing

Start by pinning the green appliqué to the center of the background fabric. Next pin the adjacent purple piece in place, extending it under the green edge by ½ inch to allow for the ¼ inch of green that will be turned under. (The outer edge of the green piece is appliquéd on top of the inner edge of the purple piece, which is not sewn separately.) Finally, pin the turquoise pieces in place. Baste all pieces carefully ½ to ¾ inch in from the raw edges. Make sure each piece lies smooth and flat. Following the directions in the Craftnotes on page 44, appliqué the pieces in this order: first the outer purple edge, then the outer green edge over the raw inner purple edge, then the inner green edges, and finally the turquoise edges.

Assembling and Quilting

Assemble the top layer first. Measure and mark the center points of two long border strips, two short border strips, and the edges of the background fabric. Right sides facing, stitch these borders to the background fabric (Figure G, page 41). To miter the corners where the borders meet, fold the background fabric diagonally at the corner, matching the unstitched ends of adjacent border strips. Stitch together diagonally as shown in Figure H, page 41. Repeat the procedure on the three remaining corners. The top layer is now completely assembled.

Put the top layer, right side down, on a flat surface and tape it there to keep it from shifting. Place the piece of batting on top of the taped-down fabric; pin batting and fabric together around the edges, keeping the batting as smooth as possible. Remove the tape and carefully trim the batting to the same size as the top layer. Place the backing piece of fabric on top of the batting, with an equal margin of batting extending all around. Baste all three layers together, beginning at the center and stitching outward in a sunburst pattern (page 45). Remove all pins.

The next step is quilting. If you wish, transfer the quilting lines to the fabric pieces using painter's chalk and a wad of cotton (photographs 1 and 2, page 40). Use white thread to quilt around the outside of all appliqués, as close to the turned-under edge as possible. If you have marked them, quilt subsequent rows following the dotted lines. (White thread is used for the turquoise appliqués, black thread for the green.) If you have decided to do the quilting freehand, work each subsequent row within each appliqué as an echo of the shape of the outside edge. Keep the rows smoothly curved; as a guide, score the fabric an inch or two ahead with the point of the needle (photograph 3). Complete stitching each row before going on to the next. Most rows should be about ½ inch apart, but you can vary the spacing from ¼ to 1 inch in order to accommodate the narrower and wider areas of the appliqués.

Finishing

To make the hanging tabs, fold the 3-by-45-inch strip of fabric in half lengthwise, right side inside. Stitch along the lengthwise edge, making a ¼-inch seam. Turn the strip right side out, and press it with an iron so the seam lies along one edge. Cut the strip into five 9-inch tabs.

Place the quilted hanging, right side up, on a flat surface. Fold the tabs in half crosswise, and spacing them evenly, pin them across the top of the hanging, raw edges even with the top edge of the border. Right sides facing, pin the four remaining border strips to the four front borders, raw edges matching. Sew each strip in place with a ½-inch seam (Figure I). Turn the back border strips to the back, pressing under ½-inch seam allowances as shown in Figure J. (It is not necessary to miter the corners on the back.) With tiny stitches, sew the folded-under edges to the back of the hanging by hand. Remove the pins and basting stitches. Slip a dowel through the tabs, and use two nails to suspend the hanging from the wall.

CRAFTNOTES: TRADITIONAL QUILTING PATTERNS

The treasury of traditional quilting patterns, some of which are shown here, is virtually limitless. But all patterns are basically a series of curved or straight lines, and even the most elaborate design can be copied with the aid of a ruler and a compass or curved objects you can trace, such as cups, saucers, or jar lids. The selection and arrangement of a pattern hinge on the quilter's skill and taste, the time available, and the shape of the fabric patches or appliques in the quilt top. Although the traditional patterns for quilting stitches have always served the practical purpose of holding the layers together, they have come to be used as a decorative element as well.

Patchwork

Patchwork, the method of sewing small patches of fabric together to form a larger piece, is a technique in which accuracy plays an important part. The fabric patches—and the patterns, or templates, from which they are cut—must be marked and cut carefully so they will fit together with precision. In addition, as many pattern edges as possible should be placed along the straight grain (lengthwise and crosswise threads) of the fabric. Patches cut on the bias tend to stretch and should be avoided. Cut patterns for patchwork from thin, stiff cardboard because you will trace them several times. If you will be cutting a large number of fabric patches of one shape, make several identical patterns. Discard worn patterns when their edges become frayed from frequent tracings. Durable patterns for small shapes can be cut from thin plastic (use the flat parts of containers).

Marking, cutting, and machine stitching:

Make sure that all patterns have a uniform seam allowance added on all sides and that your pencil point and scissors are sharp. Many quilters insist that patches should be marked and cut individually to ensure accuracy. To mark an individual patch, place the pattern on the wrong side of the fabric, and trace around it with a pencil. Use a dark pencil for light-colored fabrics, a light-colored pencil (not chalk—the line it makes is too wide) for dark fabrics. Carefully cut out the patch, following the marked line. Other quilters maintain that cutting patches individually is unnecessary, except when you are working with heavy fabrics such as corduroy or velvet. As a time-saver and to add stability to lighter weight fabrics, you can cut several patches of the same shape at one time. Triple or quadruple the fabric and pin or baste the layers together temporarily. Then trace the pattern on the top layer only, and cut all layers simultaneously. Try both methods with different fabrics, and use the one that works better for you.

When you sew the patches, pin or baste them together, right sides facing. Make sure the raw edges of the sides to be seamed are even. Stitch the seam, using the markings on your sewing machine's needle plate or the edge of the presser foot to maintain a uniform seam allowance. After each patchwork unit is sewn together, press the seams to one side (open seams weaken the construction). If you are combining light and dark fabric, press the seam to the dark side so it will not show through.

Marking, cutting, and hand stitching: Since so many seams are involved, most people use a sewing machine to do patchwork. If you sew by hand, the procedures are generally the same except that you do not have a needle plate or presser foot to measure the seam allowance. Therefore, make patterns actual size, without a seam allowance. When you trace the pattern on the fabric, you will mark the seam line instead of the cutting line. Cut out the patch outside this seam line, with a seam allowance around. When you sew the patches together, match up the marked seam line.

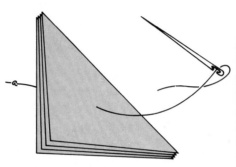

Handling quantities of patches: Once they are cut, a good way to keep a large number of patches orderly is to group them according to shape and color. Then string each group together by running a thread, knotted at one end, through the centers (above). Lift off each piece as it is needed.

Appliqué

An appliqué is a piece of fabric that is sewn onto a larger piece of background fabric. Appliqués sewn on by hand have narrow turned-under edges; so they should be cut on the bias (cross grain) of the fabric to make it easier to turn under any curved edges.

Right side up, pin the appliqué to the right side of the background fabric, smoothing it down as you pin. Then baste all around, ½ to ¾ inch in from the raw edges.

Begin with a knot at the end of the thread. Using the tip of the needle as a tool, smoothly turn the raw edge of the appliqué under 3/16 to ¼ inch (top right). With the needle, smooth and crease the turned-under edge (middle right). All-cotton fabric creases the best.

Hold the turned-under edge with your thumb just ahead of where you will be stitching. The stitch used to appliqué is a tiny, almost invisible stitch. To begin, bring the needle and thread through to the right side of the fabric, catching a few threads of the appliqué in the process. Then insert the needle into the background fabric and bring it up at an angle, ⅛ inch away or less from the last stitch (bottom right). On the right side the visible stitches are tiny and perpendicular to the edge of the appliqué. On the wrong side they are larger and diagonal.

Sharp inside and outside corners are a challenge, and it takes practice to make them neatly.

For inside corners (or concave curves), turn the edge under using the tip of the needle as usual, but run the needle around the corner several times to get the edge to stay under. Hold the turned-under edge with your thumb a bit closer to the stitches than usual. Then take several small appliqué stitches close together to keep the raw edge from popping out.

For sharp outside corners, stitch as usual to within ⅛ inch of the point of the corner. Then take two stitches in the same place at the point. Push under the raw edge of the adjacent side, with the needle tip, and make the next stitch ⅛ inch away or less.

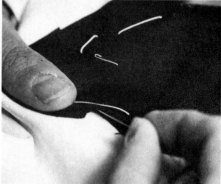

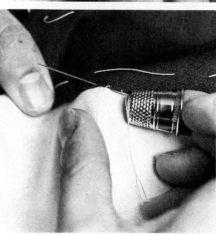

PATCHWORK, APPLIQUE, AND QUILTING

Quilting

Basting: Before you begin to quilt either by hand or machine, you should baste together the top, batting, and bottom layers so they do not shift during the quilting process. Make sure both bottom and top fabric layers have been prewashed and pressed.

Put the quilt backing, wrong side up, on a flat surface. Place the batting on top of the backing; then smooth the top layer in place. The photograph above shows these three layers. Pin the three layers together.

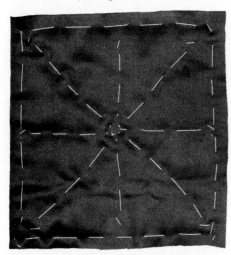

Next, baste the layers together with rows of long basting stitches. Begin each row at the center of the quilt, and stitch out to the corners and sides, making a sunburst pattern (above). Then baste around the edges. As you baste, smooth the layers and check frequently to make sure the stitches penetrate all three layers.

Quilting by hand: The quilting stitch is a running stitch—small, straight stitches in a row. You should make between five and twelve stitches per inch; the number will vary from person to person and according to the thickness of the quilt. Regardless of size, it is important that the stitches be of even length. Always start in the center of the section being worked on, and take several stitches before pulling the needle and thread through.

To quilt by hand, thread a quilting needle with a single 15-inch-long strand of quilting thread or sewing thread that has been pulled over a cake of beeswax. Gather the three-layered sandwich in your non-stitching hand, or, if you are using a frame or hoop, place your free hand beneath it.

To begin, insert the needle in the quilt top and batting about 1 inch from where you plan to make the first stitch. Bring the needle up where the first stitch will start, leaving a short tail of thread on the surface. From underneath, put your index finger against the line to be quilted. You can protect the finger from the needle point with adhesive tape. Make several running stitches in the direction opposite to the one in which you will be quilting, penetrating all three layers (above).

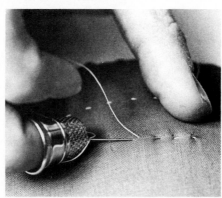

Then double back, making stitches in the right direction in exactly the same places as the first series was made (above). Having thus an-

chored the thread, snip off the tail close to the surface and continue stitching. When you reach the end of the thread or the end of the row, anchor the thread again the same way.

Another way to begin and end a length of thread is with a knot. When you begin a row, make a small knot at the end of the thread. Insert the needle from the back, and give the thread a tug from the front, forcing the knot through the bottom layer and embedding it in the batting. To end the thread, quilt to within one stitch of the end of the row; then make a small knot in the thread, close to the surface. Make the last stitch, and penetrating only the top layer and part of the batting, bring the needle up about an inch from the last stitch. Give the thread a tug, burying the knot in the batting; then cut the thread off close to the surface of the quilt.

Quilting by machine: If you quilt by machine, you will do so at home; so the portability of the project is reduced. In addition, many people find it hard to sew a smooth curve; even mass-produced quilts made by experienced sewers often have uneven curves. But if you do block-by-block quilting (page 47), the smaller units are more maneuverable than a whole quilt.

To quilt by machine, set the stitch length at 6 to 10 stitches per inch and use a No. 14 needle. Practice quilting on a test block of the same batting and fabrics that will be used in the quilt. Follow your sewing-machine manual in making adjustments in the stitch length, the thread tension, or the pressure on the presser foot, so the quilting thread will go smoothly and evenly through the thickness of the quilt. For straight-line quilting, you will find a quilting foot helpful. This attachment acts as a guide in spacing parallel rows of quilting stitches.

When you begin to quilt, start at the center and quilt outward, as in hand quilting. Always start with a full bobbin so you do not run out of thread in the middle of a row. When the quilting is finished, pull all of the ends of top thread to the back and knot them with bobbin thread ends. Trim the ends close to the knot.

Gladys Boalt's love for quilts began when her mother gave her a book about quilting. Her first quilt took her eight years to complete, but after she discovered block-by-block quilting, she became engrossed in the craft. Ms. Boalt, who studied illustration and advertising at Pratt Institute, exhibits her work at fairs, schools, and libraries, and makes quilted pillows and hangings for the Gazebo, a crafts boutique. She conducts once-a-week quilting bees at her home in Stormville, New York, and teaches quilting at nearby art centers.

A quilt with an Early American flavor decorates the bed of a colonial-style bedroom. Traditional patterns such as this Dresden-plate design add a note of warmth and coziness. Gladys Boalt made this 66-by-85-inch quilt to fit a three-quarter-sized bed, but you can adapt the design to fit a bed of any size.

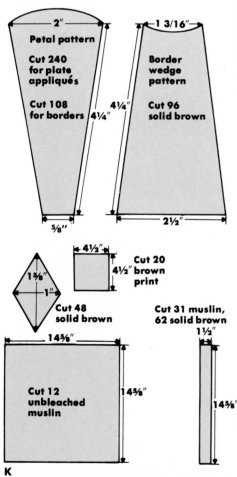

Petal pattern

2″

Cut 240 for plate appliqués

Cut 108 for borders

4¼″ 4¼″

⅝″

Border wedge pattern

1 3/16″

Cut 96 solid brown

2½″

1⅝″ 1″

Cut 48 solid brown

4½″

Cut 20 4½″ brown print

Cut 31 muslin, 62 solid brown

1½″

14⅝″

Cut 12 unbleached muslin

14⅝″

14⅝″

K

Figure K: Follow these measurements as you use a pencil and ruler to draw these pattern outlines on cardboard. But before cutting, add a 3/16-inch seam allowance on all sides, except for the top and bottom edges of the petals and wedges.

Dresden-plate quilt

The design for the Dresden-plate quilt pictured above, also known as the aster or the friendship ring, combines quilting with patchwork and appliqué to form the quilt top. Most antique Dresden-plate quilts are worked in pastel colors, but the design fits a modern decor when bright or dark-and-light colors are used. The pattern was popular in colonial times when women traded fabric scraps. An old Dresden-plate quilt might include 500 to 1,000 different fabric prints, with no two petals alike. For your quilt, you might choose, say, 20 prints, a different one for each of the 20 petals in each plate, or you might prefer to alternate fewer fabrics.

The 66-by-85-inch bedspread-type quilt shown here fits a three-quarter-sized bed and is made from 12 appliquéd squares joined with decorative strips and edged with a scalloped border. To adapt the design for beds of other sizes, add or subtract squares or strips as necessary. On page 51 are directions for measuring a bed. With these measurements in hand, juggle the number of squares and strips until you hit upon the combination that will give you the size you need. Each appliquéd block, after seaming, is approximately 14½ inches square. Finished, each set of three joining strips is approximately 4½ inches wide. The finished width of the border is 4 inches. But in determining how many strips and blocks you need to fit your bed, you must allow for a 1-inch shrinkage of each block during the quilting process; that is, it will end up being 13½ inches square. The strips too will shrink, but only slightly. By omitting the joining strips and corner squares, sewing together 24 squares in four rows of six, and then adding the scalloped border, a 62-by-89-inch bedspread, to fit a twin-sized bed, could be made. A coverlet to fit a full-sized bed would require 25 squares arranged in five rows of five, plus connecting strips, corner squares, and a border. Work out the combination on paper, and refer to the sketch later to determine the number of pieces to cut from each fabric. Adjust the amounts of fabric and batting needed, and adapt the directions that follow to conform to the measurements you need.

Materials

To make the quilt in the size shown you will need the following amounts of 45-inch-wide cotton or cotton-and-polyester fabric: 6 yards of unbleached muslin (for appliquéd squares and joining strips); 3 yards—you may use scraps from previous projects—of assorted brown prints (for plate petals and border); ½ yard of dark brown calico print (for corner squares); 2 yards of solid dark brown (for strips and border); 6 yards of a lightweight cotton fabric, such as batiste, in a small print (for the backing). You will also need a roll of double-bed-sized polyester quilt batting; tracing paper; pencil; ruler; carbon paper; scissors; thin, stiff cardboard (for patterns); straight pins; iron; quilting and sewing needles; quilting and sewing thread, or sewing thread and a cake of beeswax. For the binding, you need 10 yards of 1-inch-wide bias tape (or you can make your own from ¾ yard of fabric—see page 1704).

Block-by-Block Quilting

Although making a quilt may seem a formidable task, this particular pattern is quite easy to do. With a block-by-block quilting technique, an entire block can be assembled and quilted in a single evening.

The Dresden-plate design is formed by sewing petals together into a plate shape, then appliquéing the plate onto a plain square. Edging strips are sewn onto the appliquéd square; then batting and backing fabric are added, so each block is a tiny quilt. These are quilted separately, then joined by stitching the front layers of the blocks together by machine. The edges of the backs of the blocks are then turned under and stitched by hand. In the days when it was the practice to spread out a whole quilt or put it in a frame, blocks were sewn together to form a single large top layer. Then batting and backing fabric of the same size were added, and the quilting was done on one large piece. Block-by-block quilting is more convenient. It makes hoops and frames unnecessary, since each block can be held easily. This makes the project portable. Also, when a curved line is being quilted, the small block can be shifted around so you are always working in a comfortable direction (usually toward you).

Making the Blocks

Using the dimensions in Figure K, measure and draw the patterns directly on cardboard. Then add a 3/16-inch seam allowance on each side. Cut out the patterns along the outer lines. Edges will become worn from repeated tracings; so make several patterns of the petal, diamond, and border pieces—those that will be traced most frequently.

Figure K also gives the number of pieces of fabric to cut in each color. For how to mark and cut the pieces, refer to the Craftnotes on page 44.

When all the pieces have been cut, you are ready to begin sewing them together to form the 12 blocks. Unless otherwise indicated, all pieces are sewn together with right sides facing, making 3/16-inch seams. Press all seams to one side after each step; pressing seams open weakens the construction. For each block, make one plate by stitching 20 petal-shaped pieces together along their long sides, forming a ring. When the plate is completed, press all the seams to one side and then center the plate on a 15-inch muslin square. To center the plate appliqué, fold the square into quarters and lightly crease the folds at the center. Unfold the square and use the creases as a guide in placing the plate. Pin the appliqué, right side up, to the square; insert a pin through each petal and smooth the fabric as you pin. Following the Craftnotes on page 44, sew the appliqué onto the muslin square using appliqué stitches. Turn under the 3/16-inch seam allowance, and sew first around the inner and then the outer edges of the appliqué.

After the plate design has been appliquéd, pin four diamonds to the center of the plate, again using the creases as a guide. Then appliqué the diamonds to the muslin as you did the plates.

The feather-edged star design that Gladys Boalt used for a pillow dates back to the early 1800's and is considered one of the most difficult patterns, combining patchwork, appliqué, and quilting.

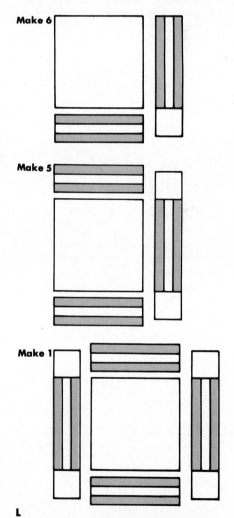

Make 6

Make 5

Make 1

L
Figure L: To make the twelve blocks required, sew the plain strip units to the small muslin squares first, in the positions indicated. Press the seams to one side; then add the strip-and-square units, following the diagrams to obtain the required number of each type of block.

47

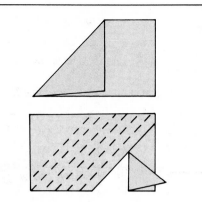

Bias strips

Bias strips of fabric, cut at a 45-degree angle across the grain of the fabric, have more stretch and give than strips cut on the straight grain; they are used to bind and finish the raw edges of a quilt. They are also used to make piping. You can purchase bias tape in widths from ½ to 1½ inches, and in solid colors as well as some prints. But for a perfect match and a custom look, make your own bias tape by piecing together strips of fabric that you have cut.

To make bias tape, fold one corner of a rectangle or square of fabric on the bias (above, top). Crease the fold.

Using the crease as a guide, mark the fabric with parallel lines the desired width of the bias strips. Cut along the marked lines (above).

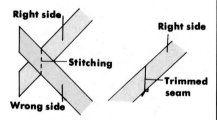

To sew the strips together to form one long strip of the required length, place the ends together, right sides facing (above, left). Then stitch along the straight grain.

When the strips are opened up, the seam will appear diagonal (above, right). Trim the seam to about ¼ inch and press it open to avoid extra bulk.

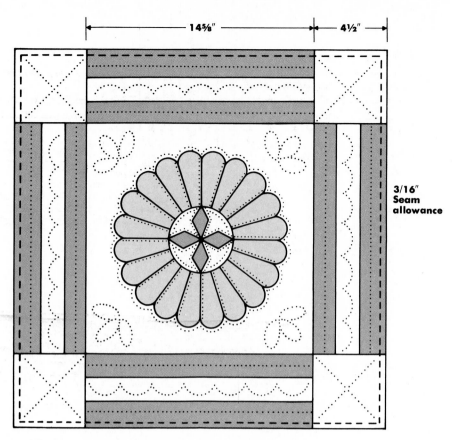

M

Figure M: For each block, quilt around the appliqués and patches as close to the seams as you can. When quilting the Xs in the corner squares, stop stitching ½ inch in from the edges so the seam allowance is left open; the last few quilting stitches can be made after seaming.

The next step is to add the joining strips and corner squares to the appliquéd muslin squares. It may seem logical to sew the strips to the sides of the muslin squares and then add the corner squares. However, this forces you to sew the corner squares into the 90-degree angle formed by the joining strips. To do this, you have to make a sharp turn exactly at the point where the seams of the strips meet—a tedious operation if you do it for all 20 corner squares, especially if you are using a sewing machine. To eliminate this, first sew the joining strips together in units of three, with one muslin strip between the brown ones. Then sew corner squares to one or both ends of some of the units. If you are making a 12-block quilt, you will have 31 strip assemblies; sew a corner square onto one end of six of these and onto both ends of seven. Finally, sew the strip units and then the strip-and-square units onto the muslin square as shown in Figure L on page 47. If you are making a quilt that is not the size shown, use Figures L and N as guides as you calculate how many strip units and strip-and-square units you will need to make the number of blocks required. (Additional blocks for larger quilts are made by repeating those in the middle vertical and horizontal rows in Figure N.)

Quilting the Blocks

Place a finished block, face down, on a flat surface. Cut a piece of batting the size of the block and place it on top. Then cut a piece of backing fabric 1 inch larger than the block on each side. (For example, if you have a 19-inch square block, make the backing 21 inches square.) Pin and baste the three layers together, smoothing out any wrinkles. Use Figure M as a guide in determining where to place the lines of quilting; draw the leaves and scallops on the fabric with a pencil. The other lines may also be drawn, but if you use the seam lines as a guide, they can easily be quilted freehand. Refer to the Craftnotes on page 45 for quilting directions, and quilt each block, working your way out from the center toward the edges. Do not quilt into the seam allowance. When all the blocks have been quilted, sew them together (Figure N) by seaming the front layers only. To prevent the batting and backing layers from catching in the seam, pin them out of the way. Place the blocks to be seamed together, right sides facing, and sew with a 3/16-inch seam.

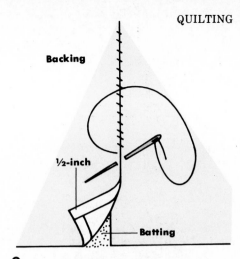

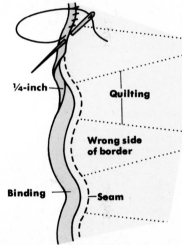

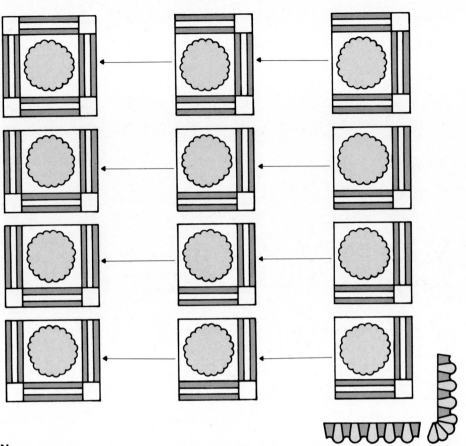

O

Figure O: Since each block was quilted separately, you will need to finish the backing seams between blocks. Overlap adjacent backing edges, folding the top edge under ½ inch. Sew with a tiny hem stitch as shown, catching only the underlayer of backing, not the filling.

P

Figure P: To finish the outer edges of the quilt, sew bias tape to the right side of the border edge, right sides facing. Then turn the tape to the back and fold the raw tape edge under ¼ inch. Sew the tape down by hand with small stitches.

N

Figure N: To put the quilted blocks together, first sew them into vertical rows of four; then sew these three vertical rows together. When you have made and quilted the four border strips, sew on the top and bottom strips first; then add the side strips.

The Border

The border is assembled in four strips, for the top, the bottom, and each side. First, the front of each strip is pieced together, then batting and backing are added. The strips are then quilted and sewn in place as were the blocks. For the front of the top and bottom border strips, sew 20 print-fabric petals together, alternating with 21 of the solid-color border petals. The top layer of each side border strip is made with 26 print petals alternating with 27 solid petals. To each end of each side border strip, add four print petals whose narrow ends have been trimmed to a width of ⅜ inch (Figure N). This forms a fan-shaped curved corner.

Pin and baste the batting and backing to each border strip as for the blocks. Then quilt each strip close to the seams of each petal (remember to quilt only to within ½ inch of the raw edges to allow for seams; put in the last few stitches after the quilt has been assembled).

Again referring to Figure N, stitch the fronts of the border strips to the block fronts, pinning the batting and lining back out of the way.

Finishing

To finish the backing, trim away excess batting so adjacent edges fit together smoothly. Overlap the edges of the backing, turning the top edge under ½ inch; hand sew the folded edge down, forming a felled seam (Figure O). Finish all edges in this way except the outside one, which is finished with a binding.

For the binding, purchase 1-inch-wide bias tape or make your own following the directions opposite. (Approximately 10 yards of tape were needed to finish the edges of the quilt shown.) Right sides facing, pin the bias tape around the scalloped perimeter of the quilt, raw edges even. Overlap the ends where they meet, turning the edge of the top end under ¼ inch. Sew the tape to the quilt, making a 3/16- to ¼-inch seam. Then fold the tape to the wrong side of the quilt (Figure P) and hand-sew the edge to the quilt back, thus encasing the raw edges of the quilt.

Karen Katz is a fabric artist who creates clothes, quilts, and quilted tapestries for individuals and for commercial reproduction. For Ms. Katz, who directs the crafts department at Marymount College in New York, creating a design and watching it develop is an exciting experience. The projects here show she has a love for luxurious fabrics, rich color, and fanciful subject matter.

Cloudy-day vest and skirt $ ◩ 👤 ⚗

Karen Katz used one of her favorite materials—satin—to add clouds and raindrops to an ordinary pattern, giving this vest flash and originality. A matching skirt with a cloud pocket completes the outfit.

For the outfit pictured, colors both vivid and pastel were used to make satin clouds that were then machine-appliquéd to a satin vest and skirt made from a purchased dressmaker's pattern. The raveled edges that are so often visible in machine-stitched appliqués can be eliminated with the glue technique described here.

Materials
To make the vest, purchase a pattern for a simple lined vest. Referring to the pattern envelope for the amounts of fabric needed, use black satin for the outside fabric; prequilted fabric for the filling (you will need the same amount as you did of the outer fabric; prequilting eliminates the need of a backing fabric); and lining fabric such as taffeta or satin. Prequilted fabric can also be used in side insets if the pattern calls for them, as in the vest pictured. For the appliqués you will need small amounts of satin in various colors that will contrast with the background fabric. Additional tools and materials needed are: a zigzag sewing machine; sewing thread in several colors similar to, but not necessarily the same as, the appliques; paper; pencil; ruler; scissors; straight pins; sewing needle; white glue; a dish for mixing the glue with water; a small pointed paintbrush; and tailor's chalk.

Making the Vest
Following the pattern directions, cut the outer fabric, the prequilted fabric, and the lining pieces. Cut the prequilted pieces from the outer fabric pattern pieces and eliminate any interfacing. Pin the outside pieces to the corresponding prequilted pieces, wrong sides facing. Baste each section together and set aside.

Enlarge the cloud designs (Figure Q), or draw your own. Cut out the patterns, and with a light colored pencil, transfer the outlines to the wrong side of the satin fabric. Then use this technique to keep edges from raveling after they are cut. Mix one part of water with three parts of white glue. Apply the diluted glue in ⅛-inch-wide lines inside the marked edges of the appliqués, letting the glue extend just over the lines. Let the glue dry thoroughly; then cut out the appliqués. The glue will hold the cut fabric threads in place.

Pin the cloud appliqués to the outer vest pieces. Arrange them as you like, singly or overlapping in groups. When you are satisfied with the design, baste the pieces in place. Set the sewing machine to a zigzag satin stitch, wide enough to cover the glued edge of the appliqués. Sew all around the edge of each cloud, through the outer fabric and the prequilted batting. When all the clouds are sewn down, you may want to add a few machine-embroidered raindrops (as on the back of the vest pictured). Next, use tailor's chalk to draw additional quilting lines across each section. The lines should echo the shapes of the clouds. Using the variously colored threads, sew along the quilting lines with a narrow zigzag stitch.

Using a long straight machine stitch, baste all around the edges of each outer vest section close to the seam line, within the seam allowance. Trim off the excess batting. Assemble and finish the vest and lining, following the pattern directions.

The Pocket

To make a patch pocket like the one pictured on the black satin skirt, cut one large cloud from satin. (Or cut two clouds, overlap them, and sew them together with a zigzag stitch along the overlapping edge; trim away any excess on the wrong side.) Cut a cloud of prequilted fabric the same size for the filling and lining of the pocket. Place the satin and the prequilted clouds together, right sides facing. Using a straight stitch, sew them together all around; make ¼-inch seams and leave a small opening for turning. Turn the cloud right side out. Fold the raw edges of the opening ¼ inch to the inside and press. Stitch this opening closed as near the edge as possible. This may be done by machine, since this stitching will be concealed with the satin stitch. Cut a small cloud appliqué from a contrasting color, coating the edges with diluted glue as for the vest appliqués. Appliqué the small cloud to the pocket, using a satin stitch of the same width as for the vest.

To finish, sew a decorative satin stitch along the edge of the top half of the pocket. Pin the pocket in place on the garment. Beginning and ending where the decorative satin stitching left off, sew the bottom edge of the pocket to the garment using the same satin stitch.

Rainbow-cloud quilt $ ⧗ ⚒

The rainbow-cloud quilt, pictured on page 52, is easily adapted to many sizes and goes together quickly. It is almost entirely stitched by machine, using a variation of the block-by-block quilting method described on page 47. The clouds, cut from rainbow-striped patchwork fabric, are backed with cloud-shaped pieces of plain fabric to form little pillows, then are sewn onto individual fabric blocks in such a way that the clouds puff up. The quilt shown measures approximately 76 inches square when finished and fits a double bed. To alter the size, add or subtract blocks (each measures 11 inches square when finished), and vary the width of the border strips. (For how to measure a bed for a quilt, see right.) Adjust the fabric requirements and the directions accordingly.

Materials

To make the 76-inch-square quilt, you will need the following amounts of 45-inch-wide cotton, satin, or taffeta fabric: about ½ yard each of eight different colors (for the squares); about ½ yard each of six different colors (for the clouds); 2¾ yards of a dark color for the borders; 6¾ yards of muslin or other inexpensive lightweight fabric (for backing the squares, borders, and clouds); and 4 yards of a color that complements the borders (for the lining). In addition, you will need: a double-bed-sized roll of batting; sewing thread; embroidery thread; sewing needle; sewing machine; large-eyed embroidery needle; cardboard for the patterns; pencil; ruler; bulldog clip; straight pins.

The Clouds

The first step is to make the pillowlike clouds. To begin, make the striped patchwork fabric from which the clouds will be cut. To do this, cut the six fabrics into strips measuring 45 inches long and about 2 inches wide. Sew the strips together with ¼-inch seams, right sides facing, forming a 45-inch-wide piece of striped fabric. For contrast, alternate light-colored stripes with dark ones. Press the seams to one side, preferably toward the darker fabric so the seam allowance does not show through. Enlarge the cloud pattern (Figure R, page 53) and cut it out of cardboard. Using the pattern, cut out 13 striped clouds (the pattern includes a ¼-inch seam allowance). To save time you can cut several clouds simultaneously. First cut the fabric into thirteen 11-by-12-inch rectangles. Place several rectangles

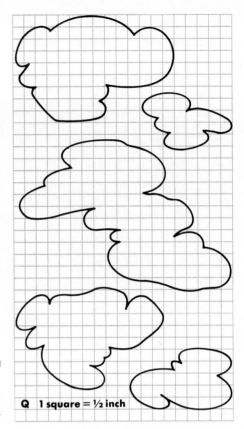

Q   **1 square = ½ inch**

Figure Q: Enlarge these cloud patterns by copying them, one square at a time, on paper that you have ruled into ½-inch squares.

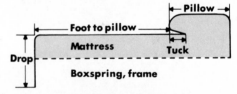

Measuring a bed for a quilt

To measure any bed for a quilt, first measure the width and length of the top of the mattress. The standard twin-bed size is 39 by 75 inches; three-quarter-bed size is 48 by 75 inches; double-bed size is 54 by 75 inches.

To the width and the length of the mattress must be added the drop—that part of the quilt that will hang over the sides and the foot of the bed. The drop may cover just the mattress and box spring, or it may extend to the floor. To make a decorative bedspread-type quilt that will be tucked under the pillow, add 8 inches to the length.

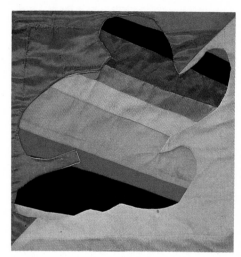

This detail of the rainbow-cloud quilt, pictured at right, shows how the pillowlike clouds puff up.

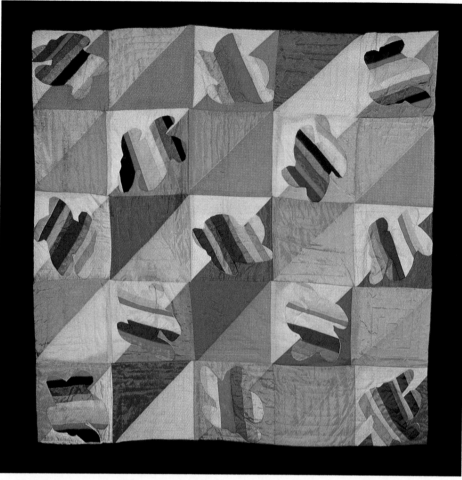

A quilt embellished with puffed-up rainbow-striped cloud appliqués was made using Karen Katz's special techniques. Block-by-block quilting makes the project relatively easy; machine stitching makes the work go fast.

in a pile with the pattern on top; hold them all together at one edge with a bulldog clip. Then cut through the several fabric layers, following the pattern edge. Handle the fabric clouds carefully after you have cut through the seams, since the thread will be unknotted.

Next, cut 13 clouds from muslin, and use one to back each striped cloud by sewing the two together, right sides facing. Make ¼-inch seams and leave a small opening for turning. Turn the cloud right side out and hand sew the opening closed with tiny stitches. You now have 13 little cloud pillows; set them aside until later.

The Squares

Cut a 12-inch square pattern from cardboard. Cut out 25 squares of fabric—about three of each color. Cut each fabric square in half diagonally, forming triangles. Spread the triangles on the floor and mix pieces of different colors to make two-colored squares. As you combine the triangles into five rows of five squares, try to form a dark-light pattern, such as the pattern of diagonal stripes evident in the photograph above. Sew the triangles back together in pairs, forming 25 squares. To do this, place the triangles together, right sides facing, and make a ¼-inch seam. Press the seam to one side, toward the darker-colored triangle.

Quilting

Arrange five rows of five squares. Every other square will have a cloud sewn onto it (see photograph above). Using pencil and ruler, mark quilting lines on the 12 squares that will remain cloudless as follows: Mark a 2-inch square at the center; then make three more concentric squares spaced about 1 inch apart. To mark the

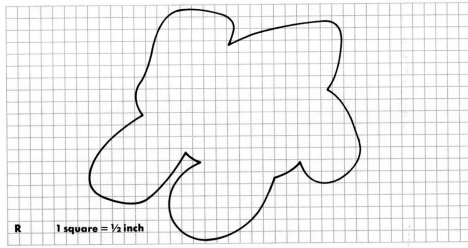

Figure R: To enlarge the cloud pattern for the rainbow-cloud quilt, copy it—one square at a time—on paper that you have ruled in ½-inch squares.

R   1 square = ½ inch

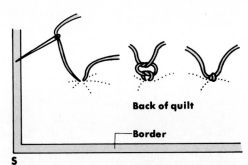

Back of quilt

Border

S

Figure S: To make a tuft in a quilt, have the lining side of the quilt face up and insert the needle from front to back, penetrating all layers. Taking a tiny stitch, reinsert the needle, and come up about ⅛ inch away from the point of entry. Tie the ends on the back of the quilt, using the square knot shown (right over left, then left over right). Trim the ends to 1 inch.

remaining 13 squares (those that will have clouds sewn on them) draw quilting lines that correspond only to the two outer quilting lines of the cloudless squares (about 2 inches and 3 inches in from the edges). Using the two-colored squares as patterns, cut 25 squares each from the batting and the muslin. Pin the three layers of each square together, and following the directions in the Craftnotes on page 45, quilt by machine along the marked lines.

When the quilting is done, sew a cloud pillow to each of the 13 lightly quilted blocks. Center each cloud on a block and pin it, face up, to the right side. Machine-stitch all around the cloud's edge, catching just the muslin lining, not the striped top, in the stitching. This is a bit difficult—you will have to keep pushing the top layer away from the needle—but the effect will be worth the trouble, with the clouds puffing up away from the background.

Assembling the Squares and Border
Arrange the blocks once more in five rows of five. You will first assemble five horizontal rows of five blocks each. To sew two blocks together, place them together, right sides facing, and sew with a ¼-inch seam through all six layers. After the five rows have been assembled, press the seam allowances to one side; then sew the rows together, placing them together right sides facing, and again making ¼-inch seams through all six layers. Press the seams to one side.

Next, add the borders. Cut two 12-inch-wide strips of fabric the same length as the sides of the quilt plus 1 inch (this will be approximately 56 inches, but will vary slightly because of the shrinkage caused when you quilted the fabric). Then for the top and bottom borders, cut two 12-inch-wide strips the same length as the patchwork top and bottom, plus 24 inches. Cut batting and backing pieces from muslin the same size as the strips, and baste all six layers together, as for the squares. Machine-quilt three parallel lines along the length of each border strip, spacing the lines 3 inches apart. Right sides facing, sew the side strips to the patchwork, with a ¼-inch seam. Press the seam allowances toward the borders. Then sew the top and bottom border strips to the patchwork and the ends of the side strips. Press the seam allowances toward the borders, and trim any excess fabric at the ends.

Piece the lining fabric together to form a single piece of fabric measuring 3 inches smaller in length and width than the quilt. Baste the lining to the wrong side of the quilt, leaving a 1½-inch margin of excess fabric all around. To hold the quilt and the lining together, the quilt is tufted, or tied, at each corner of the squares. To make a tuft, thread an embroidery needle with two strands of embroidery thread; make a tiny stitch and tie the ends (Figure S). Begin tufting at the center of the quilt and work out toward the edges.

To finish the edges, turn the edges of the front under ¼ inch, and then fold them to the back 1¼ inches. Hand-sew the folded edge to the lining with tiny stitches.

Eleane Hiller, who describes herself as an instinctive designer, is French. She left her native city of Hyeres to design clothing in Sao Paulo, Brazil, where she lived for 15 years. In 1965, she moved to New York, where she first worked as a sportswear designer. She now owns Elart, a fashion house manufacturing sportswear and accessories.

SEWING WITHOUT A PATTERN
Fabric Geometry

Beginning with a rectangular length of fabric—even an attractive bedsheet—you can sew shapes that may seem complicated but are not. The mysteries of a bias-cut apron, of a circular cape that swirls, or of a round tablecloth that completes a bedroom ensemble, are not difficult to solve.

You will not need special equipment. Pins, tailor's chalk, pencil, ruler, and scissors are sufficient for measuring and marking the fabric and cutting out the shapes. A pencil at the end of a taut piece of string makes an adequate compass for describing a circle. If you need to make an adjustment in the size of any of the garments shown here, or if you want to determine the number and size of the sheets you will need for the room ensemble opposite, it may be helpful to work out the proportions on a sheet of graph paper, making each square on the paper equal to an inch.

Bias-cut apron-shawl $ ▨ ♙ ⚵

A bias-cut fabric triangle with a lace-edged ruffle becomes an apron that molds itself to the body.

The same ruffle-trimmed triangle can also be worn over the shoulders as a casual shawl.

Making the bias-cut calico apron (above, left) is a good investment of time and energy because it can also be worn as a shawl (above, right) or as a beach skirt knotted at one side of the waist.

The triangular shape of the apron is arrived at by folding a length of material on the diagonal, cutting along the fold, and rounding off the opposite tip. The ruffle is then made with two strips of fabric taken from the material remaining after the triangle has been cut. It is trimmed with lace, gathered, and attached. The longest side of the triangle becomes the apron waist. The ruffle begins 12 inches down from the points, freeing them to serve as ties.

The triangle is cut on the bias—the diagonal of the fabric (Figure A)—which is

Figure A: To obtain the basic apron triangle, with two sides equal, from a rectangular piece of fabric, fold the fabric diagonally. Measure and mark the desired length (28 inches) from the bottom right-hand corner. To obtain two bias strips 8½ inches wide for the ruffle, measure and mark that width and twice that width along the fold line, connecting the points on the diagonal of the fabric, as shown.

The fresh-looking greenery at the windows, on the bed, and over the night table at right all were stitched from four printed bedsheets and two sheets in a coordinated solid color. These accessories were designed by Judith Hinsch; directions for making them begin on page 63.

54

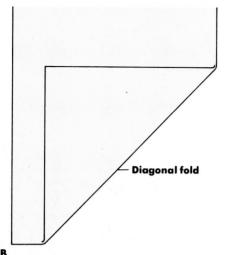

B

Figure B: Fold the apron's triangular section to the left, pin it there temporarily, and cut along the diagonal fold.

1: To attach the lace trimming, turn up the raw edge ⅛ inch to the right side of the apron and stitch it. Then sew the lace on top.

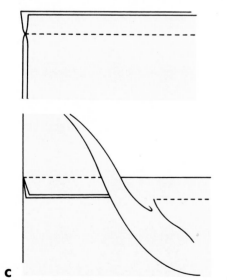

C

Figure C: A French seam encloses raw edges to provide a neat finish. First, machine-stitch the two pieces, wrong sides facing, ¼ inch from the edge (top). Trim the seam allowance to ⅛ inch. Fold along the stitched line, right sides facing, and stitch again ¼ inch from the fold to enclose the raw edges (bottom).

not the usual way to cut fabric. Woven fabric consists of two sets of threads, one running lengthwise called the warp and the other running crosswise called the weft. They cross each other at right angles. Usually fabric is cut along these straight thread lines for stability. But when fabric is cut on the bias, angling across the thread lines, it will stretch slightly when pulled. The bias cut of this apron lets it cling and mold itself to the body as it is tied into place.

You will need 1⅔ yards of material for the apron and 3¼ yards of ½-inch-wide lace for the trim. In order to cut a fabric triangle 28 inches long down the center front, not counting the ruffle, you will need material at least 45 inches wide (Figure A, page 54). The long side of the triangle measured diagonally is 56 inches.

To cut a perfect triangle from the length of fabric, fold the fabric as shown in Figure B and cut along the fold. Round off the tip, as shown in Figure A, by measuring 3 inches in from the tip on either side and cutting a freehand curve.

Ruffles are gathered strips of fabric used for trimming. By cutting them on the bias (Figure A), you can make them produce softer folds than they would if cut along the lengthwise or crosswise threads. To make a ruffle of average fullness, use a strip of fabric 1½ to 2 times the length of the edge to be trimmed. For the apron, cut two strips, each 8½ inches wide and 56 inches long. Round off one end of each strip by measuring 3 inches in from a corner and cutting a freehand curve. Join the two strips end to end with a French seam (Figure C) so the raw edges will not be

2: With right sides facing, stitch the lace-trimmed ruffle to the apron triangle ½ inch inside the latter's raw edge.

3: Fold over the ½-inch allowance twice, so its raw edge and the raw edge of the ruffle are enclosed. Then stitch close to the edge of this fold.

visible on the wrong side of the ruffle. With the wrong side of the two strips facing, stitch ¼ inch in from the edge. Trim the seam allowance to ⅛ inch, turn the fabric so the right sides are facing, and stitch ¼ inch in from the seamed edge to encase the raw edges of the seam allowances.

Making the Ruffle
It is not necessary to hem the raw edge of the ruffle before sewing on the lace trimming. Simply turn up the raw edge ⅛ inch, right sides facing, and stitch it down with invisible nylon thread (photograph 1).

To gather the ruffle, loosen the tension on the sewing machine slightly, and sew a row of stitches along the raw edge of the ruffle opposite the lace, ¼ inch in from the raw edge. Knot one end of the threads, pull the bobbin thread at the other end with one hand to reduce the length from 112 inches to 52 inches, and arrange the fullness evenly with the other hand.

Finish the raw edge of the triangle across the top and 12 inches down on each side before attaching the ruffle. If your sewing machine has a hemming foot, it will double-roll the edge for you. If not, fold under ⅛ inch of fabric and then a second ⅛ inch and stitch.

Join the ruffle to the triangle so the seam on the wrong side will have a clean finish. With right sides together, place the ruffle ½ inch in from the edge of the triangle, pin it in place, and baste it with a loose running stitch before sewing a row of permanent stitches right over the basting and gathering stitches (photograph 2). Then turn under the ½ inch of fabric twice, and stitch it down so it encases the raw edge of the ruffle (photograph 3).

Man's kimono coat $ ⊠ ☂ ⚴

The kimono, worn traditionally by men and women alike, is a loose, wrap-around robe distinguished by its wide, straight sleeves cut in one piece with the bodice, and by its sash. The word is Japanese, from *ki*, to wear, plus *mono*, meaning person or thing; the literal translation is "thing for wearing."

The kimono originated not in Japan, however, but in China. Visual documentation dates back to the third century B.C., but it is probably much older. Known to the Chinese as a *p'ao*, it was worn by them until the end of the Ming dynasty (1644). The Japanese adopted it in the eighth century. Westerners have modeled countless bathrobes, lounging robes, and beach jackets after the comfortable kimono style.

Traditional kimonos were made of exquisitely woven and patterned silks, a textile art which the Chinese discovered and began to develop more than 4,000 years ago. The most beautifully decorated and colored Japanese silk kimonos date from the seventeenth and eighteenth centuries. The kimono's style lends itself not only to silk but to any type of fabric that is supple enough to drape well, and even to some fabrics with more body.

The short kimono coat (below, right) is made of machine-washable, drip-dry cot-

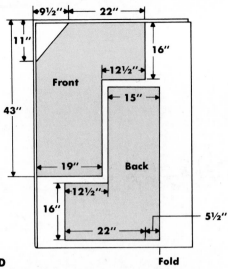

D

Figure D: Kimono sleeves are cut at right angles in one piece with the body of the coat. To cut both back and front pieces from doubled 45-inch-wide fabric so you have two of each, place the bottom of the back section in the space below the sleeve of the front section so they nest together.

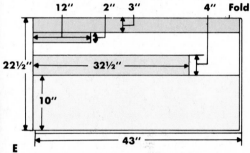

E

Figure E: To reduce the amount of stitching in the facings and sash, fold the material lengthwise and draw the front neckline facings (yellow) along the selvage side so the woven edges serve as the inside hem. Place the sash (green) along the fold so only one side need be stitched. Fit sleeve facings (blue) and back neck facing (orange) between.

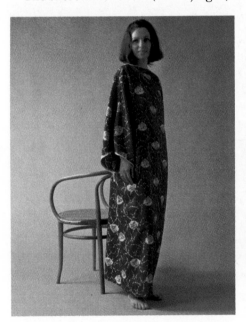

The caftan is similar in shape to the kimono but is slotted at the neck for slipping over the head.

The right-angle sleeve is the key in making a kimono coat suitable for men or women.

ton with a bold, colorful stripe, suitable for lounge wear or beach wear. It has a V-shaped neckline and a front closing with a generous overlap that is faced with the same striped cotton fabric as the coat. The sleeves stop short of the wrist and are also faced so they can be turned back. The striped pattern in itself provides an attractive border and sash. This design is only a starting point for many variations that you can make by changing the neckline, making the kimono longer or shorter, using other fabrics, binding it instead of facing it, or adding trimmings.

This kimono was made for a man according to his measurements: width of neckline across the front, 10 inches; length of arms, 25 inches, less 3 inches for adjusted sleeve length; desired coat length finished, 42 inches. Before you start this project, read the directions on page 58 for measuring accurately.

A kimono of this length requires 4 yards of 45-inch-wide material to make the two front and two back sections (Figure D) and an additional 1½ yards to make the facings and the sash (Figure E). The fabric width is sufficient for small, medium, or large sizes, providing that you lay out the pattern pieces for cutting with a minimum of waste.

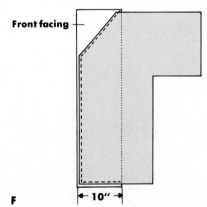

F

Figure F: With right sides together, sew the raw edges of the facings to the front sections of the kimono. Turn the kimono right side out and sew another row of stitches 2 inches from the edge—to frame the front overlap and to keep the facings flat inside. Trim off the excess fabric.

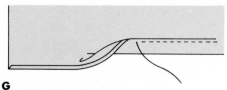

G

Figure G: To hem a raw edge by machine, fold it under ⅛ inch; then fold it again to make a hem of whatever depth you want, and stitch it along the inside fold.

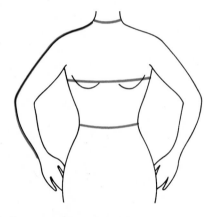

Body measurement guide

Neck: Measure around the top of the collarbone, past the point where the neck joins the shoulder, and around the most prominent vertebra at the back of the neck. The width of the neckline across the front is half of this total.

Sleeve length: Measure the length of the arm from the neckline atop the shoulder to the place where you want the sleeve to end.

Bust: Measure under the arms around the fullest part of the bust and across the shoulder blades in back; then add 2 inches for ease.

Waist: Measure from the base of the neck to a point just above the bottom curve of the spine; then measure horizontally around the torso. Hold the tape measure loosely so the finished garment will fit comfortably around the waist.

Cut off a piece of material 43 inches long for the facings and sash. Fold the remaining 4 yards in half across the width (for cutting two back and two front pieces), and pin the selvages to prevent the fabric from slipping while you are marking and cutting it. Be sure to include ¼-inch seam allowances.

Starting in the upper left corner, measure for the V-shaped neckline (Figure D, page 57). To find the sleeve length, measure along the fold from the neck point and mark off the length desired. Draw a line 16 inches long perpendicular to the shoulder to establish the depth of the kimono sleeve. Mark a second point 16 inches down parallel to it so you can rule off a straight line 12½ inches long for the bottom of the sleeve. Next, starting at the upper left-hand corner, rule off 43 inches down the left selvage for the length, then 19 inches across the bottom for the front width. Connect the points for the side seam. The back is identical to the front of the kimono in all but two respects; the neckline is measured 5½ inches straight across the base starting in the lower right-hand corner, and the bottom is only 15 inches wide. Cut out two of each piece.

The Facings and Sash

You can avoid sewing extra seams by the way you mark and cut the facings and sash pieces. Fold the remaining material in half, matching the selvage edges (Figure E, page 57). Take the front facings from the selvage side, letting the woven edge serve as the inside finish. Use the shape of the kimono neckline as a pattern for the facings, which are 10 inches wide and 43 inches long. Pin the strips, right sides together, beneath the front pieces of the kimono, with their raw edges flush against the closing edge, and cut out the neckline (Figure F, page 57). By taking the belt from the folded side, you will have only one long edge seam to sew later.

Sewing the Kimono

Sew the center back seam of the kimono (right sides facing as with all seams). If you are working with stripes, be sure to match them. Sew the front to the back at the shoulder seams, from neck edge to edge of sleeves. Join the front facings and back neck facing at the shoulder seams. Pin the right sides of the kimono and facing together. Sew a row of stitches all around the edge and trim the excess fabric (Figure F). Turn right side out and sew a second row of stitches on the right side, 2 inches away, to frame the closing and to keep the facing lying flat on the inside. Face the sleeves with the 4-inch strips of fabric. Pin the right sides together, sew around the edge, and turn; then fold the raw edge under twice and stitch around the inner edge of the facing (Figure G).

Match the angle of the underarms; then pin the front and back together completely before sewing the underarms and side seams. Carry the row of stitching from the edge of the sleeve to the underarm, and reinforce it by sewing around the curve over the first row of stitches before continuing all the way down to the hem. Turn up the hem, double roll the raw edge, and machine-stitch it (Figure G). Join the belt strips with right sides together to obtain a length of 60 inches; then sew the raw edges together along the length, leaving an opening of 1½ inches for turning it right side out. Iron the belt flat and stitch the opening closed by hand.

Contemporary caftan $ ☒ ♦ ♨

The caftan is a long, loose, shirtlike garment with long, wide sleeves, usually fashioned of striped cotton or silk. It is derived from garments common throughout the eastern Mediterranean and North African countries and, coincidentally, resembles the Japanese kimono in its basic outline. The word caftan, common to the Turks and Persians, was used originally to describe a type of luxurious coat worn by men in the eleventh century. Features of the Moroccan man's djellaba, a full, long-sleeved woolen cloak with a hood, also enter into the styling of westernized caftans.

The caftan shown on page 57 is essentially the same shape as the man's kimono coat pictured next to it, but its greater length and softer fabric give it a different look. Instead of being a coat style, sashed at the waist, it is designed to be slipped over the head. The neckline, high and round, has a deeply cut center opening in front. Bias binding is used for ornamental trimming.

The ankle-length caftan shown was made for a woman 5 feet, 6 inches in height who wears a dress size 8. Her measurements: neckline, 14½ inches; length of arms, 22 inches; desired length finished, 54 inches. (Refer to instructions on taking body measurements, opposite page.)

Making this caftan requires 4 yards of material, 45 inches wide, and at least 3 yards of ½-inch-wide, double-fold bias binding, available in any notions department. If you choose a printed fabric, allow enough extra yardage to match the repeat of the pattern. Match the print while folding the fabric to assure a continuous flow of the design across the front and back seams (photograph 4). Save the extra fabric for cutting out the facing of the neckline.

The procedures for folding and pinning the fabric, making the diagram for the caftan (Figure H), and using the neckline as a pattern for the facing are similar to those described for the man's kimono coat (page 57). To locate and measure the neckline for the front (the upper left-hand corner in Figure H), measure a distance of 4 inches across the top and 2 inches down along the left selvage. Connect the two points with a diagonal line (Figure I). Then draw a continuous curve freehand, close to the diagonal line. To ensure a smooth curve you can draw a rectangle as shown; then draw a second diagonal line in the opposite direction. Using the point where

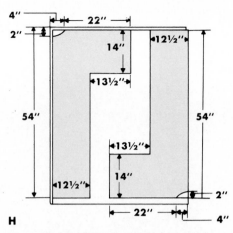

Figure H: The sleeves and body of the caftan are similar in shape to the kimono (page 57), but the neckline is round. Extra inches gained by eliminating the front overlap make it possible to lay out front and back sections along the selvages of 45"-wide material.

4: To make a caftan that has the pattern matched at the seams, match the pattern of the printed fabric (it will be repeated at regular intervals) when you fold the fabric before cutting it.

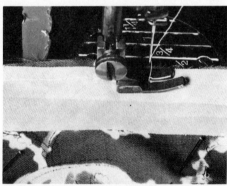

5: Use commercial bias binding to enclose the raw edges of the caftan and its neckline facing. With wrong sides together and the bias binding face down on top, stitch ¼ inch from the edge.

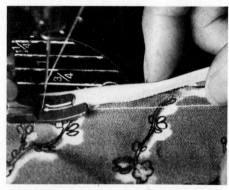

6: After sewing the first side of the bias binding (photograph 5), fold the binding over the raw edges of fabric, turn the binding edge under, and stitch along this fold, as shown.

the diagonals intersect, measure ⅜ inch down along the first diagonal line (this will be the deepest point of the curve). Draw a curve connecting this point with the upper right corner and the lower left corner. Cut out the neckline, allowing 8 inches for the center front opening. To make the back neckline, start in the lower right-hand corner, and follow the directions for the front neckline. Although the distance from the neckline over the shoulder to the tip of the sleeve is 22 inches, the same as for the man's kimono, this garment when finished seems to have longer sleeves because the woman's arms are shorter than the man's. The cut of the garment under the armpit controls the width of the garment and its comfort. As the right angle moves up and closer to the body, the width of the sleeves and the width of the sides diminish. Conversely, as it moves down and away from the body, the widths of the two increase. If the caftan sleeves are cut too skimpily, the sides of the garment will pull up whenever the arms are raised and extended horizontally. There should be no problem with a sleeve that measures at least 14 inches in depth along a line perpendicular to the shoulder line. This line corresponds to the distance between the neck point and a point about 2 or 3 inches below the bottom of the bust in average women's sizes. It is easy to make the garment smaller without narrowing the sleeves by bringing the side seams closer to the body. If you have any doubts about the measurements you want, work out the proportions on graph paper before marking the fabric.

Lay the back sections of the caftan right sides together, and stitch the center back seam; then sew the front seam in the same manner, leaving not only the neckline opening unstitched but also a few inches extra below it. Then, after you have

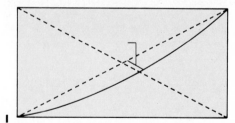

Figure I: To draw the caftan neckline curve smoothly, draw a diagonal line connecting the neckline marks (top left, Figure H). Draw another diagonal crossing the midpoint of the first, as shown above, and mark a point ⅜ inch below the intersection to locate the center of the curve. Join this point to the upper right and lower left marks with a curved line.

bound the front of the neckline, you will be able to catch the raw edges of the binding in the center front seam and avoid having to square off this binding at the point where it finishes off the neckline. Join the front of the caftan to the back, right sides together, at the shoulder seams; then pin and sew the under-sleeve seams and the side seams, using the same two steps described for the man's kimono on page 58. Join front and back facings at the shoulder seams, and finish the outside raw edge by double folding and machine stitching.

Double-fold bias binding comes ready made with one fold slightly wider than the other. The wider portion goes on the inside of the garment. Baste the facing in place along the raw edge of the neckline, wrong sides facing (photograph 5, page 59). Sew around the front closing first. Then when you finish sewing the front seam up to the neckline, you can catch the raw ends of the front binding underneath. Turn the caftan right side out, fold the binding over the raw edges of the neckline, and topstitch the binding close to the edge to completely encase the raw seams (photograph 6, page 59). To keep the front opening closed, add ties.

To make these 15-inch-long streamers from the binding material, keep the binding folded, and stitch along the open edge. Attach at the top front of the neckline. Bind the sleeves and finish the garment by turning up the hem (Figure G, page 58). Notice that the caftan can be worn backwards, as it is in the photograph on page 57, because there are no bust darts to interfere with the flow of the fabric.

This semicircular cape was cut in one piece from a 112-inch-long rectangle of wool, 56 inches wide. An angled hood can be fashioned from the remnants of the wool rectangle.

Semicircular cape with hood $ X ♦ ⚲

The cape, a type of ancient sleeveless cloak, is at its most fashionable in periods when loose garments are popular or when they are worn in layers for reasons of warmth.

To make a semicircular cape like the one shown at left, you need a rectangular piece of fabric at least wide enough to accommodate the length of the cape (the radius) and at least twice as long (the diameter).

This hooded semicircular cape, 54 inches long plus 2 inches for the seams, required a rectangular piece of fabric (wool and mohair) measuring 112 inches in length and 56 inches in width. After it was sewn, the raw edges were encased decoratively with ¾-inch-wide flat double braid. Ten yards of braid are needed to edge the cape and hood and make the ties at the neckline.

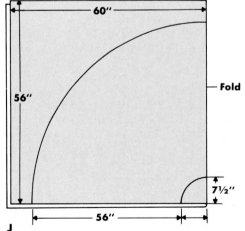

J

Figure J: To make a semicircular cape, use fabric wide enough to accommodate the cape's desired length (the radius), and at least twice its radius in length to accommodate the full sweep of a semicircle. Fold the fabric in half as shown, and mark the quarter circles with a pencil on a string, using the fold as the center line of the cape's back and the woven selvages at the bottom as the front closing of the cape.

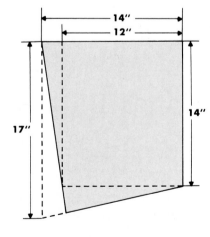

K

Figure K: To draw one side of the hood, make the top and back lines, plus three temporary lines (dashed lines above). To establish the neckline, connect the bottom right corner with the end of the 17-inch temporary line. To mark the front edge, connect the upper left corner with the intersection of the two dashed lines that meet at a right angle; then continue to the neckline. Allow a ½-inch seam allowance along top and back.

In preparation for drawing the semicircle, fold the fabric rectangle in half along the width, and pin it along the selvages and down the center to prevent the two layers from slipping. The positioning of the cape with its center back on the fold eliminates construction seams (Figure J). The selvages at the bottom of Figure J serve as the center front opening. The curve of the neckline and that of the hem fan out from the center point. The material left over after the semicircle is cut provides material for the hood, detailed in Figure K.

If you choose a napped fabric (any fabric with a one-way design, or a pile or texture that runs in one direction), the nap will run in opposite directions when you fold it, so you must then cut along the fold line and turn one of the squares upside down so all the nap runs in the same direction. Then place one square on top of the other, right sides together; pin and mark. Instead of having the seamless center fold, you will now have two raw edges to sew together to make a center back seam.

With the fabric folded as shown in Figure J, measure a distance of 7½ inches from the bottom right corner up along the center fold. Make a compass with a pencil or tailor's chalk tied on the end of a 7½-inch length of string. Hold the end of the string at the corner, and with the string taut, draw a quarter circle. Follow the same procedure to mark the hem, measured along the center fold; in this case it is 56 inches from center point to hemline. Then cut out the cape. Baste along the seam line of the neck edge to keep it from stretching out of shape.

7: With the raw edge of the cape against the fold of the braid trim, stitch the cape to the braid ½ inch from the edge, starting at the neckline.

8: Fold the braid trim over the raw edge of the cape and stitch along its edge, thus securing it to the right side of the cape.

9: Fold under the raw edge of the braid trim where it meets the starting point of the braid, at the point where the neckline and hood are joined.

The Hood

The only right angle in the side of the hood is the one formed by the top and back which are the same length—14 inches (Figure K). You will have to make three temporary lines (shown in dashed lines in Figure K) to get the correct angles for the front and neckline. Rule off the top and back lines and the three temporary lines as shown. Next, rule a line that connects the bottom right corner with the bottom of the lower temporary line—to establish the neckline of the hood. To make the front opening angle, connect the upper left corner with the intersection of two temporary perpendicular lines, and continue the line to meet the neckline of the hood. Allow an additional ½ inch at the top and back for seams. Cut two identical pieces.

Join the sections of the hood across the top and back with a French seam (Figure C, page 56); then pin the neckline of the hood to the cape, right sides together. There is always some extra fullness when an inside curve is being fitted to an outside curve; so pinch in the fullness as you pin and baste it into place before sewing a French seam for a neat finish.

The cape is bound all around with ¾-inch flat double braid in eggshell color. Such braid can be machine stitched to both sides of the garment, using colorless nylon thread. Place the cape right side up. Starting at the neckline, lay the edge of the cape along the inside fold of the braid, and stitch it ½ inch from the edge (photograph 7). Fold the free edge of the braid on top, and stitch it along the edge (photograph 8). Finish off by folding the braid under itself at the neckline where it meets the starting point (photograph 9); it will be least visible here. Hand stitch it so it lies flat (photograph 10). Stitch on the ties by hand or machine.

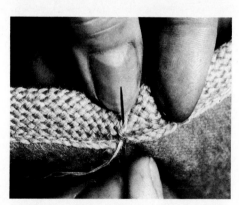

10: Stitch the folded end of the braid to the starting braid, making small stitches by hand.

Figure L: To make a wraparound skirt with elasticized waist, two shaped rectangles are stacked right sides up and trimmed as shown in the diagram. The slanted left edges are then stitched together. The bottom corners at the right are rounded off. Measurements shown are for a child's size 4, but the proportions can be adjusted to fit any size.

Wraparound skirt with tube top

The wraparound skirt with bound edges, bottom left, is proportioned for a small child, but it can also be made in women's sizes. The elasticized waistline can be tied at the side or front. The skirt is made of two rectangular scraps of cotton calico, left over from another sewing project, using these miniature measurements: 21 inches around the waistline and 9 inches long, finished. Elastic ½-inch wide makes the waistband.

Take two rectangles, each measuring at least 15¼ inches wide to provide hem and seam allowances, and 9⅝ inches long to allow the waistline casing (Figure L). Lay the rectangles wrong sides together and pin. Measure 10½ inches across the top for the waistline, and draw a line connecting this point with the bottom left corner of the rectangles. Mark off 3 inches on both edges adjacent to the lower right-hand corner. Draw a line connecting the points to round off the tip. Cut out the skirt and join the two sections with a French seam. Sew on the red bias binding, following the directions on page 59.

Measure 2 inches in from each side of the waistline, and mark each point to indicate where the elastic begins and ends. Fold the raw edge under ⅛ inch; then make a second fold to enclose the elastic (photograph 11). After stitching down one end of the elastic, sew the casing with the elastic inside. (Be careful not to stitch over the elastic.) By following this method, you will avoid having to pull the elastic through the casing after it has been sewn. Gather in the casing to fit the waistline, and stitch the elastic down on the opposite end. Sew a hook and eye to close the skirt. Stitch two ties made from the red bias binding to the front flap and at the waistline, where the flap meets the skirt.

A tube top sewn with elastic thread and a wraparound skirt elasticized at the waistline fit perfectly without a need for darts. This summer outfit could be made in any size.

11: To enclose the elastic and make the casing for the waistline of the child's skirt, fold the fabric over the elastic, as shown, and stitch.

12: To stitch the tubular top with elastic thread, hold your index finger behind the presser foot, and press down firmly against the fabric.

Elasticizing the Tube Top

To make the pert matching top, one length of fabric 42 inches long and 9 inches wide was sewn with elastic thread. The fabric's long dimension circles the torso and is seamed down the center back. Row upon row of elastic thread running around the tube gives it its stretch. The tube is 6 inches long finished; the other 3 inches were turned up to make the top and bottom hems. The red shoulder ties are made from extra pieces of the bias binding used for the skirt.

Thread the bobbin with elastic thread, winding it tightly by hand, until the bobbin is almost full. The elastic thread should come off the bobbin with plenty of stretch; so be sure the tension is tight enough. Leave your regular sewing thread on top, but set the machine for a long stitch in order to give the elastic thread as much play as possible. Turn under the raw edge 1½ inches for the top hem, and catch it in the first row of stitches. Sew the rest of the rows 1 inch apart except for the bottom which is hemmed in the same manner as the top. As you sew, hold your index finger right behind the presser foot, and press down hard against the fabric to hold it taut (photograph 12).

Quilted coverlet

Judith Hinsch has been sewing since the age of seven, when she made doll clothes. She was taught to sew by her grandmother, a professional seamstress. Judith was awarded a Homemaker of the Year award when she was graduated from high school. With additional instruction in advanced sewing techniques, she now sews all of the clothes that she and her two children need. She also designs and sews children's clothing for a shop near her home in Holliston, Massachusetts.

Bedspreads can have a tailored look with straight sides or a frilly look with flounced sides; they can be formal or informal, snug-fitting or throwlike, floor length or short on the sides. Short, loose covers, called coverlets, are often coordinated with separate skirts, called dust ruffles. The ruffle conceals the box spring. The coverlet covers the mattress on top plus overlapping the top of the ruffle by 3 inches. Printed sheets can easily be turned into coverlets.

Like any quilt, the coverlet pictured on page 55 has three layers: the top fabric, the filling or batting, and the backing. The top of the quilt was made from a twin-sized plaid sheet, the backing from a twin-sized sheet in solid green. Quilt battings are sold in standard sizes, including 72 by 90 inches, the most practical size to use for a single bed. Lightweight polyester batting is easy to work with and will remain fluffy through many washings.

To assemble the quilt, pin the three layers together on a flat surface. Place the backing wrong side up, spread the batting smoothly over it, then cover it with the fabric, right side up. The first step is to hold the batting in place with pins. Pins placed every 3 inches are not too many. Use T pins or safety pins if you find that straight pins do not hold. Begin at the center and work out towards the edges in rows parallel to the lengthwise and crosswise grains, checkerboard fashion, smoothing the surface as you pin. Then baste the layers together, using the same procedure as you did for pinning.

The design of a patterned fabric often suggests the placement of the quilting lines; here, the plaid provided the answer. Use the longest stitch on your machine for quilting. Usually eight to ten stitches to the inch set at a looser than normal ten-

13: To quilt a coverlet by machine, push down on the three layers—the fabric, batting, and backing—as they go under the presser foot.

14: To prepare the dust ruffle for gathering, stitch three rows of long machine stitches (about six to the inch) inside the ½-inch seam allowance.

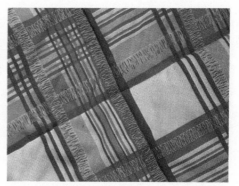

This coverlet was quilted by following the lines of the plaid. Working out from the center, first the lines were sewn in one direction, then the other.

sion take care of the bulk. Begin stitching in the center of the coverlet and move out towards the edges. First sew all the lines in one direction; then do all the cross lines to correspond with the lines in the plaid pattern. As they move under the presser foot, press the fabric layers down to lessen their bulk (photograph 13). (A coverlet larger than twin size may be too cumbersome to quilt by machine; stitching by hand is recommended.) After the coverlet has been completely quilted, lay it evenly on the bed and trim to size, 3 inches longer than the mattress on each side. Bind the raw edges together with medium-width (⅞-inch) bias binding in a contrasting color, in the manner shown in photographs 5 and 6, page 59. Be sure to enclose the edges of the batting as you stitch.

The Dust Ruffle

The dust ruffle on the bed has a center section made from an old sheet; unbleached muslin could be used. The ruffle itself, a three-sided one because the head of the bed is against a wall, was made from a twin-sized sheet. What remained from the sheet was used for the pillow cover, page 65.

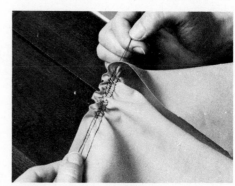

15: To gather the dust ruffle, pull the ends of the three bobbin threads with one hand while gathering the ruffle with the other hand.

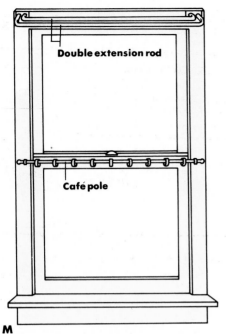

M

Figure M: Accurate measurements are the key to well-fitting café curtains. Mount the curtain rods first; then measure for each section of the curtain.

Two sets of café curtains topped with a valance, all created from printed bed sheets, make a distinctive window treatment.

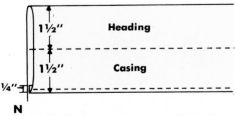

N

Figure N: To make a casing for a café curtain rod, allow 3 inches for the top hem. Fold and press it. Turn under the raw edge ¼ inch and hem it. Make a second line of stitching along the center of the hem. Slip the rod into the casing and gather the curtain along the rod.

To make the center section for the dust ruffle, spread the sheet over the box spring, taking advantage of the 1-inch finished hem by placing it at the head flush against the edge. (If you are using muslin, finish this edge with a double-stitched hem.) Cut the sheet to fit the perimeter of the box spring, allowing an extra ½ inch for seams on both sides and at the foot of the bed. Round off the corners.

Measure from the top of the box spring to 1 inch from the floor to establish the finished length of the dust ruffle. (The one pictured is 14 inches.) Allow an extra ½ inch for the top seam and 2 inches for the bottom hem. Measure the perimeter of the box spring on the three sides to be ruffled and allow 1½ times its length for the dust ruffle before gathering. Cut out enough sections of solid-color sheeting to equal this total.

Sew three rows of long running stitches along the top of the ruffle material, instead of the conventional two rows, to prevent the thread from breaking under the weight of the fabric (photograph 14, page 63). Keep rows inside the ½-inch seam allowance. Join the sections but be careful not to catch the ends of the gathering threads in the side seams because you will need to pull them later. Hem the raw edges at each end, as described on page 58, making two ¼-inch folds.

Starting at the head end of one long side of the bed and with right sides together, pin the dust ruffle to the center section, following the rounded corners at the foot. Pull up the gathering stitches (photograph 15, page 63) until the ruffle fits around the box spring and the fullness has been distributed evenly all around. Sew the ruffle and center section together. Trim the seam allowances and press them towards the center section so they will lie flat when the dust ruffle is placed on the box spring. Place the dust ruffle on the box spring again, pinning up the hem to clear the floor. Take it off the bed, turn under the raw edge of the hem ¼ inch, then stitch the finished hem as indicated by the pinning. The hem will be a little less than 2 inches deep.

Café curtains with valance $ ▨ 大 ⚑

Café curtains (left) are short, straight-hanging rectangles or squares of material designed as window treatments for casual room settings. When used to curtain double-hung windows, they are commonly hung in tiers of two or more pairs, one tier covering the upper half of the window, another the lower. A valance usually completes the ensemble. A valance is a very short borderlike curtain hung at the top of a window frame to provide a decorative heading for the tiers. When the top of the window is treated with tiers and a valance, a double extension rod is used to accommodate both. To hang correctly, both valance and the top tier should cover the curved ends of the rods and reach the wall. Each lower tier is suspended on a single rod which is slipped through rings sewn onto the top of the curtain.

Measuring and Cutting

Two sets of café curtains and a valance were made to decorate the standard double-hung window pictured. A double extension rod supports the valance and top tier, and a café pole and rings support the lower tier (Figure M).

One double sheet provided enough material for the window pictured, as well as the top pair of cafés for another window, not shown. The bottom set of cafés came from a twin-sized sheet needed in part for the ruffle described above. The other valance came from the remnants of the double sheet used for the tablecloth described opposite. Windows vary so much from house to house that you will need to plot the measurements for your windows on graph paper to get the most out of each sheet.

Allow the following measurements for each of the curtains: 1-inch side-seam allowances, 2-inch bottom hems, and a width equal to that of the window itself. Each pair of café curtains will therefore be twice as wide as the window, enough to make them hang with generous folds. When you are making two or more tiers of curtains, add 3 inches to the vertical measurements to allow for the tier above to overlap the one below. Since each piece will vary in proportion only slightly, write the position of the piece in pencil on the back of the fabric.

To make a top hem with a casing, allow 3 inches. Fold along the 3-inch line, wrong sides together, and press it. Turn under the raw edge ¼ inch and stitch it (Figure N). Make a second line of stitching halfway along the center of the hem. The rod slips into the casing and the curtain is shirred along the rod, creating fullness and a decorative heading. The valances, 11 inches deep when finished, and the top tier of curtains have casings made the same way.

When curtains are hung from rings that have either been clipped on or sewn, only a 1-inch hem allowance is needed on top. Check the length of the curtains by hanging them up and pinning the hem before sewing it.

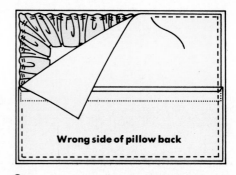

Wrong side of pillow back

O

Figure O: To match the right sides of the ruffle and pillow cover, sandwich the ruffle, face down, between the front and back sections of the sham, which are placed right sides facing. After the sham is sewn and turned right side out, the front of the ruffle will frame the front of the sham.

Ruffled pillow cover

A sham is about the easiest type of decorative pillow cover to make and its closure is just a simple overlap in the center of the back. The material for the front and two back sections of the sham, at right, was left over from the green sheet used to make the dust ruffle on the box spring (page 63). The sham's plaid ruffle is a remnant of the twin sheet used to make a pair of café curtains (opposite).

Measure the length and width of the pillow to be covered over the fullest part, and add 2 inches extra for ease and seam allowances. Cut one piece to these measurements for the front of the sham. To make the back, measure two sections of the same length, but only half the width, and add 1¾ inches to allow for the center hem. Cut out the two pieces. Hem one side of each small piece by turning the raw edge under ¼ inch, stitching it, then turning and stitching again to make a 1½-inch finished hem. Pin the sections together with hems overlapping so that the total area of the pillow back measures the same as the front piece.

A 3-inch ruffle of pleasing fullness is twice the perimeter of the sham. The strips for it should be cut on the bias (Figure A, page 54). Cut strips 4 inches wide, including 1 inch for seams. Join the strips to make one continuous ruffle piece, using French seams to enclose the raw edges (Figure C, page 56). Now turn up the bottom edge of the ruffle ¼ inch, then another ¼ inch, and hem it. Sew two rows of gathering stitches along the top of the ruffle, keeping both rows within the ½-inch seam allowance. Then gather the ruffle to fit the perimeter of the sham.

To assemble this pillow sham, sandwich the ruffle between the front and back sections of the sham (Figure O). First, place the front section right side up and pin the ruffle on top, matching raw edges. Then place the back pieces on top of them, face down. Pin them all together and sew around the perimeter ½ inch from the edge. Turn the finished sham right side out and insert the pillow through the back opening.

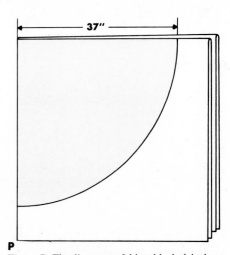

The pillow cover, made from remnants of the other projects described here, coordinates the printed and solid-color fabrics of the bedroom ensemble.

A round tablecloth

To find the measurements of a floor-length tablecloth, measure the diameter of the table top, and measure the drop from the edge of the table top to the floor. Double the latter measurement, add the table's diameter, and you have the diameter of the circular cloth. Divide the diameter in half to obtain the radius. The radius of the tablecloth shown in the room setting on page 55 is 37 inches. You can eliminate seams entirely by using a sheet. To gain a little extra material, open the sheet's hem and press with a steam iron to remove the creases.

To cut out the circle, fold the sheet carefully into quarters and pin the edges to prevent them from slipping. Starting in the corner (Figure P), measure and mark the radius, allowing an extra inch for the hem. Using a pencil held taut at the end of a measured piece of string, draw the curve. Cut along this line through all four layers of sheeting. Finish by machine hemming (Figure G, page 58).

37"

P

Figure P: The diameter of this tablecloth is the diameter of the table top plus twice the height of the table. Half this total is the radius. Fold the sheet in quarters, mark the radius, draw a quarter circle with a pencil compass, then cut all four layers along that line.

EMBROIDERY
Stitch Imagery

Solweig Hedin studied textile design at the Institute of Textiles and the School of Arts and Crafts in her native Sweden. She teaches embroidery and other needlework skills in New York City and is a free-lance needlework designer, artist, and consultant. The co-author and designer of Creative Needlework, *she also exhibits her work in craft shows.*

Embroidery, the art of stitching decorative designs by hand or machine on textiles or leather, encompasses a great variety of techniques and materials. The basic materials most commonly used are cotton, linen, wool, silk, leather, and some synthetics; but unusual substances, such as gold and silver, precious stones, pearls, beads, and feathers can be employed to achieve spectacular effects.

Because there are so many kinds of embroidery techniques, it is difficult to classify them. A good deal of overlap exists, since one technique may influence another. Many of the same stitches can be used in several techniques and worked in different materials, according to the type of embroidery. For example, the satin stitch can be employed in crewel-work and hardanger, two quite dissimilar embroidery techniques.

Historically a popular craft, embroidery is rapidly coming back into favor today. It is a relaxing, creative pastime with an end product that carries the mark of the creator's personality. In fact, some men are taking up embroidery for this very reason. It is also inexpensive and easy to learn, strong factors in its appeal to children.

The following brief summary of some of the major embroidery techniques include easy ones as well as some that require a skill and patience not as much in evidence now as they were 50 or 100 years ago when people had more time. The following projects, however, help you to develop the basic skills of the craft and are within the capabilities of the modern embroiderer.

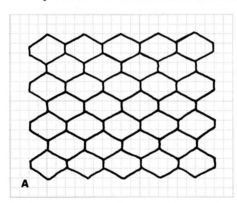

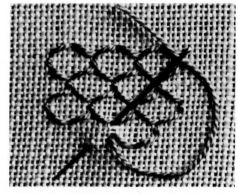

Figure A: In this simple black work filling pattern (a repeated design used to fill in an area), each blue square equals two fabric threads.

The pattern in Figure A, left, is shown worked in backstitch on even-weave fabric. See page 68 for a description and photograph of black work.

Counted-Thread Embroidery

This technique requires an even-weave fabric (also called even-count fabric), so named because it has an equal number of horizontal and vertical threads per inch.

The stitches are worked by referring to a chart that is in the form of a grid. The squares of the blue grid in Figure A correspond to the threads of the background fabric. The embroiderer counts the squares on the chart, then makes the stitch by counting the appropriate number of threads on the fabric (see photograph). A square may represent one, two, or more fabric threads for a variety of reasons depending on the fabric, the type of thread used, and the design. Embroidery techniques employing counted-thread principles are needlepoint, hardanger, cross stitch, black work, and some forms of white work (see page 68).

This is a portion of Solweig Hedin's 36-by-36-inch square wall hanging, worked in silk and rayon threads and fabrics. Directions and a photograph of the piece in its entirety are on page 73. The basic design idea of appliqueing and embroidering small circles within a large circle adapts well to a number of useful items. A bedspread or a tablecloth would look dramatic with this design at its center or cushions and curtains may be coordinated by applying only a few small circles.

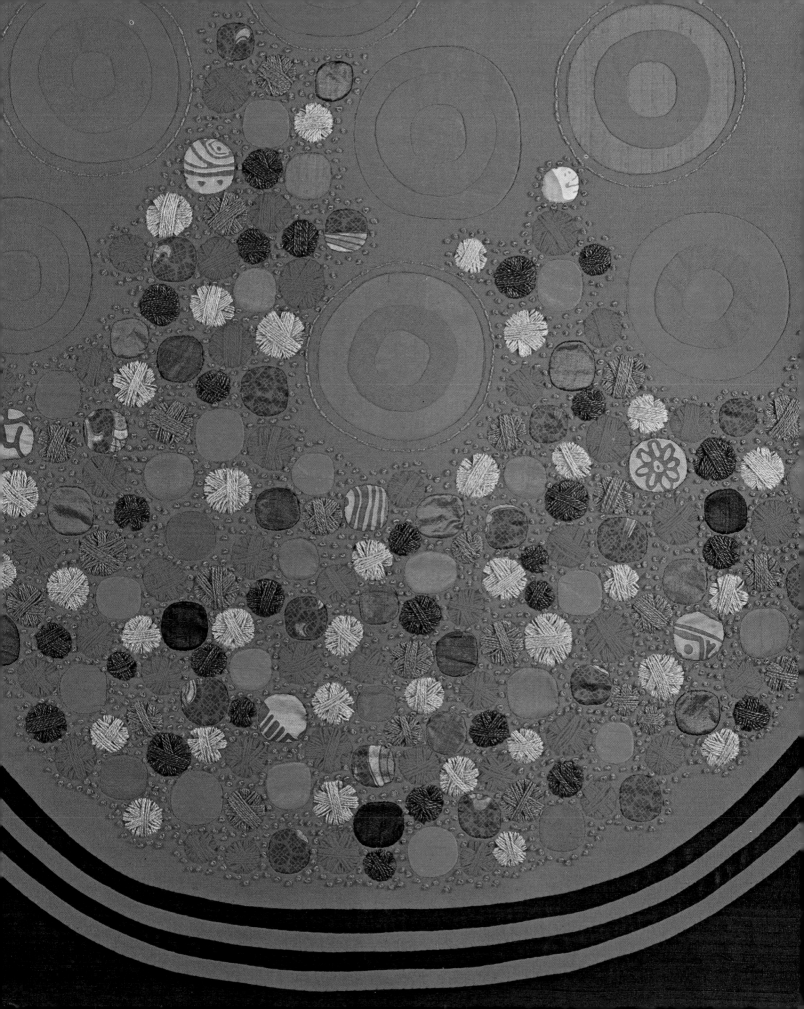

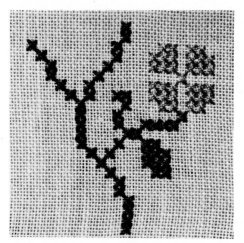

Use the cross stitch for geometric designs like this flower worked on even-weave fabric using No. 3 and No. 5 pearl cotton.

Sixteenth-century coif (top left) and matching forehead cloth were embroidered in the black work technique using black silk on white linen.

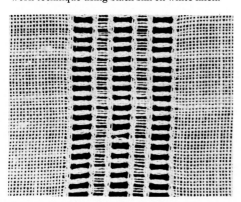

Open-weave areas are achieved by withdrawing fabric threads, as in this drawn-work embroidery.

Cross Stitch Embroidery

Embroiderers usually combine the cross stitch with other stitches, but you can work an entire piece of embroidery in this stitch alone. The regularity of the stitch is more easily accomplished by carrying it out on an even-weave fabric. Owing to its regular and geometric construction, cross stitching looks best if the design is rather formal or has a motif that repeats itself several times.

Black Work

As the name suggests, black work was traditionally done using black silk thread on white or natural-colored, evenly woven fabric. Black work originated in Spain and was brought to England by Catherine of Aragon in 1501. It reached its greatest popularity in Elizabethan times, when it was widely used for embroidering fine linen neck ruffs and frilled shirt cuffs. Black work, when done in a double running stitch (Holbein), is completely reversible (see Figure E, page 74), and thus it was especially suited for items on which the stitches were visible from both sides. As clothing styles changed, exposing more and more shirt, entire sleeves, stomachers (garments worn over the chest and stomach), and bodices—in addition to coifs (caps; photograph left center), gloves, and handkerchiefs—were embroidered with increasingly elaborate black work patterns. Delicate, formalized flowers and leaves, outlined and filled in with lacy geometric patterns of counted stitches, later embellished coverlets and cushions. The striking effect of black work is achieved by the weight or tone of the filling patterns and the interrelationship of dark, medium, and light patterns within a design. Black work is also known as Spanish work and Black and Gold, because of the frequent addition of metallic threads as highlights. Directions for black work projects begin on page 74.

White Work

Traditionally worked in white or off-white threads on a white or natural-colored background fabric, white work comprises a number of different stitches and techniques. White work needs a contrast of texture and perfectly worked stitches to bring out its full effect. The subtle, monochromatic color scheme of white-on-white can be worked to advantage in pulled work—in which the fabric threads are pulled by the stitching thread (see photograph below), drawn work—in which fabric threads are cut and withdrawn to form open areas (see photograph below left), and hardanger, a form of drawn work (see "Embroidery" on page 78).

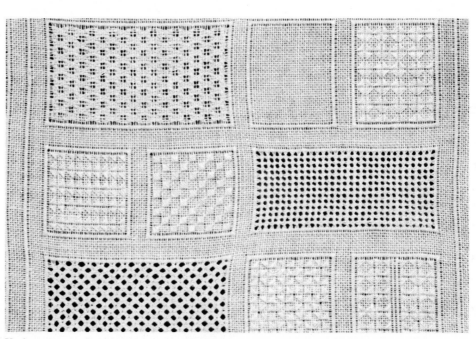

Various textures, intricate designs, and lacy openings are created by the pulled-thread technique on even-weave linen, as shown in this detail of a white-work sampler.

This flower was done in free-motion embroidery on a straight-stitch sewing machine.

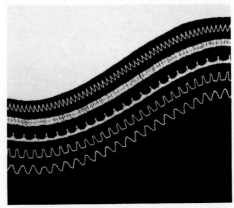

These five decorative stitches can be done on most modern sewing machines.

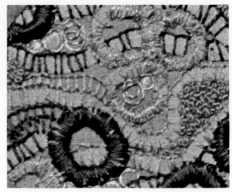

An interesting effect is achieved in this mixed-media embroidery by using rayon and metallic threads to work French knots, satin and blanket stitches. Background fabrics and circular shapes are Indian raw silk and linen.

Machine Embroidery

Anyone who owns or has access to a sewing machine can discover how easy it is to decorate clothing, cushions, tablecloths, and placemats. Shown above right are some of the many decorative stitches obtainable with a zigzag sewing machine or one with zigzag attachments. If you don't have one of these types, don't despair; free embroidery, or free-motion embroidery, can be done on a regular, straight-stitch machine. The photograph above left shows a flower worked on a straight-stitch machine in free embroidery. Simply remove the presser foot, and lower the feed dog teeth (see the manufacturer's operating manual). This allows "free motion," meaning the stitches can go in any direction.

Shown here is a portion of a hanging in mixed-media technique on linen background fabric. The embroidery uses linen and silk threads; the padded circles are appliques cut from the linen fabric.

Silk thread in white and gold combines with beads on a rayon background in this unfinished work. Paper inserted under the circles done in long satin stitches creates a raised effect.

Mixed Media and Creative Stitchery

The mixed media method either uses several different materials in the same piece of embroidery (such as silk and linen yarn, illustrated above), or combines two techniques (applique and embroidery, for example, pages 72 and 73) or both. Creative stitchery uses traditional stitches and techniques in nontraditional ways; for instance, working a delicate technique such as black work in heavy yarn, thus achieving a totally different effect from that of the past. Creative stitchery, therefore, also includes mixed media. Today, many designers draw from the vast heritage of embroidery techniques to cover a surface with the glowing colors and textures of various materials. New and unusual combinations of materials are a natural result of the availability of a wider range of fabrics and threads than were available to our ancestors. Natural and synthetic fabrics and yarns of all weights and thicknesses, beads and buttons, sequins and feathers, are laid one upon another. The stitches secure these various materials or stand on their own as design. Areas are raised and given dimension by padding with paper, fabric, or cotton. Fine gold or silver thread may be combined with coarse unspun yarn. In the mixed media method, apply yarn, fabric, and whatever other materials you choose in the same way that a painter would apply paint.

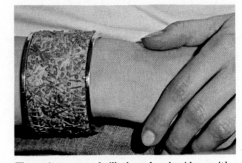

The artist wrapped silk thread embroidery with tiny yellow glass beads around a silver cylinder to make this unusual bracelet.

Fabrics

There are many factors that enter into choosing a background fabric: the intended use for the finished product, the embroidery technique, and the kind of yarn or thread you will work with.

For items that will receive a lot of wear, use a sturdy, closely woven fabric such as linen, cotton, denim or a synthetic or a blend. Wall hangings can be worked on loosely woven, delicate, or even gauzy fabrics. Even-weave fabric is used for counted-thread embroidery (see page 66). In general, use lightweight cottons, linens, wools, synthetics, organdy or silk for delicate stitchery; use medium and heavyweight linen, burlap, wool, synthetics and blends for the more substantial stitching. Of course, you can modify these guidelines somewhat if you are experimenting with mixed media or doing creative stitchery. Unless otherwise specified, when cutting the fabric, be sure to leave at least a 2-inch margin on all sides for blocking and mounting.

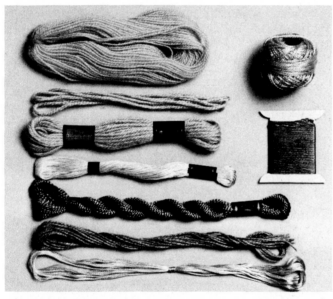

Left top to bottom: crewel yarn, Persian yarn, tapestry yarn, six-strand cotton embroidery floss, pearl cotton No. 3, linen yarn, silk floss. Upper right: pearl cotton No. 5. Lower right: rayon floss.

Yarns and Threads

In general, relate the yarn to the fabric; fine threads and yarns go with lightweight fabrics, heavy ones with heavy fabrics. If the finished article will receive wear and tear (cushions, chair seats, some articles of clothing), use sturdy, tightly twisted yarns such as wool (crewel, tapestry, Persian), some synthetics (such as acrylic yarns), and linen. Six-strand cotton embroidery floss—a basic embroidery thread—matte cotton, and pearl cotton are suitable for embroidering items of clothing such as blouses, shirts, sweaters, and blue jeans; handkerchiefs; household articles such as tablecloths, napkins, and pillows; and wall hangings. Reserve metallic threads, silk or rayon floss, and novelty yarns such as raffia, plastic straw, and bouclé for hangings.

Needles

Needles should be slightly thicker than the thread or yarn being used, to allow the thread to pass through the fabric easily and without fraying. The eye of the needle should be just large enough to receive the thread without forcing it. Crewel needles are of a medium length with a long eye and are used for most embroidery threads. But many embroiderers prefer chenille needles, which are shorter and heavier than crewel needles and have a very long, wide eye. Tapestry needles have a blunt point and a large eye and are useful for counted-thread embroidery (see page 66) and for whipped and woven stitches that are worked on top of the surface of the fabric.

Hoops and Frames

A hoop or frame, although optional, will make most forms of embroidery easier. Beginners are especially urged to use a hoop or frame, as it stretches the fabric taut and prevents puckered, uneven stitching. Hoops consist of two concentric wood or metal rings. They come in many styles, from the ones held in the hand to those with stands that rest on a table or the floor.

To secure fabric in a hoop, lay the cloth on the smaller ring; place the larger ring on top of it and press down. To prevent pressure marks when embroidering delicate fabrics, lay a few sheets of tissue paper over the fabric before placing the outer ring over it. Then tear a hole in the paper, exposing only the area of the fabric to be embroidered.

Professionals prefer a frame because it eliminates completely the pressure marks caused by a hoop. To use a frame, prop it against the edge of a table and rest the bottom edge in your lap. If you are working on a large hanging, you can construct a frame the size of the finished piece from artists' canvas stretcher strips. Hammer the strips together to form a frame of the size and shape required, making sure the corners are square. Place the fabric face down on a flat surface with the frame centered over it; staple or thumbtack the fabric to the back of the frame, stretching the fabric evenly. Block and frame it on the same strips when it is finished.

Thimbles and Scissors

Some embroiderers find a thimble indispensible, whereas others feel it's a nuisance. A thimble should fit the middle finger of the right hand (if you are right-handed) and be made of metal rather than plastic. Be sure that the surface indentations are deep enough to prevent the end of the needle from slipping when you use the thimble to push the needle through.

Embroidery scissors are small, with narrow, pointed, sharp blades. They are necessary for ripping out mistakes and should be used for this purpose only. Use good fabric shears or household scissors to cut the background fabric.

ATERIALS AND HOW TO USE THEM

Transferring the Design

Most designs are transferred directly onto the background fabric. Needlepoint and counted-thread embroideries are exceptions and are usually worked from a chart (see page 66). The first step in transferring is to make a paper pattern the desired size of the design. There are several ways of doing this. If the design is already available in the correct size, simply place a piece of tracing paper over it and trace its outlines. If it is larger or smaller than you need, have it photostatically enlarged or reduced (photostat services are listed in the telephone book) and make the tracing from the photostat. Or, enlarge the design by copying it on a grid as described on page 117. The next step is to transfer the tracing paper pattern onto the fabric. There are several ways to do this, depending upon the type of fabric and how often the pattern will be used.

Dressmaker's carbon: This is used for smooth-surfaced medium weight and heavyweight fabrics. Place the carbon paper face down between the tracing and the fabric and then trace the design through with a dull hard lead pencil.

Direct tracing: Use this procedure when the design is small and the fabric is of a light color and weight. Tape the tracing, which has been marked in heavy, dark lines, on an artist's light box or a well-lit window pane, and then tape the fabric on top. The light shining through the pattern and the fabric will enable you to trace the design directly onto the fabric with a soft pencil.

Transfer patterns: These are commercially available and normally can be reused several times. They are good on smooth-surfaced fabrics but do not work successfully on textured fabrics, coarse wools, or velvets. Pin or tape the fabric to your ironing board. Tape the transfer, face down, on the fabric. Set your iron to "low" or "rayon" and use a firm stamping motion to transfer the design. Lift a corner of the transfer to see if the design has transferred satisfactorily. After you have completed the stamping, run the iron lightly over the transfer, and quickly remove it.

Transfer pencil: You can make a transfer pattern of your own by using a transfer pencil, also known as a hot-iron pencil. On the wrong side of your tracing paper pattern, go over the lines of the design with the transfer pencil. Pin or tape the tracing paper face down on the fabric. Use as you would a transfer pattern, above.

Basting stitches: Use this method for soft, fluffy fabrics, such as sweater knits, or very heavy or textured fabrics. Pin the tracing paper pattern to the right side of the fabric and with sewing thread of a contrasting color baste around all the design outlines, using small running stitches. Carefully tear away the paper and work your embroidery stitches right over the basting stitches.

Starting the Yarn

Starting the yarn with a knot is fine for a wall hanging; on objects that will be used a lot and washed frequently, do not start off with a knot. Instead, anchor the end of the thread with a few running stitches (tiny straight stitches in a row). Anticipate the direction in which you will be embroidering and make the running stitches in a place where they will be concealed by subsequent stitches.

Finishing

Washing and Pressing: If finished embroidery is soiled, wash with mild soap flakes in lukewarm water. Roll in a towel and let dry. Place face down on thick towel, cover with damp pressing cloth, and press with warm iron. If fabric still appears puckered, block as directed below.

To Block Embroidery: Use a soft wood board larger than the piece to be blocked. Place a piece of aluminum foil the size of the background fabric on the board. This prevents the wood from staining the fabric, prevents water absorption, and serves as a pinning guide. Stretch the fabric taut over the foil. Tack down the corners to the board with rustproof thumbtacks or pushpins. Tack down the centers of each side; keep stretching the fabric evenly. Continue placing tacks halfway between the previous tacks until they are about one-half inch apart. With warm water and a clean sponge, saturate the embroidery and background. Press paper toweling on it to remove excess. Allow to dry, away from heat and sunlight for 24 hours. Unpin.

Mounting

First Method: For this simple method you need a needle and thread or sewing machine, wooden doweling, and a length of yarn (optional). First, trim the background fabric if the edges are uneven. Make narrow hems at the sides by turning the edges under ¼ inch twice. Stitch a hem about 1 inch wide (the size depends upon the thickness of the dowel) at the top, leaving ends open (figure A). Cut a length of dowel about 2 inches longer than the width of the hanging, and insert in hem. Attach a length of yarn to the dowel at the top or simply suspend embroidery from the dowel itself. If it is hanging smoothly, make a narrow hem at bottom. If you find that the hanging is curling or buckling, add weight to it by sewing another wide hem at the bottom and inserting another dowel.

Second Method: To prepare embroidery for framing, stretch it on a board after blocking it. You will need heavy cardboard or ½-inch thick insulation board, straight pins, masking tape, and a staple gun (optional). Cut the board slightly smaller than the space at the back of the frame; allow ⅛ inch to ⅜ inch for heavy fabric. Place embroidery face down on a flat surface, and center the board on top. Fold fabric margins to the back, and insert straight pins into each side to secure fabric temporarily (figure B). Check to make sure that the threads of the fabric are even with the edges of the board. Tape top and bottom edges of the fabric to the board; trim fabric at corners if it seems too bulky; then tape down the sides (figure C). If the board is at least 3/16 inch thick, you can insert staples into the edges of the board, spacing them ¼ inch apart. This forms a more permanent mount, as the tape may dry up with time, allowing the fabric to sag.

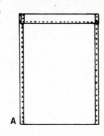
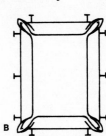
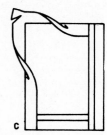

Embroider a flower applique ¢ ⧄ 👫 🎨

In the past, when embroidery included gold, lace, and jewels, much of it was reused when the original article was discarded. In addition, embroiderers often worked elaborate motifs on fine linen, which were then cut out and applied to velvets and brocades, fabrics unsuitable for a direct application of stitches. Today, using the same method, you can decorate lush velvets or stretchy knits, patch blue jeans, liven up tote bags, and personalize blouses and jackets. This way furnishes an excellent introduction to embroidery for the beginner.

The flower motifs on this page are done in basic embroidery stitches. You can practice on a piece of fabric and, when satisfied with the result, cut it out and sew it to whatever you wish to decorate.

Of course, if the background fabric permits, and if you feel sure of yourself, you may embroider the motif directly onto the fabric.

Making the Applique

You will need: tracing paper; dressmaker's carbon paper; straight pins; a pencil; closely woven mediumweight fabric such as cotton or linen; an embroidery needle; and yarn (six-strand cotton embroidery floss or wool yarn such as crewel or Persian yarn). First trace one of the actual-size motifs from the photographs below, or use one of your own. Transfer the motif(s) to the fabric using dressmaker's carbon paper (see the Craftnote on page 71). Place the fabric with the designs on it in a hoop or on a frame, following the directions in the Craftnote. Using your own colors or those shown in the photographs, embroider the motifs using the stitches listed below (see Embroidery Craftnotes: Stitches, pages 88 to 91; the numbers following the names of the stitches refer to their sequential numbers in the Craftnotes): straight stitch (2), backstitch (3), satin stitch (6), lazy daisy (12), coral stitch (28), and French knot (29).

When you have completed a flower to your satisfaction, cut it out carefully, allowing for ¼ inch beyond the outline for the single flower. For the group of flowers (top, left) cut out in a square or oval shape, leaving the background fabric visible. Pin and baste the embroidered applique on the article you wish to decorate. Sew the applique to the article with thread to match the embroidery or the fabric. Using a tiny buttonhole stitch (see Embroidery Craftnotes, Figure 27, page 90), cover the edge of the applique completely.

This plain sweater owes its new personality to the embroidered rose, which was carefully attached using a buttonhole stitch.

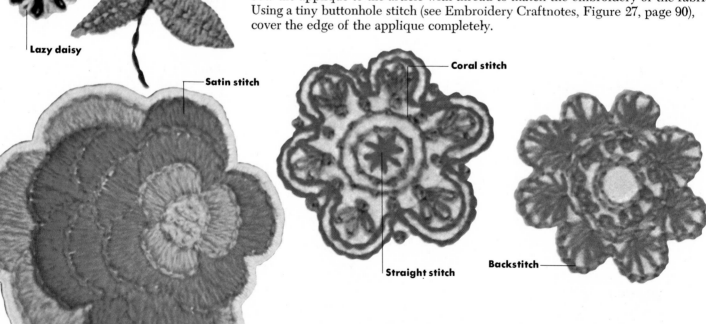

French knot

Lazy daisy

Satin stitch

Coral stitch

Straight stitch

Backstitch

Full-size photographs show embroidered flowers from which you may trace your patterns. The flowers are worked in these basic embroidery stitches: straight stitch, back stitch, satin stitch, lazy daisy, coral stitch, and French knot.

Circles within a circle

$ ● 🧍 🦀

The large, colorful mixed media piece pictured on page 67 utilizes the two needle-craft techniques of embroidery and applique. Since the finished work was to be displayed as a hanging, I was free to use delicate silk and rayon yarn and fabric. I find these materials particularly appealing because of their luxurious sheen and luminosity. The directions that follow are for a 36-by-36-inch hanging. If you are embroidering something that will require frequent laundering, such as a bedspread or tablecloth, stay with machine-washable materials such as cotton and linen fabrics, and use six-strand cotton embroidery floss or No. 3 pearl cotton. If you wish to adapt the design area to fit a larger or smaller area, refer to the entry "Applique," page 16.

Materials
As with all embroideries this large, it is best worked on a large frame. I suggest that you buy two pairs of 36-inch-long canvas stretcher strips, on which you can stretch the fabric and see the entire work at all times. When the embroidery is complete, it will already be mounted and ready for framing. You will also need two yards of 45-inch-wide background fabric in blue, one yard of 45-inch-wide red fabric; ¼ yard of 45-inch-wide fabric or 1/3 yard of 36-inch-wide fabric in magenta; scraps of fabrics in other colors (see photograph on page 67) for the small appliques; rayon floss, six-strand cotton embroidery floss, or No. 3 pearl cotton for the embroidery; sewing thread to sew on the appliques; sewing and embroidery needles; thimble, scissors; an electric iron. You may work with the colors shown, or choose your own to match your decor.

Making the Hanging
To begin, stretch a 40-inch square of blue fabric onto the frame (see Craftnotes, page 70). Cut a 32½-inch-diameter circle from red fabric (see Figure B for how to draw large circles). This is the first applique. Turn the edges of the circle under ¼ inch and press with an iron. Pin and baste the applique to the center of the stretched background fabric. Since this applique is so large, baste carefully, making sure it lies absolutely flat. Using matching sewing thread and a sewing needle, sew all around the folded applique edge with tiny overcast stitches. Then, from the remainder of blue fabric, cut a 31½-inch-diameter circle, and from the center of this cut a 29½-inch circle to form a 1-inch-wide ring. Fold and press ¼ inch under all around both outside and inside edges, forming a ½-inch-wide ring. Pin and baste to the center of the first large circle; sew on as before. The next applique is a smaller ring. From the center of the 29½-inch blue circle cut a 27½-inch circle, which will leave you with a 1-inch-wide ring. Apply as for the first ring.

The next step is to apply a series of seven circular shapes (magenta color), and then a ring on top of each of them. Cut seven 5-inch-diameter circles from magenta fabric. Fold the edges under ¼ inch and apply to the large red applique, arranging them at random in the upper half of the circle. For the ring at the center of each of the circles, cut a 3½-inch circle from red fabric, and from the center of this cut a 1-inch circle, to form a 1¼-inch-wide ring. Apply to the circles as directed above. For a special effect, I embroidered a row of backstitches in orange (see Embroidery Craftnotes, Figure 3, page 88), around some of the magenta circles.

Fill in the bottom section and the spaces between the 5-inch circles with circular shapes ranging in size from ½ inch to 1¼ inch in diameter. About half of these are appliques cut from the fabric scraps. The rest are satin stitches (see Embroidery Craftnotes, Figure 6, page 88), worked in four layers of about six stitches each (Figure C). When all the small circular shapes are completed, work orange French knots (see Figures 29a and 29b, page 91) between them.

If necessary, wash and press or block, and mount (see Embroidery Craftnotes, page 71).

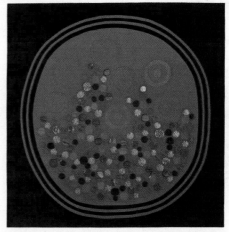
Full view of Solweig Hedin's mixed media wall hanging shown in close-up on page 67.

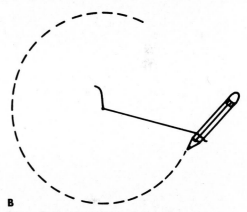

B

Figure B: To draw a large circle, make a compass using string, a ruler, and a pencil. Tie the pencil to one end of a piece of string the same length as the diameter of the desired circle. Measuring from the pencil, mark half the width of the circle on the string and tie a knot at this mark. For instance, for a 20-inch circle, measure and mark off 10 inches. With one hand hold the knot on the fabric where the center of the circle is to be. Holding the pencil in a vertical position in your other hand, pull the string taut and mark the circle.

C

Figure C: Detail showing how overlapping layers of satin stitch form a circle.

73

Marion Scoular, a graduate of London's Royal School of Needlework, is a nationally known lecturer and teacher of hand embroidery. She owns and operates the Robin Hood Wool Shop in Clemson, South Carolina where she teaches, specializing in counted-thread embroidery and canvas work. Author of a correspondence course in black work for the Embroiderers' Guild, Marion travels extensively, lecturing and conducting workshops.

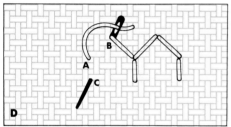

Figure D: Backstitch: Work from right to left, following the filling pattern. Bring needle up at A, insert at B, bring up at C. Form the next stitch by reinserting needle at A.

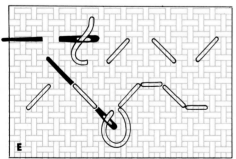

Figure E: Double running or Holbein stitch: Work from right to left. Work a row of running stitches over two fabric threads, under two threads, over two threads, etc., following the chart for the filling you are working (top). When the row is complete, turn work around and return, stitching (also on the right side of the fabric) over the threads that were stitched under previously (bottom). The number of threads covered by one stitch can vary throughout the overall design but will always be the same in one filling.

Black work tissue covers

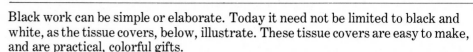

Black work can be simple or elaborate. Today it need not be limited to black and white, as the tissue covers, below, illustrate. These tissue covers are easy to make, and are practical, colorful gifts.

Materials and Basic Procedures

Fabric: Black work is a counted-thread embroidery technique (see page 66) that must be done on an evenly woven fabric. Even-count fabric is necessary in order to avoid distortion of the fillings. For instance, on fabric with more vertical threads per inch than horizontal threads, the fillings will be elongated. I suggest that you use finely woven hardanger fabric (22 threads per inch), Aida (usually 8 to 11 threads per inch), or Monkscloth (16 threads per inch). These fabrics are available at well-stocked needlework shops. More widely available fabrics that make good substitutes are burlap (usually 13 threads per inch), or coarse linen or wool. Remember that since the fillings are worked by counting threads, a finer fabric will reduce the scale of the fillings, and a coarser fabric will enlarge the scale.

Thread: For black work embroidery in which an airy, lacy effect is desired, use a fine thread. I especially recommend six-strand cotton embroidery floss for the beginner, since it is easy to handle. No. 8 pearl cotton may also be used. For the more experienced needleworker, silk and rayon floss (which also come in six strands) may be used. Rayon and silk are a bit more difficult to work with, but the rich effects obtainable are worth it. Separate the six strands, and use the correct number for each filling as specified in the project directions that follow. The more strands in the needle, the darker the filling will appear.

Covers for pocket pack of tissues, done in the black work embroidery technique.

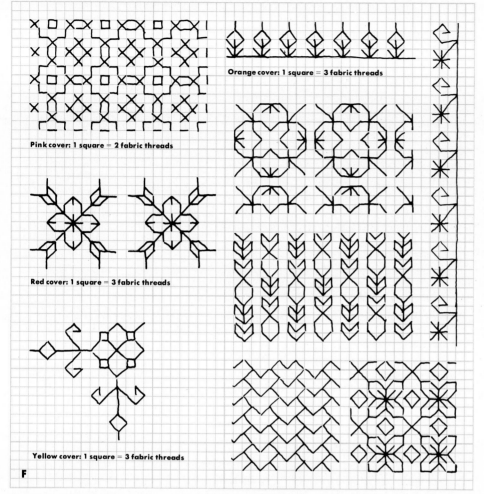

Pink cover: 1 square = 2 fabric threads

Red cover: 1 square = 3 fabric threads

Yellow cover: 1 square = 3 fabric threads

Orange cover: 1 square = 3 fabric threads

F

Figure F: Filling stitch patterns for tissue covers, page 74. For patterns used in the covers shown, the number of background fabric threads represented by each square on the blue grid is specified. If you want to use one or more of the other patterns, count each square on grid as two or three fabric threads, depending upon the type of effect you desire. Bold designs should be worked over three threads; a more delicate result is obtained by counting each square as two threads.

Needles: A blunt-pointed tapestry needle is used for this type of embroidery. See Embroidery Craftnote on needles, page 70.

The stitches: Only a few basic stitches are actually used to create the various filling patterns. Two of these are the backstitch and the cross stitch (see Embroidery Craftnotes: Stitches, page 88). The backstitch (Figure D) and the double running stitch (Figure E) are shown here on even-weave fabric. Most fillings use the backstitch; the cross stitch appears only when there are crosses within the fillings (as for the pink cover pattern, Figure F, and patterns 7, 8 and 12, Figure K). The double running or Holbein stitch is reversible and is used mostly for items where both sides are visible.

Making the Tissue Cover

I worked the tissue covers on even-count fabric with 24 threads per inch, using either two strands of six-strand cotton embroidery floss or its equivalent, one strand of pearl cotton No. 8, in a No. 24 tapestry needle. You may use the colors shown or any combination that pleases you. Start with a piece of fabric 6-by-7½ inches; fold it and secure the folds by making a row of double running stitches. To mark the vertical and horizontal centers, fold the fabric in half in both directions; and baste as shown in Figure G. Choose a filling stitch pattern from Figure F. After marking the boundaries as in Figure H, embroider each of the top sides, centering the design and repeating it from edge to edge. Sew ends together and finish, following Figure I; insert the packet of tissues.

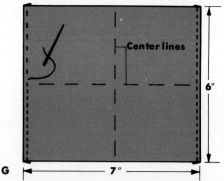

G

Figure G: Fold under ¼ inch and crease the short sides of a 7½-by-6-inch piece of fabric. The piece will now measure 7 by 6 inches. Using one strand of No. 8 pearl cotton or two strands of six-strand cotton embroidery floss, work a row of double running stitches over three fabric threads, two threads in from the fold. Fold fabric in half lengthwise. Unfold, and following the fabric grain, baste along the fold to mark the center. Fold fabric again crosswise, and mark the center with basting stitches.

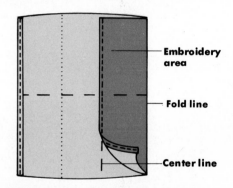

H

Figure H: With wrong sides facing, fold the fabric once more as shown, and match the rows of double running stitches with the second line of basting. The folded edges will overlap slightly. Unfold and baste along crease. Choose a border or motif from Figure F, above left. Embroider the design within the area marked by the double running stitch and last line of basting. Remove basting.

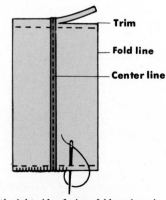

I

Figure I: With right sides facing, fold again as in Figure H. Stitch ends together, taking ½-inch seams. Trim seams to ¼ inch and finish seam edges with the buttonhole stitch. Turn right side out, gently poking out the corners with either blunt-pointed scissors or a crochet hook.

"Barnes Owl" worked by Maggie Barnes in black work technique using contemporary colors. Marion Scoular, who designed the outlines of the owl, chose this piece as an example of good distribution of light, medium, and dark-toned filling patterns.

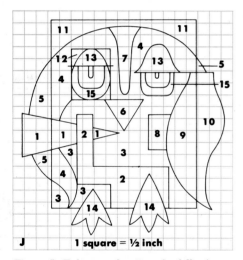

Figure J: Enlarge owl pattern by following the directions on page 117. Each area is keyed to the numbers indicating the specific filling patterns shown in Figure K on the page opposite.

Black work owl

I originally designed the black work owl and gave only the outline to my students, who then filled in the areas with black work filling stitch patterns of their choice. Maggie Barnes produced the hanging you see here. The project directions that follow allow you to duplicate the owl exactly. If you wish to create an original work, follow the suggestions at the end of the project directions.

Making the Owl

Before beginning, read Materials and Basic Procedures for the tissue covers, page 74. It will give you information on fabric and yarn substitutions, needles, stitches, and working from a chart. The owl was worked on white even count fabric with 24 threads per inch. The finished size is 12 inches square, but cut the fabric 16 inches square to allow a 2-inch margin on each side for blocking and mounting. See Embroidery Craftnotes: Preparation and Techniques, page 87 for starting and finishing yarn, threading the needle, and working with a hoop. Maggie used six-strand cotton embroidery floss in brown and gold, with the strands separated into one or two to work the various fillings and outlines. Use a No. 24 tapestry needle for the filling stitches. For the outlining, which will not always follow the weave of the fabric, use a pointed needle, such as a No. 5 crewel or a No. 25 chenille needle.

In the design pattern (Figure J), each square on the blue grid equals ½ inch. To start, enlarge the design (see Craftnotes on Enlarging Patterns, page 117). Using the enlarged paper pattern, transfer the outlines of the design to your fabric, with dressmaker's carbon paper (see Craftnotes, page 71).

Place fabric in a hoop or on a frame as directed on page 71. Using the number of strands specified in Figure K, embroider the areas of the design with the various filling stitches. The areas on the pattern (Figure J) are keyed to the numbers identifying the filling stitches in Figure K, page 77. Directly below each filling stitch you will find information indicating the number of strands of floss to use. For instance, the beak is worked in filling pattern 6 with two strands of floss in the needle. The best place to start is the center of each area to be filled. It is easier first to establish one or two complete sections in the center and then branch out, repeating the design until the entire area is filled. Fit the pattern into the corners where outlines converge. When you have completed the fillings, embroider the pupils of the eyes in satin stitch with two strands of brown floss; then outline the areas of the entire design with outline or chain stitch (see Craftnotes: Stitches, pages 88 through 91).

Wash, press, or block the finished embroidery, and then mount it on a 12-inch-square board as directed in Embroidery Craftnotes, page 71.

To Create Original Designs

If you would like to create your own black work owl, follow the directions above, but change the color and number of strands of threads specified, the color of the background fabric, or both. For instance, try a reverse effect, with a light colored thread and dark background.

To vary the design even more, simply transfer the outlines of the owl to the fabric and use other black work fillings shown on page 77. If you really feel daring, make up your own design. Transfer the outlines to the fabric, and use whatever fillings you like. Once you have done black work, you may even decide to invent a few filling stitches of your own. The only rules to remember are to count carefully and to choose fillings that will work well within the outlined shapes, following the suggestions below. The shapes of the design should be large enough for the fillings to show to advantage. Use simpler fillings for small areas, and save the more elaborate ones for large areas. Fillings have different visual effects—their tones vary from dark to light. Close your eyes slightly when looking at the fillings

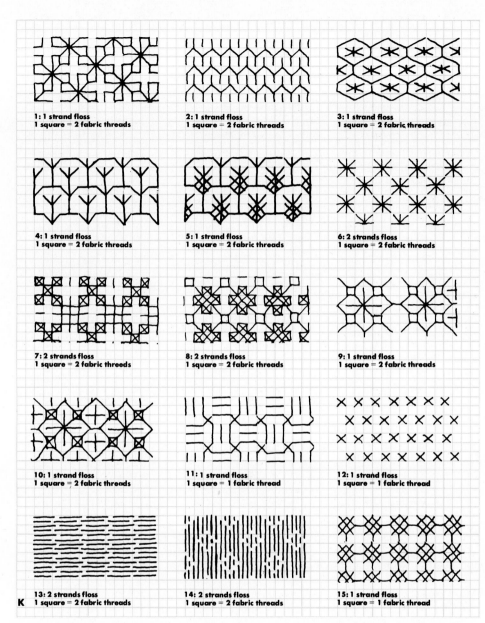

1: 1 strand floss
1 square = 2 fabric threads

2: 1 strand floss
1 square = 2 fabric threads

3: 1 strand floss
1 square = 2 fabric threads

4: 1 strand floss
1 square = 2 fabric threads

5: 1 strand floss
1 square = 2 fabric threads

6: 2 strands floss
1 square = 2 fabric threads

7: 2 strands floss
1 square = 2 fabric threads

8: 2 strands floss
1 square = 2 fabric threads

9: 1 strand floss
1 square = 2 fabric threads

10: 1 strand floss
1 square = 2 fabric threads

11: 1 strand floss
1 square = 1 fabric thread

12: 1 strand floss
1 square = 1 fabric thread

13: 2 strands floss
1 square = 2 fabric threads

14: 2 strands floss
1 square = 2 fabric threads

15: 1 strand floss
1 square = 1 fabric thread

K

Figure K: Filling stitch patterns for the black work owl shown on page 76. The number of strands of embroidery floss to use for each pattern are given in addition to the number of fabric threads each blue square represents.

illustrated above; you will notice how some appear darker than others. A good black work design balances these tones within the design. To help decide on the positions of the filling patterns, try the following method: Place a piece of tracing paper over the design. Using a pencil, color in the areas with light, medium and dark tones, distributing them evenly throughout the design. When the various tones are arranged to your satisfaction, refer to the pencil sketch as a guide in choosing your light, medium and dark fillings. If you want to use a particular filling, but it is not the right tone, varying the number of strands of yarn in your needle will change the apparent tone of the filling. Use only one strand for a light filling, and three, four, or more strands for a darker one. Plan your design carefully, try out the stitches you want to use on another piece of the fabric. Ripping out stitches will make the fabric look worn, and it is easier to erase on paper than to cut out carefully counted stitches.

L

Figure L: When working black work embroidery, you need not limit yourself to flat design. Tonal effects, as illustrated above, may be obtained by working a filling pattern in part of an area, then simplifying the pattern, gradually lightening it.

77

HARDANGER EMBROIDERY
Scandinavian Handwork

Hardanger, also known as Scandinavian embroidery, is characterized by geometric patterns formed with open squares and embroidered blocks. These effects are achieved by stitching over some fabric threads while other threads are cut and withdrawn, as they are in other forms of drawn-thread embroidery. The photograph opposite, a detail of hardanger embroidery, shows the embroidered blocks that surround the cut-out squares.

Hardanger is named for a district in southwestern Norway, where people use this form of embroidery to decorate both household and personal linens. Embroidery artist Rita Tubbs' painstaking re-creation of an heirloom Norwegian costume is pictured below; it was copied from a costume left to her by her mother, a native of

Marion Scoular, a graduate of London's Royal School of Needlework, is a nationally known lecturer. Marion teaches hand embroidery in Clemson, South Carolina, where she maintains her Robin Hood Wool Shop.

This Norwegian costume is a replica of an authentic heirloom. The apron border, collar and cuffs have been worked in a particularly intricate design of classic white-on-white hardanger embroidery which gives a lace-like appearance to the even-weave linen.

Namdalseid, Norway. Rita worked hardanger embroidery on the collar and cuffs of the blouse and the border of the apron. Hardanger is traditionally worked in white thread on white even-weave linen as shown in the costume, in contrast to the silk on gauze used in an ancient form of white-on-white work done by the Persians. Although white thread on white fabric is still considered classic hardanger, colorful threads and fabrics began to be used in the early nineteenth century.

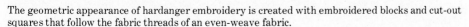

The geometric appearance of hardanger embroidery is created with embroidered blocks and cut-out squares that follow the fabric threads of an even-weave fabric.

Stitch key

 Satin stitch

⚛ Woven bar

✿ Vertical lace filling

O Picot

Materials and Basic Preparation

Hardanger fabric with an even weave (having the same number of threads per inch horizontally and vertically) may be used for hardanger embroidery. In fact, you can order an even-weave cotton fabric called hardanger cloth from mail order needlework shops such as Lee Wards, 1200 St. Charles St., Elgin, Ill. 60120, and Meribee, 2904 W. Lancaster, Fort Worth, Tex. 76107. I used it for all of the projects that follow. In addition to the hardanger cloth, you need: a blunt size 22 tapestry needle; one ball No. 5 pearl cotton thread for the satin stitch blocks, and one ball No. 8 pearl cotton thread for the filling; and sharp-pointed embroidery scissors. For instructions in basic embroidery techniques and information about the preparation of the work, see Embroidery Craftnotes, page 87.

Three-Step Procedure

The geometric pattern of hardanger embroidery is accomplished in three separate steps (Craftnotes opposite). The first step is to embroider the satin stitch blocks. Photograph 1 (below) shows satin stitch blocks worked in a diamond shape. These blocks must be worked first because they are not only decorative but they also serve as a reinforcement for the ends of the threads that are, in the second step, cut out and withdrawn. Photograph 2 shows the same diamond motif with the threads cut out. The third step is to decorate the exposed threads with a needlewoven bar (photograph 3) and to decorate the holes with lace filling (photographs 4 and 5).

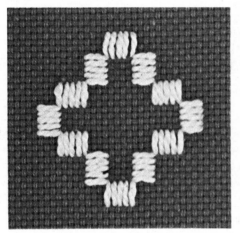

1: The first step in hardanger is to work the kloster or satin stitch blocks, 5 stitches over 4 threads each, placed here to form a diamond.

2: The second step is to cut and withdraw fabric threads, where they are supported by kloster blocks, creating holes and exposed threads.

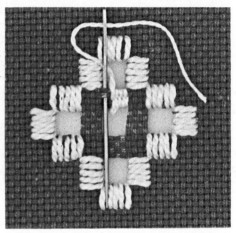

3: The third step is to decorate the exposed horizontal or vertical threads by weaving each group into a bar using the needleweaving stitch.

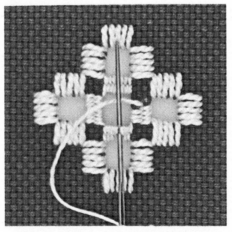

4: When you have woven to the middle of the fourth bar, pierce the center of the previous bar to start a stitch called vertical lace filling.

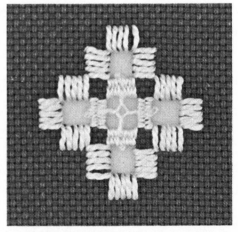

5: This diamond motif has woven bars with vertical lace filling and picots, small loops made with the embroidery thread.

CRAFTNOTES: STITCHES

Hardanger embroidery is worked in three steps. The first step is to stitch the satin stitch blocks (Embroidery Craftnotes, page 88), called kloster blocks, which outline the squares to be cut out, securing the ends of the cut thread. The blocks are stitched over an even number of fabric threads and are made up of the number of fabric threads plus one (usually 5 stitches over 4 threads). The second step is to cut the fabric threads. If vertical threads, called warp, are protected by a kloster block, then warp threads are cut leaving only horizontal threads called weft. If weft threads are protected, then weft threads are cut leaving only warp. If both warp and weft are cut, a hole is created. The third step is to decorate the threads exposed after cutting with woven bars, picots, and lace filling.

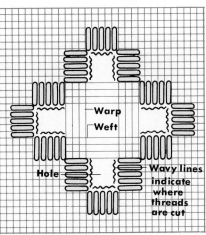

All threads to be withdrawn are cut before any are pulled out. On wrong side with embroidery scissors, snip threads at right angles to the kloster block supporting them (as shown above, along zigzag line). When all cut threads are withdrawn from the diamond motif, five holes are created. The hole in the center is created by removing the warp threads from top to bottom and the weft from right to left.

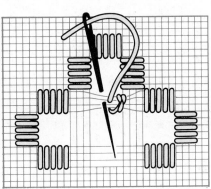

To decorate exposed fabric threads with a woven bar, use the needleweaving stitch. Place the needle under two fabric threads, then over two threads (above). See photograph 3, opposite.

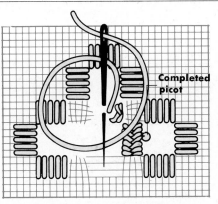

To make a picot, a small loop made with the embroidery thread, on a woven bar; needleweave to the center of the exposed threads, then bring the thread around to the front and under the needle (above), and pull the needle through. Continue needleweaving to the end of the bar.

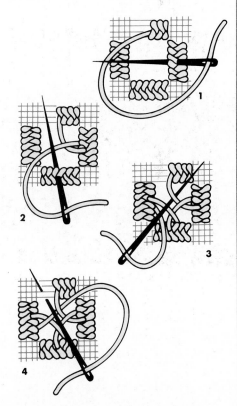

To fill the open areas with vertical lace, work to the middle of the fourth bar and make a stitch piercing the center of the last bar completed (1 above). Continue around the four bars piercing the center of each (2 and 3 above). Continue weaving the fourth bar (4 above). See photographs 4 and 5, opposite.

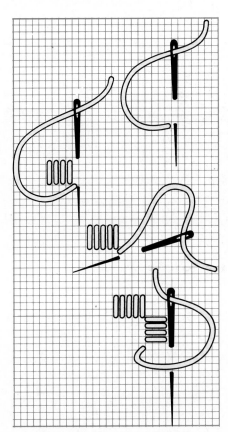

To stitch a kloster block, work 5 stitches over 4 threads (above). Make the stitches along the warp, if warp threads are to be cut and withdrawn. If weft threads are to be cut and withdrawn, make stitches along weft. Complete all kloster blocks before cutting any threads.

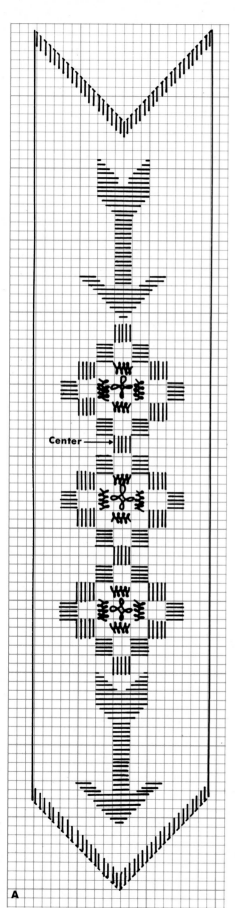

The center three motifs of this bookmark are outlined with kloster blocks whose open spaces are worked with woven bars and lace filling; the arrows are worked in satin stitches.

A bookmark

To make the bookmark pictured above, you need two pieces of hardanger cloth 3 by 10 inches. I chose pale yellow cloth and gold thread, but the color combination is optional. On one piece of fabric find and mark the center. Following the diagram (left), and using No. 5 pearl cotton thread, start stitching the first kloster block in the center and work from the center of the design down and then back up (Figure A). All blocks are five stitches over four threads. Complete all the kloster blocks (Craftnotes, page 81) for the three diamond-shaped motifs. The next step is to work the arrows in satin stitch also (see Embroidery Craftnotes, page 88). The placement of the arrow is shown in Figure A. When all the satin stitching is completed, cut and draw the threads (page 81). Using No. 8 pearl cotton thread, work four woven bars with a vertical lace stitch (page 81) in the center cut-out space of each motif.

To finish, place the embroidered fabric face down on the second piece of hardanger cloth. Baste the two pieces of fabric right sides together and machine stitch approximately six threads away from the widest part of the design along the two long sides, thus forming a long tube. Trim the seams to ¼ inch and turn the tube right side out. Press it lightly with a steam iron set on "cotton," laying the embroidery side face down on a towel. To finish each end, start at left edge and work a row of buttonhole stitches (Embroidery Craftnotes, page 90) picking up four horizontal threads of the fabric for the first stitch. Then, working left to right, descend one thread of the fabric with each stitch until the center, then begin ascending one thread until the edge is reached. Trim the fabric close to the buttonhole stitch.

Figure A: The hardanger embroidery bookmark shown at left, is started at the center kloster or satin stitch block, as indicated on this pattern, near the center of the fabric.

Wine place mat and napkin $ ● ⅄ ⅋

The dark red fabric provides an interesting background for the hardanger embroidery shown below. A detail of this place mat is shown on page 78. This type of embroidery is practical for a place mat and napkin set because, although it looks delicate, it withstands both machine washing and tumble drying on gentle cycles. To iron, place the dampened mat embroidery side face down on a towel, then press with iron set on "cotton."

To make the place mat, cut a piece of hardanger cloth 13 by 18½ inches. Using No. 5 pearl cotton thread, begin the satin stitch blocks 1¼ inches in from the edge of the center of the shorter side (Figure D, page 84). The last stitch of one block and the first stitch of the next block share a hole. The satin stitch bars in each of the four corners are 13 stitches over 4 threads. Work the kloster blocks along each of the four sides following the pattern (Figure D, page 84). There are 55 satin stitch blocks on each short side (not counting the corner bars), and 87 satin stitch blocks along each long side. When the outer row is completed and you have met the starting block, work the decorative inside row using a double running stitch ("Embroidery," page 74). There are 8 fabric threads between the row of satin stitch blocks and the row of double running stitches.

This attractive place mat and napkin are coordinated with the same hardanger embroidery border design; the corner motif is more elaborate on the place mat.

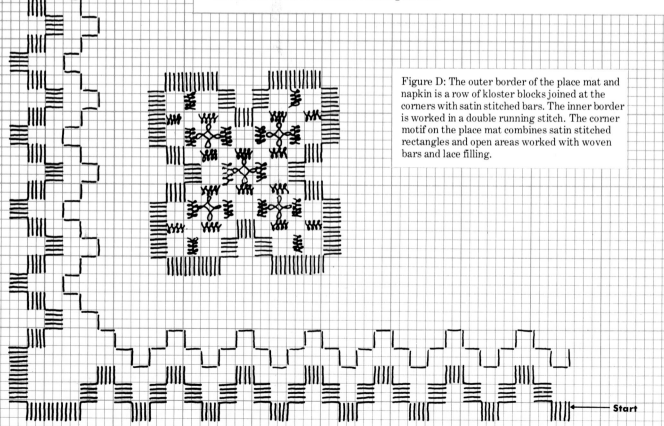

The motif in the lower right corner of the place mat is 12 threads above and 12 threads in from the double running stitch row. Start the outer satin stitch bars, which are 13 stitches over 4 threads, 12 threads above the uppermost double running stitch (Figure D). The inner satin stitch blocks are 5 stitches over 4 threads. After the satin stitch blocks are completed, the threads inside each block are cut and pulled. The threads that are exposed are worked with bars and lace filling (Craftnotes, page 81) following patterns indicated in Figure D.

To make the matching napkin, cut a piece of hardanger cloth 13½ inches square. Begin the satin stitch blocks 1¼ inches in from the edge following the same pattern for the borders used for the place mat except there will be 55 satin stitch blocks between the corner bars. A decorative row of double running stitch is placed 8 threads in from the satin stitch row. The corner motif (Figure E) is 12 threads in and 12 threads above the uppermost stitch of the double running stitch row. The motif is made up of five groups of 4 satin stitch blocks. The threads are cut from the center of each of the five squares formed and only the middle square is worked with lace filling. To finish place mat and napkin, turn raw edges under ⅛ inch and fold again so that the fold lies along same thread as the outermost satin stitches and hem.

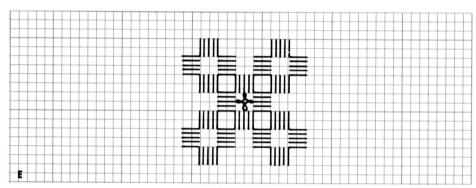

Figure E: The corner motif for the napkin, a simpler version of the one for the place mat, is placed 12 threads in from the row of double running stitches.

Figure D: The outer border of the place mat and napkin is a row of kloster blocks joined at the corners with satin stitched bars. The inner border is worked in a double running stitch. The corner motif on the place mat combines satin stitched rectangles and open areas worked with woven bars and lace filling.

D

Start

White place mat and napkin $ ● ♦ 🏃 ✂

This lovely place mat and napkin have been worked in the traditional hardanger of white stitching on white fabric. The edging of Italian hemstitching, a decorative openwork hem, and fringe, complement the hardanger embroidery. The openwork for the hemstitching is cut and withdrawn first, the hemstitching is worked next, and then the hardanger embroidery is worked.

Rita Tubbs became interested in traditional hardanger embroidery because she was intrigued by her mother's Norwegian costume. In her search for hardanger information, she consulted a Norwegian friend in Atlanta, Georgia; found a book on hardanger embroidery in a Danish shop in Solvang, California; and had a woman from the Hardanger area of Norway work a sampler of the embroidery to use as a reference. After she successfully copied the costume shown on page 79, Rita then designed this place mat and napkin set in traditional white-on-white hardanger.

To make the place mat, cut a piece of hardanger cloth 14 by 18 inches. Since the hemstitching is part of the design, it is easier to do it first but the fringe is left to last. Starting at the lower right corner, measure 1 inch in from the edge to allow for

Rita Allgood Tubbs, born in China of missionary parents, graduated from the University of Alabama with a degree in clothing, textiles and related arts. A member of the Georgia and Dogwood Chapters of the Embroiderers' Guild of America, she teaches hardanger embroidery in Atlanta and Marietta, Georgia. Her embroidery has won many awards.

The delicate beauty of traditional white hardanger embroidery worked on white even-weave fabric is illustrated by this place mat and matching napkin.

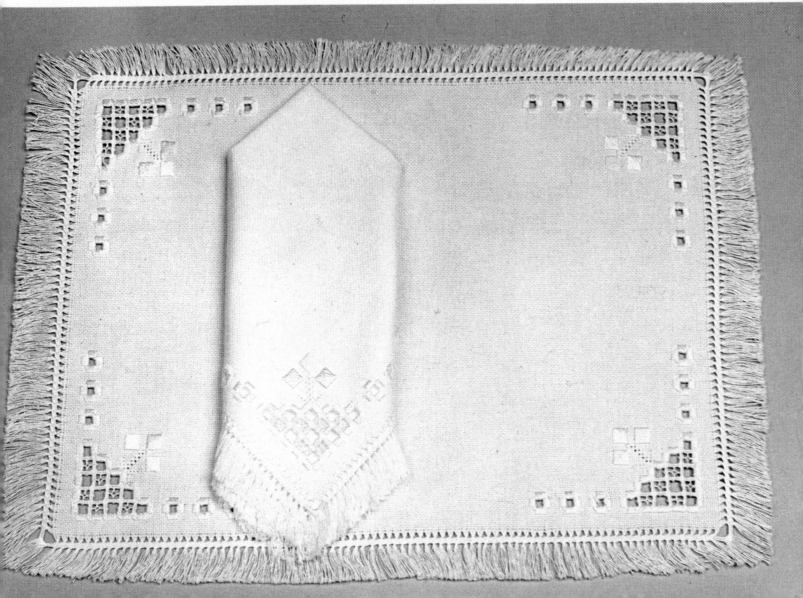

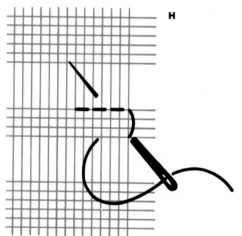

Figure G: Start hemstitching in the bottom right corner of the open mesh. Secure the thread with several running stitches, then take a stitch under the first 4 vertical fabric threads.

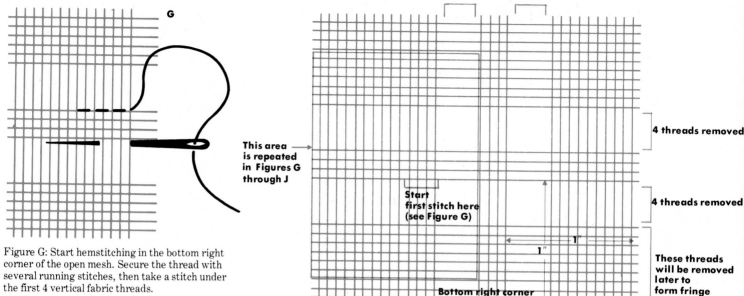

Figure F: To begin the hemstitching pictured on page 85, an open mesh 1 inch from the edge along each of the four sides is formed by withdrawing 4 threads from each side of a 4-thread group.

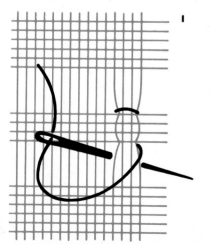

Figure H: To bind the four threads together at the bottom open mesh, take a stitch across them and bring the needle up at the upper edge of the horizontal 4-thread group.

fringe and pull out 1 thread (Figure F). Count 4 threads toward center and pull out the next thread. Now remove 3 threads on each side of this group of 4 threads. Repeat this procedure on each of the sides of the place mat, leaving an open mesh (Figure F). To begin hemstitching, fasten thread by taking a few running stitches in the fabric between the two spaces where the threads were withdrawn (Figure G). Insert the needle, right to left, under the first 4 threads in the lower space. Bind these 4 threads together by taking a stitch back over them, bringing the needle out in the upper space at the left of the same 4 threads (Figure H). Then bind them together in the upper space by taking a stitch back over them (Figure I) and bring the needle out again at the left of the same 4 threads in the upper space. Repeat the process, inserting the needle from right to left under the next 4 threads of the lower space (Figure J) and proceed as before, binding 4 stitches together first at the bottom and then at the top. At the corner (Figure K), weave a bar over the 4 horizontal threads (Craftnotes, page 81), and then buttonhole stitch (see Embroidery Craftnotes, page 90) around small woven square to turn corner. Next, turn the place mat so that the left side becomes the bottom and weave another

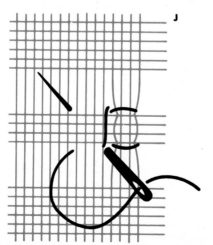

Figure I: Take a stitch in front of the same 4 threads (as in Figures G and H). Bring the needle out again at the top to the left of the threads to bind them together.

Figure J: Take a stitch at the bottom of the next group of 4 vertical threads to bind them together after bringing down the thread from the top of the previous group of 4 threads.

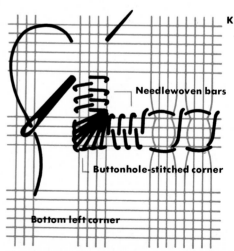

Figure K: To bridge the corner, work a needlewoven bar between hemstitching and corner, buttonhole stitch in corner, a needlewoven bar; then take a stitch over first 4 threads of left side.

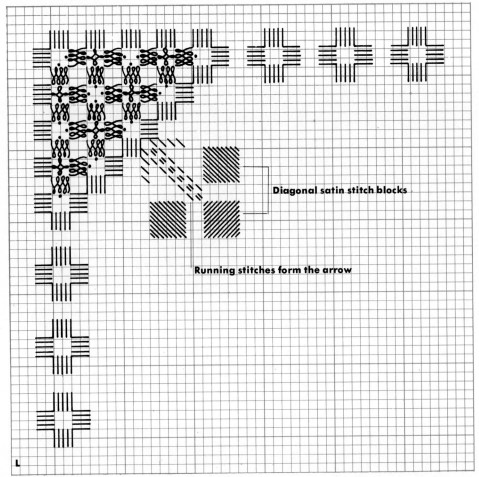

Diagonal satin stitch blocks

Running stitches form the arrow

L

Figure L: This corner motif is repeated in each of the four corners of the white place mat but in only one corner of the matching napkin. The 3 diagonal satin stitch blocks and the arrow are worked after the kloster blocks, cutting, and lace filling are completed.

bar (Figure K). Continue the hemstitching along each side. Do not pull remaining threads from hemstitching to edge of fabric (to make fringe) until the embroidery is completed.

The place mat is now ready for the hardanger embroidery. Work the kloster blocks starting in the corner 8 threads up from the hemstitching. Make 5 satin-stitched blocks, 4 threads apart. Repeat this vertically, starting in 8 threads from the hemstitching on the left side and leaving 4 threads between blocks. To complete the third side of the triangle and the 3 squares on either side of the triangle, follow the klosters as indicated in Figure L. When all the kloster blocks are completed, carefully cut the threads from the 3 squares on either side of the triangle. Then cut the threads from the squares that form the triangular motif.

To finish the embroidery, make woven bars of all the exposed threads in the triangle (Figure L), and stitch the picots shown (Craftnotes, page 81). Then work vertical lace filling in the squares as indicated. To complete the motif, make small diagonal running stitches over 2 threads in the shape of an arrow. The center row of stitches is worked with a double thread. Work the three blocks shown in diagonal satin stitch. Repeat this motif in each corner of the place mat.

To make the matching napkin, cut a piece of hardanger cloth 18 inches square. Hemstitch as you did the edge of the place mat (page 86). Make the same triangular corner design as for the place mat, but in one corner only. Finish both place mat and napkin by pulling out remaining threads of the marked-off inch on each side between hemstitching and edge (Figure F). This will form the fringe.

EMBROIDERY CRAFTNOTES: PREPARATION AND TECHNIQUES

Threading the needle and handling yarn lengths

Cut yarn 18 to 24 inches long; a longer strand might fray by the time you reach its end. To thread the yarn: Fold back a few inches of yarn at one end of strand to make a loop.

Pull loop taut around the head of the needle (above, left), and pinch this fold with thumb and forefinger. Slip loop off needle and push the pinched fold through the eye of the needle (above, right).

Starting and finishing yarn

When starting a length of yarn, knot the end and insert the needle in the fabric so the knot lies on the wrong side. When you reach the end of a yarn length, weave the thread under a few stitches on the wrong side, and clip the end close to the fabric. Begin subsequent new threads by weaving them under the nearest few stitches on the wrong side.

Working with a hoop

Each time the needle is inserted, it goes in vertically with a jabbing motion. Keep one hand above the standing floor hoop and the other below it, as shown in the drawing.

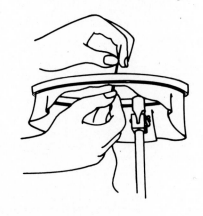

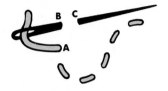

1. Running Stitch: Bring needle up at A, down at B, up at C. Space between stitches should be equal to their length.

2. Straight Stitch ▉: Worked the same as running stitch, but the stitches are longer. May be worked in rows, at angles, or at random.

3. Backstitch: Work from right to left. Bring needle up at A; insert at B; bring it up at C, and draw thread through. Go back; insert in front of A, and complete figure. Be sure the stitch lengths are uniform.

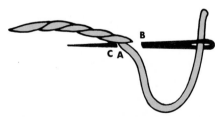

4. Outline or Stem Stitch: This is a basic stitch used to embroider lines, outlines and the stems of flowers. Start at top or bottom guide line. Bring needle up at A; insert at B at a slant as shown; bring up at C, and pull yarn through. Always keep the yarn on the same side of the needle.

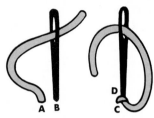

5. Seed Stitch ▉: Small stitches randomly placed. Come up at A, go down at B, a small distance away. Come up at C and go down at D, crossing the first stitch diagonally.

6. Satin Stitch ▉: A plump, solidly filled figure is created with this stitch. Outline the area to be worked with small Backstitches (3), to keep the edge even. Come up at A; draw yarn through. Go in at B; pull yarn through. Continue, placing stitches side by side across the design just outside the outline stitches. Keep the stitches close and their direction uniform.

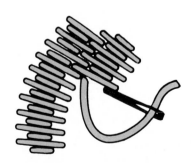

7. Long and Short Stitch ▉: Resembles Satin Stitch (6) and is used to create a solid filling. Alternate long and short Satin Stitches, as shown, placing them side by side. In the next row, a long stitch goes below a short one.

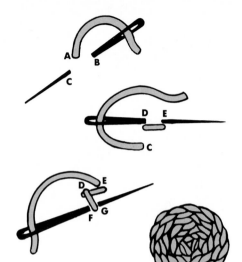

8. Raised Rose ▉: Bring yarn up at A, and with needle at a slant, go in at B; come up at C; pull yarn through. Go in at D; come up at E; pull yarn through. Go in at F; come up at G; pull yarn through. Work a spiral of Outline Stitches (4) around triangle formed by first three steps.

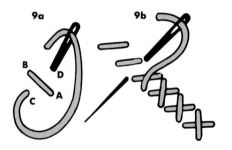

9a   9b

9. Cross Stitch: To make a single Cross Stitch, bring needle up at A; insert at B, up at C, and in at D, as in figure 9a. Be sure B and C, A and D are parallel. To make a row of Cross Stitches, work a row of slanting stitches from right to left, or left to right. Then work back across row, slanting stitches in the opposite direction, as in figure 9b. In a group of Cross Stitches, be sure the top stitches always slant in the same direction.

Note: Stitches worked best when fabric is stretched tautly in a hoop are indicated by the symbol ▉.

STITCHES

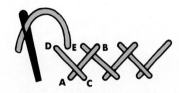

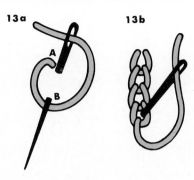

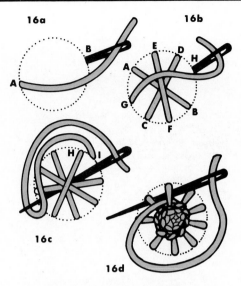

10. Herringbone Stitch: Row of slanted stitches crossed at top and bottom. Following the drawing, bring needle up at A, in at B, up at C, in at D, up at E, and continue.

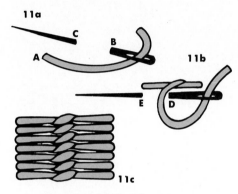

11. Roumanian Stitch: Bring needle up at A; pull yarn through. Go in at B and up at C, with thread below needle as in figure 11a. Pull yarn through. For second part of stitch, insert needle at D; bring out at E (figure 11b). Pull yarn through. Continue as from A. Result is shown in figure 11c.

13. Chain Stitch: This stitch is also used for a decorative outline. Bring needle up at A; lay a loop of yarn on the fabric. Hold the loop while you insert the needle back at A and bring point of needle up at B, with loop held under point (figure 13a). Draw yarn through. Form remaining loops in same manner, always inserting needle where it emerged from last stitch (figure 13b). Anchor last stitch of chain by inserting the needle below its loop.

14. Open Chain: Made in the same way as the Chain Stitch (13) except the top of the loop is open. Finish off as for Chain Stitch.

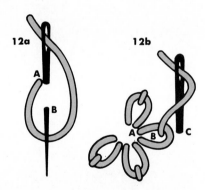

12. Lazy Daisy or Detached Chain: Bring the yarn up at A; make a loop and hold down loop with thumb. Insert the needle back at A and bring it out over the loop at B. Pull yarn through. Next, anchor the loop by inserting the needle at C and pulling the yarn through to the underside. May be worked separately as in figure 12a, but most often worked in a circle to form petals of a flower (figure 12b).

15. Twisted Chain: Same as Open Chain (14), with a twist at the top of the loop.

16. Whipped Spider Web ⊞: Work spokes with chenille or crewel needle. Bring needle up at A; insert at B, bisecting circle as in figure 16a. Bring needle up at C, pull yarn through and insert at D; up at E, in at F, up at G, and down at H, following figure 16b. Bring needle up at I (figure 16c). Change to tapestry needle. Slide tip of needle under all the threads where they cross at the center and loop the yarn over and under the needle tip as in figure 16c. Tighten yarn, forming a knot at the center, and the ninth spoke. To whip the spider (figure 16d), slide needle counterclockwise under two spokes of yarn (do not catch the fabric); pull yarn through; slide needle back under the second of these spokes and then under the spoke ahead, as shown. Pull yarn through. Continue in a spiral until the circle is filled.

17. Woven Spider Web ⊞: This differs from Whipped Spider Web (16) in that the yarn is woven over and under single spokes counterclockwise. Work Whipped Spider to completion of center knot; then weave yarn under first spoke, over second, under third, continuing until circle is filled.

18. Backstitched Chain: Work a row of Chain Stitch; finish off. Using a contrasting color yarn, if desired, Backstitch (3) through it, as shown.

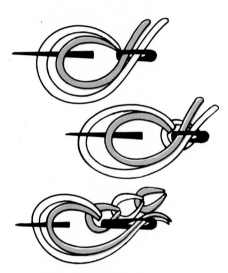

19. Magic Chain: Chain worked with two colors of yarn in the same needle. Thread needle with first and second colors, and proceed as for Chain Stitch (13), but loop only first color under the needle for the first stitch. For the second stitch, loop the second color under the needle. Alternate this pattern in subsequent stitches.

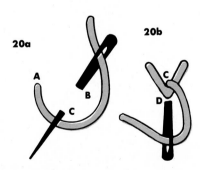

20. Fly Stitch: Like the Lazy Daisy Stitch (12), but open at top. Bring needle up at A; insert at B, and come up at C with the thread looped under the needle, as in figure 20a. Pull yarn through. Insert needle at D (figure 20b) to secure the loop.

21. Open Attached Fly Stitch: Like Fly Stitch (20), but anchored by a long rather than short stitch. Work from top to bottom.

22. Closed Attached Fly Stitch: Worked in the same manner as Open Attached Fly Stitch (21), but with the stitches close together and the connecting loops short.

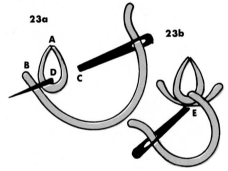

23. Wheat Ear Stitch: Combination of Lazy Daisy Stitch (12) and Fly Stitch (20). Bring needle up at A, form loop of desired size, and reinsert needle at A, as in Lazy Daisy Stitch (12). Bring the needle up at B and draw through. Insert needle at C and come up at D with yarn under needle (figure 23a). Pull through. Anchor at E (figure 23b).

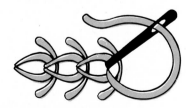

24. Attached Wheat Ear: Complete Wheat Ear (23) through D, but do not anchor at E. Instead, make loop of next Wheat Ear, and then end by anchoring as in Wheat Ear.

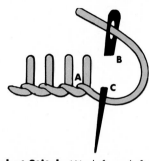

25. Blanket Stitch: Work from left to right. Bring needle up at A. Loop yarn in position shown, insert needle at B with point coming up at C and the yarn looped under needle. Draw yarn through. Repeat B-C across. This stitch can be used as a filling or to form outlines.

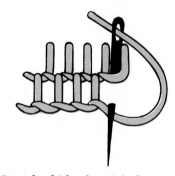

26. Attached Blanket Stitch: Joined rows of Blanket Stitch (25). Work row of Blanket Stitches. Finish off. Starting at the beginning of the row, work second row in bottom loops of first row. Work additional rows the same way.

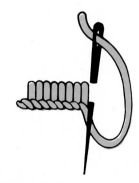

27. Buttonhole Stitch: A closed Blanket Stitch (25). Proceed as for Blanket Stitch, but space stitches close together, as shown.

TITCHES

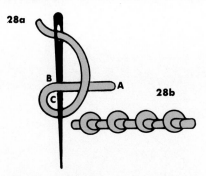

28. Coral Stitch: Series of attached knots. Come up at point A. Hold yarn to the left; go in at point B, and come up at C with yarn under the needle. Draw knot tight. Lay thread to the left for next stitch. Continue as for B and C. Figure 28b shows a row of completed Coral Stitches.

29. French Knot: Come up at the point where the French Knot is to be. Form loop around needle, and insert needle vertically into or just next to same point. Pull loop tight around needle. Hold yarn with left thumb, pull needle through (figure 29a). Figure 29b shows enlarged finished French Knot.

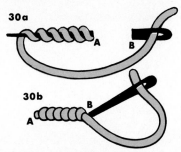

30. Bullion Stitch: Bring needle up at A. Insert needle at B and bring out near A; do not pull needle all the way through. Twist thread 6 times around point of needle as in figure 30a (the coils, when pushed together, should equal the distance between A and B). Holding coils and needle securely with thumb and forefinger, draw needle through fabric and coils. Carefully pull thread to tighten stitch so knot lies flat against the fabric (knot will flip over). Reinsert needle in B (figure 30b).

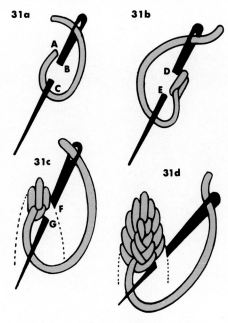

31. Closed Cretan Stitch: Closely spaced, elongated loops that overlap. Work from top to bottom. Bring the needle up at A, in at B, and up at C with the yarn looped under the needle (figure 31a). Pull yarn through. Insert needle at D, and come up at E with yarn under the needle as in figure 31b. Pull yarn through. Next stitch, F to G (figure 31c), will begin just below and to the right of B. Pull yarn through, and continue. Increase the length of the stitches as you work downward (figure 31d).

32. Open Cretan Stitch: Same as Closed Cretan Stitch (31), but with space between them.

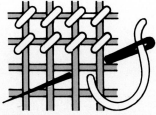

33. Simple Trellis : Trellises are squared filling stitches and consist of a combination of couching with preceding stitches. To couch means to tack down long threads with small stitches. Use long Straight Stitches (2) to lay evenly spaced trellises of yarn across area to be worked. Then couch intersections with small diagonal stitches as shown here.

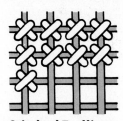

34. Cross Stitched Trellis : Worked as Simple Trellis (33), except the yarn is couched at intersections with small Cross Stitches (9).

35. Simple Diagonal Trellis : Lay vertical and horizontal yarns as in Simple Trellis (33). Then lay diagonal yarns. Couch intersections with small diagonal stitches.

36. Cross Stitched Diagonal Trellis : Lay yarns as in Simple Diagonal Trellis (35). Work diagonal rows of Outline Stitch (4), slanting in opposite direction from the first diagonals. Couch with Cross Stitches (9) where diagonals intersect.

The young girl in the silhouette on the wall, Becca Read of Putney, Vermont, stitched the sampler (dated June 19, 1800) on the table. The sewing basket, needlecase, scissors, and brass eyeglasses belonged to Sally Steele George of New Sharon, Maine. The tin spool holder, clamp-on iron pincushion, embroidery hoop, and Shaker darning egg date from the nineteenth century. Everything shown is from the collection of Glee Krueger of Westport, Connecticut.

SAMPLERS
Xs Make the Message

Bernice Barsky of New York designs handcraft projects for magazines and yarn companies. On one assignment, she adapted pre-Columbian textile designs to make needlepoint kits for the Metropolitan Museum of Art. She enjoys translating needlecraft directions written in French and Italian, owned a yarn shop for ten years, and has been a mechanical draftsman and technical editor. Bernice studied at the Pratt-New York Phoenix School of Design, The Fashion Institute of Technology and Mechanics Institute in New York, and the Philadelphia College of Textiles and Science.

The kind of needlework samplers that are being worked today—with pictorial scenes, alphabets, numerals, verses, and borders of flowers done mostly in cross-stitch on even-weave fabric—evolved largely in America and England during the period between 1750 and 1840.

Before then, as far back as Elizabethan times, a sampler was a collection of many different embroidery stitches worked on a long, narrow strip of handwoven linen. Stitches, especially those that were new or particularly difficult, could be referred to as necessary. Samplers of lace patterns and knitting stitches were made for the same reason, also being worked in long strips.

Many samplers of the late eighteenth and early nineteenth centuries were done by children remarkably young, during their school years and even before. This was a time when a young girl's education consisted mainly of mastering needlework, etiquette, and religious beliefs. Samplers were exercises in embroidery skills, of course, but they also tested to some extent a child's neatness, spelling, and knowledge of the Bible. In samplers made by older girls in certain finishing schools, the influence of a few teachers can be found in the similarity of the designs and verses. Some of the more elaborate samplers took months and even years to complete.

The earliest American sampler still in existence, now displayed in Pilgrim Hall at Plymouth, Massachusetts, was made around 1640 by Loara Standish, daughter of Captain Miles Standish.

A detail of the bottom section of a sampler made by Lois Tillson in 1760 is one of the earliest samplers to show an umbrella or parasol (held by the middle figure in the pink dress). Stitches include: two-color rice, cross, satin, oriental, outline, and eyelet. The sampler is American and possibly was done in Massachusetts.

Below: This small ruffled sampler was made in England by Ann Ward in the nineteenth century. The stylized floral and animal motifs and the central verse are done in red cross-stitches on a bleached linen ground. The sampler is 6 inches high by 6⅝ inches wide, with a ¾-inch ruffle added.

An English sampler fragment depicting the Garden of Eden, 9 inches high by 8¾ inches wide, is stitched with silk threads on a linen background. The fig leaves on the figures of Adam and Eve are worked in a detached buttonhole stitch and attached separately. The sampler dates from 1727.

Antique Samplers

The antique samplers and fragments of samplers on these pages are from the collection of Glee Krueger of Westport, Connecticut. Mrs. Krueger was on the staff of the Art Institute of Chicago and is the author of a book on New England samplers. The samplers shown here date from the seventeenth, eighteenth, and nineteenth centuries and were worked in America, England, and Canada.

An example of embroidery done on perforated or punched paper is this ribbon-backed bookmark worked in wool, silk twist, and steel beads. The inscription reads: "Presented to Mrs. Ruth Goodale by Mager John Button living in Canada aged 81 years Sept. 1853/Remember me." The bookmark is 2⅝ inches high by 8¼ inches wide.

Young boys stitched samplers too—George Parker, born May 30, 1791, made this sampler in 1799 in Bradford, Massachusetts. He worked with silk floss and twist threads on linen; the sampler is 12½ inches high by 11 inches wide.

An embroidered pincushion 2⅛ inches square commemorating the marriage of Queen Victoria to Prince Albert, February 10, 1840, was stitched by a child in England's Cheltenham Female Orphan Asylum. One side proclaims that "A virtuous woman is a (crown) to her husband." The silk cross-stitches are on a gauze ground, with silk tassels at the corners.

A pegboard sampler

Cross-stitching a name in big block letters across a pegboard is a good way for a young child to practice embroidery. On graph paper, plot the child's name in Xs to determine how much pegboard you will need. Pegboard holes are spaced 1 inch apart, and one cross-stitch will use four holes—two across and two down. A short name, such as Jackie, will fit on a board 12 by 36 inches, as pictured below, left. A longer name will need a longer board; a two-part name can be stitched in two rows on a wider board.

Have the pegboard cut to size; then spray one side with two coats of white enamel. Heavyweight rug yarn (one skein) and a blunt tapestry or rug needle with a large eye make the stitching go quickly and easily.

Stitching on pegboard is good practice for the proper two-handed method of embroidering. One hand is held on top of the work and the other hand below; the needle is passed through the work from one hand to the other (photograph 1). When fabric is used, this results in smoother stitches and causes less distortion of the weave than inserting the needle in and out of two points in a single motion.

Making knots at the ends of threads is not a good idea on fabric because the knots show through and cause bumps, but there is no problem when the fabric is a stiff sheet of pegboard (photograph 2). Ends too short to be knotted can be taped down.

When the cross-stitches are done, hang the pegboard and insert hooks to hold his or her paraphernalia.

Jackie now has a special place to hang her hats, and she can proudly say it is a sample of her embroidery talents. The pegboard was sprayed with white enamel; the cross-stitches are made with brightly colored rug yarn.

1: Jackie works intently on her pegboard sampler, using two hands to pass the needle back and forth, while Trin looks on.

2: Knots can be used to end a length of yarn on the back of the pegboard because they do not show or cause bumps. Short ends can be taped flat.

Hoop-framed samplers

Using gingham or dotted swiss as a background fabric lets a beginner count checks or dots instead of counting threads when she makes a sampler. And embroidery hoops made of colorful plastic or natural wood can be used as frames when the embroidery is done. For these reasons, hoop-framed sampler pictures done on either fabric are ideal projects for children.

A round hoop 8 inches in diameter, preferably with a screw-type adjustment, is a good size for small, inexperienced hands. A hoop works well for embroidery of this size because the fabric does not need to be moved. For larger samplers, a frame is preferable; moving a hoop from one area to another could damage stitches caught under the top hoop. Choose either a tapestry (blunt) or a chenille (pointed) needle, and use six-strand embroidery floss, pearl cotton, or light-to-medium weight yarn.

Cut a 12-inch square of gingham (⅛-, ¼-, or ½-inch checks) and a square of the same size from a man's white handkerchief to use as the lining. Put the two layers of fabric between the hoops and pull them taut (photograph 3, page 98).

Following one of the cross-stitch charts on page 98, or any chart for a simple design that can be contained within the hoop area, locate the center of the chart and the center of fabric. Then decide where to start the first stitch (photograph 4, page 99). If the design is at all complicated, it is best to start in the center and work out toward the edges. On simple designs such as those shown here, you can work from

Jennifer used dotted swiss instead of gingham so she could follow the dots as she worked the stitches of her flower with variegated floss.

Trin didn't stop with a purple chick; she added a stretch of grass and a flower to her gingham-background sampler picture.

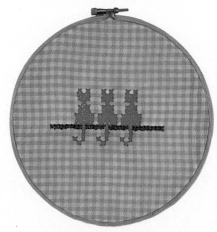

Grace embroidered a trio of cats on ⅛-inch gingham checks. She gave the design a personal touch by providing them with a fence to sit on.

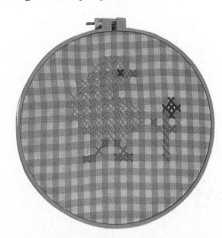

Joanna followed a chart to make her cheery yellow chick, then added her own flower design. The basic charts are given in Figure A, page 98.

CRAFTNOTES: STITCHES

Cross-stitch
Make a row of evenly spaced, slanting stitches, starting at the lower right corner and working from right to left. Work back, completing the Xs. Be sure that all top stitches cross in the same direction and that all stitches meet at the corners. (Cross-stitches may be worked from left to right, if that is more comfortable for you.)

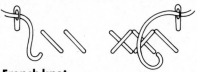

French knot
Wrap the thread several times around the needle, holding the thread taut. Insert the needle close to the starting point; pull it through slowly and keep the knot close to the surface.

Straight stitch
Bring the needle through at one end, and insert it at the other end, making a single stitch. Carry the needle under the fabric to the start of the next stitch, leaving space between the stitches.

Stem stitch
Working from left to right, take regular, slightly slanting stitches along the line of the design. Bring the thread through on the left side of the previous stitch, and keep it below the needle.

Filled-in running stitch
Run the needle over and under the fabric, making the upper stitches equal or unequal lengths as needed. Work back, filling in the spaces.

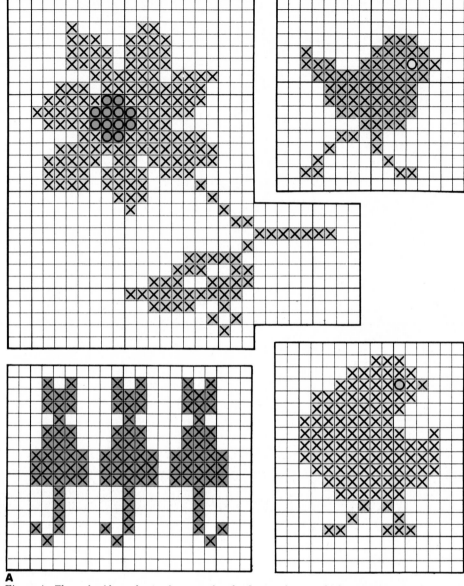

Figure A: The embroidery charts above are for the flower, the two chicks, and the trio of cats that appear on the hoop-framed samplers, page 97. Cats and chicks are stitched on the denim patches, page 100, and a lone cat is stitched on the sampler on page 101.

3: Joanna makes sure that both layers of fabric, the gingham and the lining, are unwrinkled and taut in the hoops.

the top down or, for that matter, in any direction. If you find the fabric needs to be moved on the hoops in order to center the design, do so as soon as the basic motif or a key part of it is completed (photograph 5).

Add extra designs to fill in the background if you like, when you are sure the main design is centered. If the fabric stays in the hoops in a wrong position for any length of time, you may need to iron it before repositioning it. Iron the cross-stitches on the wrong side, face down on a terry cloth towel, to avoid flattening them.

To thread thick yarn through the needle, pinch the yarn around the needle below the eye (photograph 6) and push the eye onto this doubled end (photograph 7). To secure an end of yarn, pull it through a few stitches on the back; do not make knots. If the end is very short, unthread the needle and push it through a few stitches until the eye aligns with the end of the yarn. Then thread the yarn through the eye and pull the needle through (photograph 8).

When the embroidery is finished, round the corners of the excess fabric and gather up the edges (both layers together) with basting stitches, pulling the excess inside the hoop on the back. Secure the gathering stitches. Hang the hoop on a hook, using a length of matching yarn or ribbon.

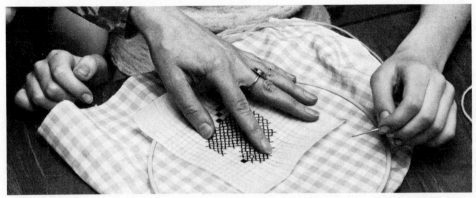

4: Craftswoman Bernice Barsky shows Joanna how to center her design on the fabric. With the first stitch in place as the starting point, Joanna will simply count the Xs in each row of the chart and fill in a corresponding number of squares on the gingham.

5: Grace shows her first cross-stitch cat. If she finds that the design is off-center, she can unscrew the top hoop and move the fabric.

6: To thread sport-weight yarn through the eye of the tapestry needle, first pinch it tightly around the needle, leaving an end an inch or so long.

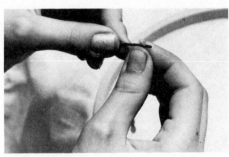

7: Then slide the yarn off the needle without losing the crease; push the eye of the needle onto this loop and pull the loop through.

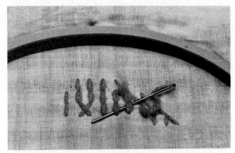

8: To secure a short end, work the unthreaded needle under a few stitches until you align the eye with the yarn end, thread it and pull it through.

Joanna concentrates as she checks the chart for the number of stitches she still must make in the body of the chick.

Trin holds her hoop with one hand and passes the needle from the back to the front through the same hole as the neighboring stitch.

Next, she passes the needle in the opposite direction. This two-step method results in uniform stitches and does not pull the fabric.

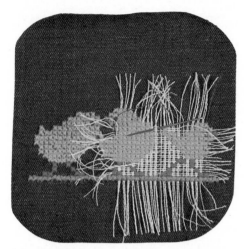

9: Baste cross-stitch canvas onto the denim patch, embroider through the patch and over the canvas meshes (as you would over threads of even-weave fabric), then gently pull out the canvas threads with your fingers or tweezers.

An iron-on denim patch, embroidered with a pair of fat cats, can be used to decorate a book bag or a pair of jeans. Variegated embroidery floss can give the cats a sun-dappled look.

A patch of denim

Counting threads on an iron-on denim patch would be virtually impossible—but it is possible to embroider such a patch with cross-stitches, and to keep those stitches as straight and even as though you could count the threads. The secret is cross-stitch canvas. It looks like a thin penelope needlepoint canvas, with a dark vertical thread every five meshes to help you keep count. You simply baste this cross-stitch canvas on top of the denim patch (or any other uneven-weave or hard-to-count fabric); then work your stitches through both layers. Count the threads of the canvas as you would count the threads of an even-weave fabric, and make the cross-stitches over the meshes, keeping them even but not too tight. When the embroidery is finished, cut off the excess canvas and gently pull out the threads from underneath the cross-stitches (photograph 9). To avoid crushing the stitches, use a terry cloth towel as a press cloth when you iron the patch onto a tote bag or jeans.

Design your own sampler

Many things can be translated into charts for samplers—drawings from a child's coloring book, photographs from a magazine, a fabric print, needlepoint charts, greeting card designs. The personalized sampler shown on the opposite page is an invitation for a boy named Richard to visit his grandparents; the elements could be modified to make such a sampler appeal to any child. In this case, the fabric was pulled taut and thumb-tacked to the back of a canvas-stretcher frame from an art store; this kept it smooth while it was being worked. The finished sampler can be displayed in a picture frame under glass if that is desirable.

To create your own design, use graph paper to trace the design—the transparent kind used by draftsmen is ideal. Or you can hold ordinary graph paper up to a window and trace the design behind it. Still another alternative that works well with simple, large designs is to make your own graph on tracing paper; then outline the shape and fill in with Xs. Square off any rounded edges to fit into the squares of the graph paper and simplify complicated designs. Trace on the wrong side of the graph paper so that if you must erase, you will not erase the graph lines. You can vary the size of the design by changing the size of the graph paper (how many squares it has per inch) or by plotting each stitch over more than one square. For example, wide cross-stitches can be made one square high and three squares wide; tall stitches can be one square wide and two squares high.

When planning a sampler with several motifs, use thread to baste the outlines of the major elements on the fabric. This helps you visualize how the finished sampler will look, and you can rearrange motifs before they are stitched. Remove the basting threads after the embroidery is completed.

The background fabric can be any cloth with an even weave, such as linen, hardanger cloth, loose-weave wool, panama cloth, *aida* cloth, or *herta* cloth. The thread can be one or more strands of pearl cotton, six-strand embroidery cotton, crewel wool, tapestry yarn, or silk or metallic threads. Check your local art needlework shop, or order from the mail-order sources listed on page 102.

The sampler shown on page 101 has an actual design area 12 by 16½ inches. It is worked primarily in crewel wools and the background fabric is hardanger cloth. Charts for the alphabet and major design elements are given in Figures B and C, pages 101 and 102. The basic stitch is cross-stitch; the dark blue tree tops are straight stitch; the border has an inner row of stem stitch and two outer rows of cross-stitch. The roof of the house is half-cross-stitch (four threads high by two threads wide); the doors and windows are small cross-stitches (two threads square) surrounding large cross-stitches (four threads square). The alphabet, small sailboat, birds, and animals are worked in small cross-stitches (two threads square), the house, cars, truck, train, large boats, airplanes, and green trees are large cross-stitches (four threads square).

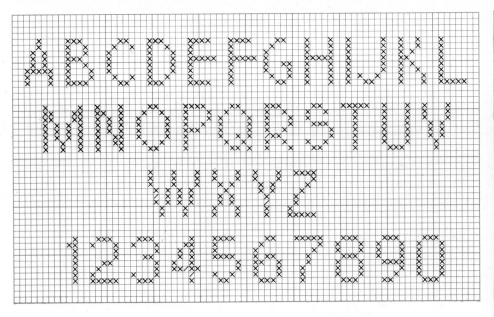

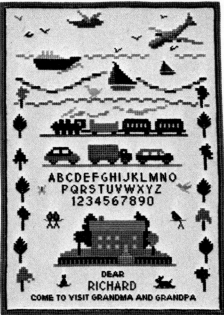

Richard will remember this invitation to visit his grandparents for years to come, since it will hang in his room. Many different elements of interest to him make this sampler very personally his.

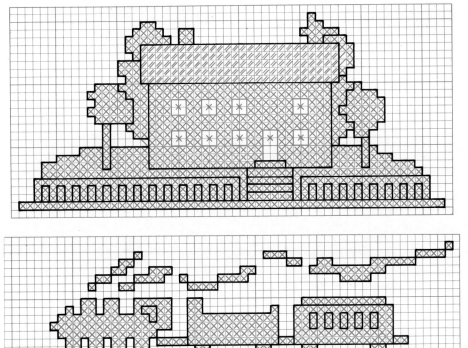

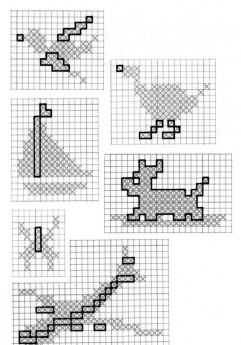

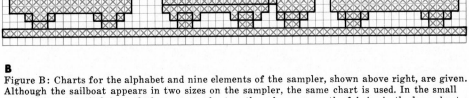

B

Figure B: Charts for the alphabet and nine elements of the sampler, shown above right, are given. Although the sailboat appears in two sizes on the sampler, the same chart is used. In the small boat, each cross-stitch is worked over a two-by-two-thread square on the fabric; in the large boat, each stitch is worked over a four-by-four-thread square. This technique can be used with any chart to reduce or enlarge the size of the motif. Charts for six other elements used on the sampler are given in Figure C, page 102.

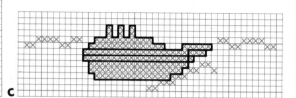

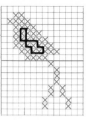

Figure C: Charts for additional elements used in the sampler on page 101 are given above.

Perforated-paper sampler ¢ ⏰ 🧍 🧵

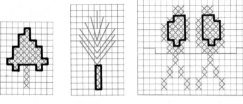

Janet Fiori of Sea Cliff, New York, is a free-lance designer who specializes in doing embroidery on perforated paper, although she does many other types of stitchery as well. Her designs have been published and she teaches this Victorian craft to women's groups and children in her neighborhood.

Samplers, bookmarks, and greeting cards embroidered on perforated paper instead of cloth were popular during the nineteenth century, but their popularity so waned that by the late 1940s this special-purpose paper was no longer made. An example of an old perforated-paper bookmark is shown on page 94.

The paper is again available and this almost-forgotten needlecraft is being revived. You can order sheets of the perforated paper from Sewmakers Incorporated, 1619 Grand Avenue, Baldwin, New York 11510. The traditional way to embroider on the special paper is to stitch in the design only, leaving the cream-colored background unworked.

The sampler pictured at left is embroidered with three strands of six-strand embroidery cotton in five colors: light, medium, and dark green; medium and dark coral. The filled-in running stitch alphabets (top) are dark green; the cross-stitch alphabets (bottom) are medium green; the single motifs between the alphabets combine light green and light coral; all other stitches are either medium green or dark coral. Charts for the alphabets, borders, and single motifs are given in Figure D; refer to the color photograph, left, for their placement.

Stitching on perforated paper is much like stitching on fabric, with a few exceptions (photographs 10 and 11). Because the paper is stiff, you cannot crush the sides to reach the center or put the paper in a hoop, although you can tack it to a frame. The paper does not ravel, so finishing the edges is unnecessary. Select a blunt, slender needle with a long eye. Use two separate motions to make a stitch—do not work the needle in and out of two holes in a single motion. Work evenly and do not pull the stitches very tight. Use thread no thicker than three strands of embroidery cotton to avoid tearing the holes, and stitch over loose ends in back to hold them rather than make knots. When crossing from one letter to the next on the back, use a diagonal stitch to minimize show-through.

This alphabet-and-borders sampler is stitched in soft shades of green and coral on perforated paper. As shown, the overall size is 11 by 14 inches (157 by 201 holes), but you can combine the various elements in Figure D to make a larger or smaller sampler. The top alphabets are worked in filled-in running stitch; the bottom alphabets are done in cross-stitch (see Craftnotes, page 97).

Suppliers
Mail-order sources for background fabrics, threads, and other embroidery supplies:

Judy's Originals, 182 Mt. Bethel Road, Warren, N. J. 07060

Boutique Margot, 26 West 54th Street, New York, N. Y. 10019

Alice Maynard, 724 Fifth Avenue, New York, N. Y. 10019

Lee Wards, Elgin, Ill. 60120

Merribee, 2904 West Lancaster, P. O. Box 9608, Fort Worth, Texas 76107

10: The design elements are done in cross-stitch (top) and filled-in running stitch (bottom). The back side of the paper is less smooth and shiny than the front side.

11: Cross from one letter to another on the back side with a diagonal, rather than a horizontal, stitch to minimize show-through. Indicate the center of the sheet with pencil lines on the back.

D
Figure D: Charts for the alphabets, border designs, and single motifs for the paper sampler are given above; combine them any way you like or follow the color photograph opposite for placement. The filled-in running stitches for the top alphabets cross over one or more holes to give letters the proper slant and height.

NEEDLEPOINT
A Stitch in Time

Although Ella Projansky embroidered as a child, she became interested in needlepoint only a few years ago. Not satisfied with commercial needlepoint designs then available, she designed her own. A shop proprietor liked them and asked her to design for the shop. Mrs. Projansky did custom designing for several years before deciding to open her own studio and showroom, needlepoint things unlimited, in White Plains, New York. Mrs. Projansky teaches needlepoint at Craftsmen Unlimited in Bedford Hills, New York, at continuing education classes in Chappaqua, New York and at her studio when she is not designing for ella projansky's needleworks, inc., a mail-order business.

Needlepoint, a form of needlework that was popular in the sixteenth century, is much in vogue again—and for good reasons. Among them are needlepoint's portability, the beauty of readily available materials, the great fun to be discovered in creating an attractive design with your own stitches, and the enormous range of practical applications. Needlepoint, no longer limited to filling in the background of a pre-worked floral motif, has gained recognition as a modern, adaptable, creative form of graphic art.

What Is Needlepoint?

Basically, needlepoint is a method of completely covering an open-weave fabric with yarn. The fabric is called canvas and there are two types—mono-canvas, made with single horizontal threads crossed by single vertical threads, and penelope canvas, which has pairs of horizontal threads crossed by two closely woven vertical threads. Both come in tan or white. White is usually considered easier on the eyes for marking and counting, but use whichever you think more comfortable. The size or gauge of needlepoint canvas is designated by the number of meshes per inch (photograph 1). A mesh is one intersection of horizontal and vertical threads. The basic needlepoint stitch (Craftnotes, page 116) is worked over one mesh. A 10-mesh canvas, for example, has 10 mesh to the inch, hence 10 stitches to the inch. The fewer mesh to the inch, the larger the stitches become, so fewer stitches are needed to cover a given area. When there are more mesh to the inch, stitches are smaller, and more are needed to cover the canvas. Mono-canvas is available with 10, 12, 14, 16, 18, 20 or 24 mesh to the inch. Penelope canvas is described with numbers, such as 10/20; the first represents the number of mesh to the inch if a pair of canvas threads are treated as one, and the second represents the number of mesh if the canvas threads are worked separately. Small stitches dividing such pairs of threads are called petit point. The most commonly used sizes of penelope canvas are 10/20, 11/22, 12/24, and 14/28. It also comes in 3½, 4 and 5 mesh- the rug canvases. In rugs the double threads are usually not separated as for petit point but are used double to give strength to the widely spaced mesh.

At one time canvas was made of linen, hemp and even silk, but today only cotton is used. The consistently high quality of canvas made in France makes it superior to other canvas. It costs more, but it is not a good idea to economize on needlepoint materials; poorly made canvas tears at the wool, and the limp threads that result make uneven stitches. The hours of work that you put into a needlepoint project and the years of enjoyment you will have from the finished product make quality materials worthwhile.

1: Canvas, the loosely woven fabric on which needlepoint is worked, comes in a variety of sizes designated by the number of mesh (intersections) per inch. From top to bottom above, pictured actual size, are 18-mesh canvas, 14-mesh canvas, 12-mesh canvas, 10-mesh canvas, and 5-mesh penelope (double-thread) canvas. The latter is also known as rug canvas.

A monogrammed pencil holder keeps pencils and markers neatly at hand in Mrs. Projansky's work area, which is backed by a splendid array of Persian yarn. For this craftswoman, the great range of colors in the raw materials serves as an inspiration for new needlepoint designs.

2: Depending on the mesh of the canvas selected, different weights of yarn are used. Shown above from left to right are two-ply Persian yarn, three-ply Persian yarn, and rug yarn.

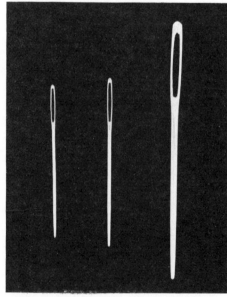

3: Among tapestry needles available are, from left to right, a No. 20 needle, used for two-ply Persian yarn, a No. 18 needle, used for three-ply Persian yarn, and a Smyrna or rug needle, used for heavy-weight rug yarn.

Other Materials

Yarn used for needlepoint must be strong enough to withstand the wear-and-tear of being pulled repeatedly through the canvas openings and still look beautiful when the needlepoint is finished. Knitting wool does not work because it is too elastic (an advantage in knitting but not in needlepoint) and because it is made of short fibers that fray quickly. Yarn used for needlepoint must have long fibers; there are several that work well. Persian wool is a loosely twisted three-ply yarn (photograph 2). Each ply is made of two strands twisted together; the plies can be used separately or together. As a three-ply yarn, Persian wool covers 10-mesh canvas well; two plies are suitable for 12- or 14-mesh canvas. Tapestry wool is a single-ply yarn made of strands more tightly twisted; they cannot be separated easily for use in a fine-mesh canvas, but the yarn is fine for 10-, 12- or 14-mesh canvas. Crewel wool, a fine embroidery yarn, is made of two strands tightly twisted together; it is used primarily for 16-mesh or smaller mesh canvas, but several strands can be used as one for working larger mesh. Rug wool is a thick, three-ply, rough-textured wool that covers large-mesh canvas quickly. Cotton, silk, rayon, and metallic threads can be used to add interest to a needlepoint work but are best confined to small areas to provide highlights since they do not wear as well as wool.

Tapestry needles—long-eyed needles with blunt points that do not split the yarn or the canvas—are used for needlepoint (photograph 3). They range in size from a No. 13 needle, the largest, to No. 24, the smallest. The eye of the needle should be slightly wider than the yarn is thick, but slim enough to slide easily through the canvas openings. A No. 18 tapestry needle works best for 10- and 12-mesh canvas, a No. 19 or 20 for 14-mesh canvas, and a No. 24 needle for 24-mesh canvas. A No. 13 needle (also known as a rug needle) is used with rug yarn on large-mesh canvas.

In addition to canvas, yarn, and needles, you will need: a tape measure or ruler for measuring the canvas; small, sharp scissors for cutting yarn and stitches; large shears for cutting canvas; graph paper for working out designs; a fine-tip, waterproof marker for marking guidelines and the center of the canvas; and 1-inch-wide masking tape for binding edges. If you use a thimble for other needlework, you will probably want to use it for needlepoint.

Preparing the Canvas

Canvas is sold by the yard, or fraction of a yard, and is available in widths from 18 to 60 inches. To determine the size of the canvas you need, add 2 inches to each side of the finished project for the seam allowance and blocking (squaring up the work). Cut the canvas, and fold strips of masking tape over the raw edges to keep the canvas threads from raveling or catching at the yarn. Selvage edges do not need to be bound with tape.

There are two ways of marking a needlepoint design on the canvas; you can plot each stitch on a graph-paper chart, or you can paint the design directly on the canvas. Graphing is most suitable for geometric designs, lettering, and repeat patterns. Each square on the graph will equal one stitch on the canvas (Figure D, page 109); the needlepoint is worked by counting the squares on the graph and working that number of stitches on the canvas. Painting the canvas is a good technique for more intricate designs; it gives you an accurate guide right on the canvas. If you have chosen a design that you would like enlarged or reduced, you can take the picture to a shop that makes photostats (they are listed in the Yellow Pages) and have a positive stat made that is exactly the size you want.

To transfer any design on the canvas, put the canvas over the pattern, and outline the major areas with a waterproof marker. To fill in the color, use a waterproof medium because the canvas will be dampened for blocking, and a water-soluble color might run and stain the wool. Oil paints and acrylic paints can be used since both are waterproof, but felt-tipped markers are easiest to use. Check them first, however; water-resistant does not mean waterproof. Color a small piece of canvas with the marker, let it dry, wet it, and rub it. If the color comes off on your finger, it will ruin the finished needlepoint. If you only have markers that are not waterproof, spray the canvas with an acrylic fixitive before you start to stitch. It is not necessary to color an area completely; a piece of yarn tied to the area will serve as a color reminder.

Stitching

For stitching, thread the needle (Figure A) with a length of yarn. Do not knot the yarn. Put the needle through from the front of the canvas about an inch from the place where you want the first stitch to be. Hold the yarn in place behind the canvas. As you work the first stitches, catch the end of yarn in the back so it will be secured (photograph 4). (The end that sticks out in front will later be snipped off in back.) To end a length of yarn, run the needle through the back of the stitches for about an inch (photograph 5), and snip the yarn off close to the stitches. Start and end all subsequent yarn lengths by weaving the needle under the stitches horizontally or vertically. When making stitches, work gently, allowing the yarn to rest on the canvas threads without being pulled taut. The yarn may become twisted as you work. If this happens, let it drop freely from the canvas, and it will untwist itself.

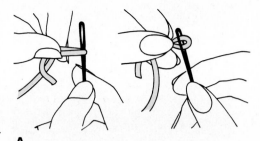

A
Figure A: To thread a tapestry needle, fold one inch of yarn over the needle and pull taut (left). Pinch this fold with the thumb and forefinger, slip it off the needle, and push the pinched fold through the eye of the needle (right).

4: To start the yarn, put the needle and yarn through the canvas from the front, about an inch from where you will make the first stitch. As you work the first stitches, catch the yarn on the back so it will be secured.

5: To end a length of yarn, thread it through stitches on the back of the canvas for about an inch horizontally or vertically, not diagonally. The stitches will hold the yarn; cut off any yarn that is left over.

Blocking

Blocking is done to smooth and straighten a finished needlepoint canvas that may have been stretched or pulled out of shape during the stitching. You will need rustproof push-pins or tacks; a ¾-inch-thick piece of plywood or insulation board that is larger than the worked needlepoint; brown wrapping paper; aluminum foil; a waterproof marker; a ruler; a T-square or right-angle; and a towel. Cover the board with aluminum foil to protect it. Place the brown wrapping paper on top of this. Using the waterproof marker, draw a rectangle the size that the finished needlepoint should be. Mark the center of each side on the paper and on the needlepoint. The needlepoint can be washed at the same time as it is blocked. Soak it in cold-water soap and water for 3 minutes. Rinse until the water is clear; do not wring. Roll tightly in a towel until excess water is absorbed. Place the worked needlepoint face down if it is tent stitches, face up if it is decorative stitches, on the paper-covered board. The two-inch border of canvas that was included in the original measurement of the canvas is used now for tacking. Tacks should not go into worked needlepoint.

Your objective is to line up the needlepoint with the outline. Tack at the center of the top and bottom; then tack the center of each side, stretching the needlepoint as necessary to fit the marked outline. Check the corners with the square or right-angle. Continue stretching and tacking opposite points around the work until the entire border is tacked at one-inch intervals. Keep the board flat to avoid sagging. Let it dry thoroughly—at least 24 hours, and up to three days if the air is humid. Then you can remove the tacks, and protect it with spray-on stain repellent.

Frames

Many experienced needlepointers like to use a frame because it holds the canvas taut, making the stitching go faster and more smoothly. The taut canvas also makes counting threads easier. The part of the canvas not being worked is kept rolled up and stays clean. However, most lap frames are not particularly portable and are cumbersome for the needlepointer who likes to carry work around. Floor frames are a great convenience for the needlepointer who wants to work in the comfort of home. Frames are essential for rug making because the frame helps support the weight of the rug canvas. For any other needlepoint project, the use of a frame is optional. Directions for mounting the canvas come with the frame.

Opportunities are unlimited for personalizing in needlepoint; start with a monogram and you will soon be creating your own designs.

Gingham pencil holder $ ◪ 🚶‍♀️🚶 🐭

Making a monogrammed pencil holder will give you a personal yet simple introduction to needlepoint. It uses only variations of the basic needlepoint stitch—the tent stitch—as detailed in the Craftnotes on page 116. To cover an 18-ounce can, you will need a 14-by-8-inch piece of 10-mesh canvas and three-ply Persian yarn in the following amounts: 20 yards of light blue; 13 yards of dark blue; 11 yards of white; 4 yards of red; and 1 yard of black. Cut your canvas to size, and bind the edges with masking tape to protect the yarn and prevent raveling. Draw the outline of the finished needlepoint—10 inches by 4⅛ inches for the 18-ounce can—on the canvas with a marker. (If you prefer a can of a different size, measure height and circumference, and add at least 4 inches to each dimension to get the size of the canvas needed.) Measure and mark the center of the outlined needlepoint area (Figure D); this is where you will center the middle initial if you are using three initials. If you use only two initials, place them on either side of the center mark. Next, draw a horizontal line about 2½ inches long through the center point, and place the body of the letters on this line letting the descending parts of the letters go below the line as necessary. This places the initials slightly above the center of the worked needlepoint, and makes the ladybug more visible.

Thread a No. 20 needle with an 18-inch length of red yarn using only two of the three plies, and make your initials with the continental stitch following the alphabet in Figure D. Then, continuing with two plies of yarn and using the basket weave stitch, fill in the ladybug following the graph pattern also in Figure D. Next, fill in the gingham background, again using the basket weave stitch. Finally, make the red border with one row of the continental stitch. When the needlepoint is complete, block the canvas, following the directions on page 107.

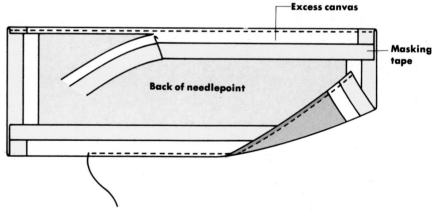

B

Figure B: Fold the excess canvas on the top and bottom to the wrong side, and stitch between the first and second rows of needlepoint stitches; trim to within ¼ inch of the folds and sides.

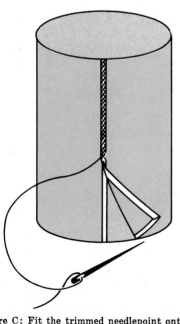

C

Figure C: Fit the trimmed needlepoint onto the can, and fold back the ¼-inch allowance at the sides. Close the seam with a cross stitch (Craftnotes, page 114).

To finish the work, fold back the excess canvas at the top and bottom, and machine-stitch it between the red border row and the first blue row (Figure B). (If you are sewing by hand, use carpet thread, a strong, waxed cotton thread.) Cut off excess canvas ¼ inch from the stitching. Except for a ¼-inch allowance on each side, trim the excess canvas from the sides. Fold the allowance back. Fit the needlepoint onto the can, and stitch the two edges of canvas together where they meet (Figure C) using a cross stitch with the top stroke going from lower left to upper right (Craftnotes, page 114). Put a 3-inch circle of felt, cork, or cardboard inside the can to protect the pen and pencil points.

Figure D: You can use appropriate letters from the alphabet opposite to make any needlepoint monogram or name. Each square represents one stitch on the canvas. To position initials on the gingham pattern (upper right), draw a horizontal line through the center point. Let the body of the initials rest on this line with only descenders going below.

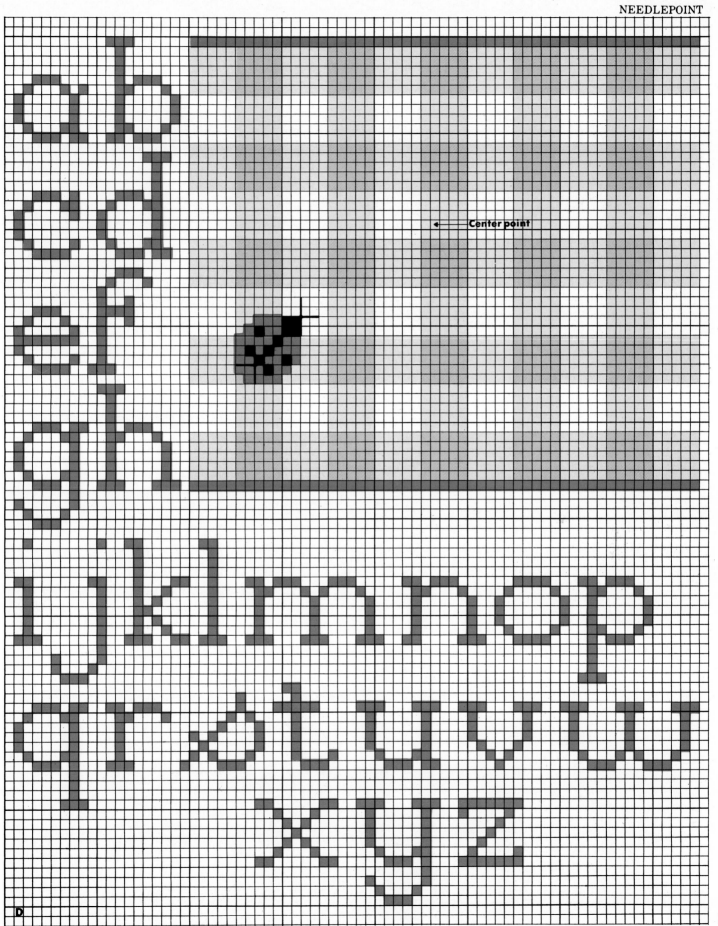

Center point

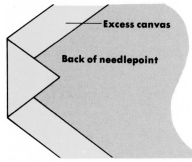

F

Figure F: After cutting the border edges of canvas to the same width, start mitering a corner by folding the point toward the center of the back of the canvas so the fold line is at the corner stitch of the needlepoint.

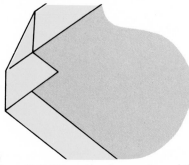

G

Figure G: Fold one side edge over toward the center of the board so that the excess canvas does not show on the front of the needlepoint.

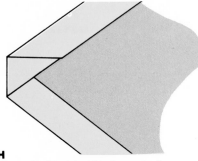

H

Figure H: Pin this side edge to the foam-core board to keep it in place.

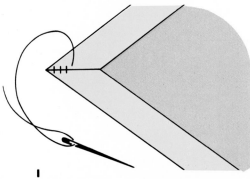

I

Figure I: Fold the other side; stitch the diagonal seam at the corner, unraveling a thread from left-over canvas to use for sewing.

A simple mirror (available at variety stores) becomes an important room accessory when framed with a 2½-inch-wide needlepoint design.

Frame yourself $ ▯ ♣ ⬚

What prettier way is there to see yourself than framed in needlepoint? To make a mirror frame, you will need: ½ yard of 10-mesh canvas; three-ply Persian yarn in the following amounts—79 yards of pink, 15½ yards of purple, and 8½ yards of red; a 5-inch-square unframed mirror (available at variety and department stores); a 9-inch-square of foam-core board (available at art supply stores); a 9-inch-square piece of felt in a harmonious color; and white glue.

The Willow Stitch Border

The frame is worked in the willow stitch which is made by weaving twisted yarn into a double brick stitch background (see Craftnotes, page 114). Cut a piece of canvas 13 inches square and bind the edges with masking tape. Measure to locate a 5-inch square in the center and mark its outline with a marker. This area is left blank; when the needlepoint is finished, the mirror will be glued here. Work the double brick stitch background 24 threads wide around the 5-inch square. Around this, work four rows of the continental stitch. The yarn that is worked into the double brick stitches to make the willow stitch is woven in this order: one pink, one red, one pink, five purple. Repeat this six times down the frame; then end with one pink, one red, and one pink. Block the needlepoint; do not trim the excess canvas.

To make the frame rigid, put white glue on the back of the 5-inch-square of empty canvas, and center it on the 9-inch-square of foam-core board, thus gluing it in place. Miter the corners of the canvas around the back of the foam-core board (Figures F, G, H and I). Secure the canvas to the board by lacing the canvas edges together (Figure J) starting from the center of opposite sides and working toward the right. Then turn the canvas around, and lace the other half from the center to the right. Repeat for the sides. When the lacing is complete, take the tape off the edges of the canvas. The adhesive that remains will help keep the sewing threads in place. The outside four rows of continental stitches should cover the sides of the foam-core board which is about ⅜ inch thick. Put glue on the empty canvas and on the back of the mirror, and glue the mirror in place. Cover the mirror with a piece of paper; then weight it down with a telephone book or brick until the glue dries.

Making Twisted Cords

To give a finishing touch to the mirror, make twisted cords in red and purple to border the mirror, and one in pink to border the frame. To estimate the amount of yarn needed for each color of cord, allow three times the circumference multiplied by the number of strands used. Thus, for the red and purple cords, the circumference of the 5-inch mirror is 20 inches, times three is 60 inches, times the two strands used is 120 inches, or approximately 3½ yards of each color. The pink cord, which goes around the 9-inch-square frame, is twice as thick. The circumference is 36 inches, times three is 108 inches, times the four strands used is 432 inches, or 12 yards. (These yarn amounts are included in the yarn estimates given above.)

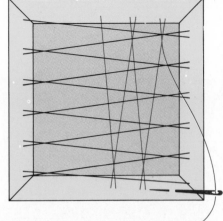

J

Figure J: To secure the canvas on the foam-core board, lace opposite edges of the border together on the back, starting at the center and working toward the right, then turn the canvas around and lace the other half from the center to the right.

K Figure K: It takes two people to make a twisted cord; each ties the ends of two strands of yarn to a pencil with a slip knot and twists the pencil clockwise until the strands are completely twisted.

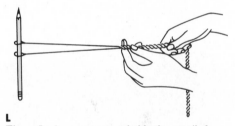

L

Figure L: As your partner holds the pencil, free the looped center and slide one hand down the yarn, stopping at short intervals to let the yarn below your hand twist by itself. When you reach the pencil, tie each end with a bit of yarn below the knot; then untie the knots.

Making a twisted cord requires two people. For the red and purple cords, cut the 3½ yards of yarn in half. Keep the two strands together, and tie each end to a pencil using a slipknot. To keep the yarn taut, each person should hold it just below the pencil with one hand, and twist the pencil clockwise with the other (Figure K). Both people must twist the pencil clockwise. When the entire length of yarn is twisted, loop the middle over a door knob or chair spindle. Bring the two pencils together, and slip both loops onto one pencil. While one person holds the pencil, the other takes the yarn by the center thus folding it in half. This person slides one hand down the yarn, releasing it at short intervals and letting the yarn twist by itself (Figure L). Once this is done for the entire length, a bit of yarn tied below the slipknots will secure the twist so the pencil can be removed and the slipknots untied.

The pink cord is made the same way but is twice as thick. Cut the 12 yards of yarn into quarters. Take the four strands and make a twisted cord as described above.

To sew the red and purple cords onto the mirror, use 2 plies of yarn in the same color and a sewing needle. Find the center of the purple twisted cord, and stitch this to the upper left corner of the mirror. Sew half of the cord along the top and down the right side of the mirror; sew the other half down the left side and across the bottom. The cords will meet at the bottom right corner. Tie them together, and separate the plies to make fringe. Repeat for the red cord. The pink cord is sewn onto the edge of the frame in the same way, but when the two halves meet at the lower right corner, overlap them slightly and tack the ends to the back of the frame stitching them to the canvas. To make the back of the frame neat, cut a piece of felt 9 inches square, and stitch it to the last row of continental stitch on all four edges.

A commercially-made acrylic shag rug is given a new look with a needlepointed border that has been sewn onto a shaved area of the rug.

A needlepoint rug

Many experienced needlepointers yearn to make a needlepoint rug that might become a family heirloom but shy away from what they imagine to be an enormous project. To needlepoint an entire rug, even a small one, is, indeed, a time-consuming undertaking. The rug pictured above, however, is an ingenious combination of needlepoint with a commercially-made acrylic shag rug. It gives you much of the satisfaction of making a needlepoint rug without all that work.

For this project, you will need: a 2-by-3-foot rug with a jute or burlap backing (avoid latex as it is difficult to sew through); ¾ yard of 36-inch-wide heavy cotton or lightweight burlap for lining; and carpet thread (a heavy-duty sewing thread) to attach the lining. (The commercially-made scatter rug that is sold as a 2-by-3-foot rug actually measures 23 by 34 inches.) To make the needlepoint border, you will need: ¾ yard of 36-inch-wide 10-mesh canvas; approximately 500 yards of three-ply Persian yarn; and a No. 18 tapestry needle. To estimate the amount of yarn needed in each color, allow half the total amount, 250 yards, for the background color, and divide the remaining yarn by the number of colors used in the pattern. The rug pictured above was worked in four shades of lavender and two of green; it required approximately 42 yards of each of the six design colors plus 250 yards of beige for the background.

Figure P: This needlepoint design fits along one long side and two short sides of the rug. The other long side is simply a repeat of the design for the long side given here.

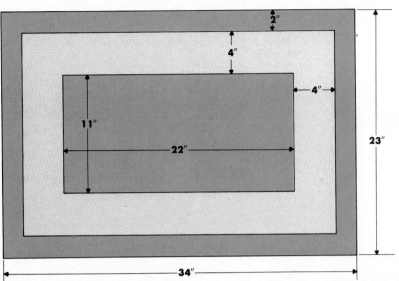

Q

Figure Q: The needlepoint border fits into the bald area; the rug pile is left at the original height in the center rectangle and along the 2-inch-wide outside border.

To avoid counting stitches (difficult on an intricate floral pattern), paint the canvas following the drawing in Figure P and the directions on page 106. The rug is made in two steps: first the needlepoint is worked on a piece of canvas; then it is sewn to the shag rug. The finished needlepoint makes a 4-inch-wide border, measuring 19 by 30 inches on its outer edge. Do not cut out the blank canvas in the center of the design until the needlepoint work is completed and blocked. To do the needlepoint, outline the butterfly and leaf shapes with the continental stitch, and fill them in with the basket weave stitch; then fill in the background with the basket weave stitch. Block the completed needlepoint following the directions on page 107. Then cut away the excess canvas allowing a 2-inch border inside and outside the worked area. Fold back this excess canvas, and miter the corners (see Figures F, G, H and I).

To prepare the shag rug for its new border, mark the 4-inch-wide border where the needlepoint will go, leaving a 2-inch-wide border of shag (Figure Q). Cut the shag down to the rug backing in this 4-inch-wide area with a pair of scissors. To get this area as flat as possible, use an old safety razor with a new blade to shave the remaining stubble. Place the needlepoint border in this bald area, and stitch the last row of needlepoint stitches to the rug backing, using heavy-duty sewing thread and making small stitches by hand. To make a lining to protect the rug, cut a piece of lining fabric 24 by 35 inches (the rug measurement plus ½ inch on each side for a seam allowance). Fold under the seam allowance, and press with a steam iron. Pin the lining to the back of the rug, and sew around the entire rug using the heavy-duty sewing thread and making small stitches by hand.

A decorative stitch in needlepoint may cover more than one intersection of canvas threads at a time, thereby appearing to be raised, and it may go in any direction including vertical and horizontal, having been stitched across the canvas threads rather than across the intersection of those threads. Where stitches must share the same hole, the new stitch should enter from the front of the canvas, if possible, so the existing stitch is not split by the needle.

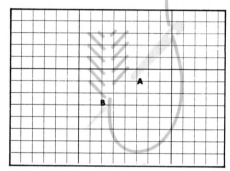

Kalem Stitch

This stitch sequence consists of two rows of diagonal stitches each over two intersections, one row with stitches slanting up to the left, and the other slanting up to the right, sharing the same center hole. Work down from the top of the row to the bottom. Put the needle in at A, and bring it out at B.

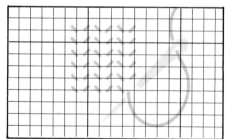

Reverse Tent Stitch

This stitch is worked the same as the Kalem stitch, but each stitch covers only one intersection.

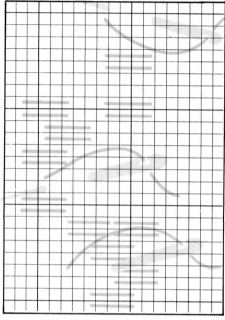

Double Brick Stitch

This stitch sequence consists of rows of two stitches over four threads, each pair of stitches staggered in bricklayer fashion. Work two stitches over four threads of the canvas, skip two spaces, work two more stitches in line with the first two. When the first row is completed (top drawing), start the second row below the top stitches in the first row, staggered two spaces to the right (center drawing). The stitches in the third row share a hole with those in the first row. Turn the canvas upside down so the needle can go into the shared hole from the front (bottom drawing).

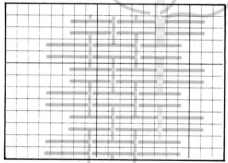

Willow Stitch

Work the double brick stitch. With the needle threaded with another color, anchor the yarn at one side of the canvas. Twist the needle until the yarn is taut (about 10 times), and, being careful not to split the yarn of the brick stitches, run the yarn under the bricks, not under the canvas. Secure at the other side.

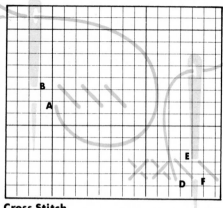

Cross Stitch

Working from right to left, bring the needle up at A and down at B (upper left), for the first stroke. Then, starting from the left bring the needle up at D, down at E, up at F to make the cross stroke (lower right).

Reverse Smyrna Cross Stitch

Work an upright cross stitch over two threads (left). Over the upright cross stitch, work a diagonal cross stitch (right), with the top stroke slanting from lower right to upper left.

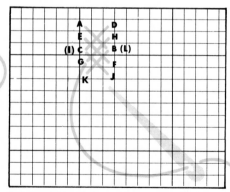

Encroaching Cross Stitch

This stitch pattern consists of cross stitches over two canvas threads, each stitch beginning in the skipped mesh of the preceding stitch. Bring the needle up at A, down at B, up at C, and down at D for the first cross stitch. Start the second stitch in the space left by the first (E). Bring the needle down at F, up at G, down at H. The third stitch shares a hole with the first; come up at I (also C), down at J, up at K, down at L (also B).

DECORATIVE STITCHES

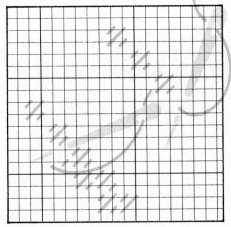

Mosaic Stitch

Worked diagonally, this stitch sequence consists of three diagonal stitches, the first over one mesh, the second over two, the third over one (upper right). In succeeding rows, the small stitches share a hole, and the long stitches are worked into the spaces that remain (lower left).

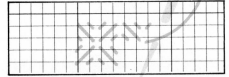

Reverse Mosaic Block

This is the mosaic stitch sequence worked into a block. The four long stitches of the block share the center hole.

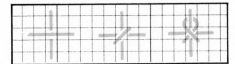

Knotted Upright Cross Stitch

This sequence starts with a cross stitch over 4 threads (left). The needle is then brought up in the center hole, below the horizontal stitch and to the left of the vertical. It is brought under the vertical thread and across the intersection, then to the back of the canvas to the right of the vertical and below the horizontal stitch.

Reverse Mosaic Block with Upright Cross Stitch

The combination of the reverse mosaic block and the upright cross looks like this.

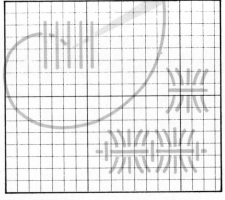

Sheaf Stitch

Make five upright stitches over four horizontal canvas threads. Bring the needle up in the middle space of the canvas behind the canvas, and slide it under the stitches to the left and out (top). Bringing the needle across the stitches to the right, return the needle to the middle space behind the stitches and pull taut (center). Sheaf stitches share top and bottom holes at the start and finish of each unit. An upright cross stitch between sheaves completes the pattern (bottom).

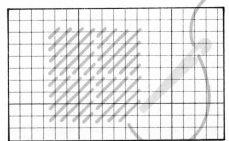

Scotch Stitch

This stitch sequence of graduated diagonal stitches forms a square. Starting at a corner, the first stitch should cover one mesh. Succeeding stitches cover two, three, four, three, two, and one mesh. All stitches slant in the same direction, from lower left to upper right.

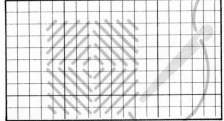

Reverse Scotch Stitch

This is worked the same as the Scotch stitch above, but with adjacent units slanting in opposite directions.

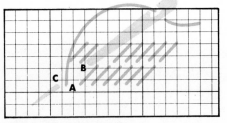

Oblique Gobelin Stitch

This stitch sequence is formed of rows of stitches that cover the same number of canvas threads (from two to six). Bring the needle up at A, down at B, up at C. The top of one row and the bottom of the next row share a hole. This stitch may be worked horizontally or vertically.

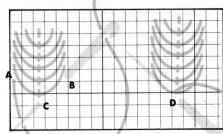

Fly Stitch

This stitch must be worked from the top of the row to the bottom. Bring the needle up at A, down at B, up in the center at C, down again at D. Repeat for each stitch. Use small slanting stitches as necessary to fill in at the beginning and end of each row.

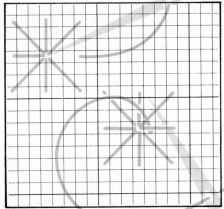

Small Whipped Spider Web

Use a long strand of yarn, and make eight spokes that share a center hole and form a square (top). Bring the needle out to the front as close as possible to the center. Carry the yarn under two spokes and back over one (bottom). Continue around until all eight spokes are completely covered, giving corner spokes one or two extra wraps of yarn.

CRAFTNOTES: THE BASIC NEEDLEPOINT STITCH

The basic needlepoint stitch is called the tent stitch. The name comes from the Middle English word **tenter** which meant a stretching implement or frame, similar to the frame on which needlepoint was then worked. The smallest unit in needlepoint, the tent stitch, is a flat, even stitch covering just one intersection of canvas threads. Every tent stitch slants in the same direction—from lower left to upper right—so every tent stitch is identical.

But there are several variations in the making of tent stitches. Although the stitches look identical from the front of the canvas, how they are made determines what they will look like from the back. The continental stitch is the tent stitch worked in a line, either horizontally from right to left (as illustrated); vertically from top to bottom; diagonally downward to the left or the right; or diagonally upward to the left. On the back, the continental stitch makes long slanting stitches that cover the canvas fairly well. This stitch is used primarily for outlining and is not recommended for fill-in work because it pulls the canvas out of shape.

The basket weave variation is worked diagonally and gets its name from the woven pattern that appears on the reverse side; the direction of the work is changed with each row. Since stitches that run in only one direction tend to pull the canvas askew, the basket weave variation is the best to use for filling in the canvas with tent stitches. Such stitches do not pull the canvas out of shape and actually reinforce the weave of the canvas threads. To follow the grain of canvas with basket weave stitches, it is necessary to differentiate between vertical and horizontal mesh. This is determined by the top thread of the intersection. Hence, a vertical mesh has a vertical thread on top, a horizontal mesh has a horizontal thread on top. Rows of stitches covering the vertical mesh are worked downward, from the top left to the bottom right, and rows of stitches that cover horizontal mesh are worked upward from the bottom right to the top left, thereby filling the entire area. It gives a heavy padding to the work and does not pull the canvas out of shape.

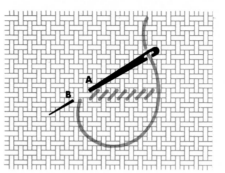

The continental: To work this variation of the tent stitch, put the needle in at A, and bring it out at B, so the yarn covers one intersection of canvas threads.

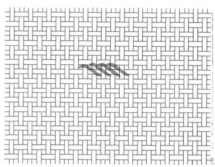

Seen from the back, the continental stitch makes long slanting stitches that cover the canvas fairly well.

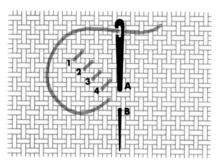

The basket weave: In this variation, rows covering vertical mesh are worked diagonally downward, the stitches made in the numbered sequence shown. Put the needle in at A, and bring it out at B so the yarn covers one vertical mesh.

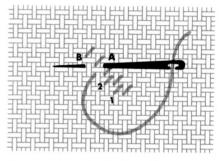

Rows covering the horizontal mesh on the basket weave variation are worked diagonally upward, the stitches made in the numbered sequence shown. Put the needle in at A, and bring it out at B so the yarn covers one horizontal mesh.

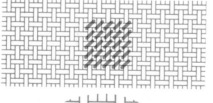

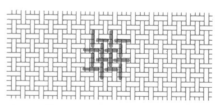

The basket weave stitch gets its name from the woven pattern that it forms on the back of the canvas.

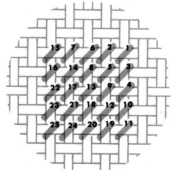

To fill an entire area with basket weave stitches (top), work the stitches following the numbered sequence shown in the magnification (bottom).

CRAFTNOTES ON ENLARGING PATTERNS

Throughout *Hand and Needle Arts,* patterns are reproduced for you to copy. To make a pattern full size, follow the system described here for enlarging the grid imposed on the heart pattern.

The system is really very simple. The small grid in the book must be translated onto a grid with larger squares that you will make; the design (in this case, the heart) will be copied onto this larger grid. The size of the enlarged grid you make will depend on what the pattern is for. For example, for a pillow pattern the grid will have much smaller squares than will a grid for a tablecloth or a bedspread. A gauge is given with each pattern printed. Draw the squares of the large grid you prepare to the size given by this gauge.

Before you cut your pattern, be sure an allowance has been made for seams.

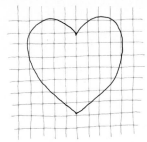

Above is the pattern of a heart as it might appear in this book. The grid placed over it is divided into small squares that actually measure ⅛ inch. All the patterns in *Hand and Needle Arts* use grids of this size. On page 22, the pattern for Charlie Chaplin is reproduced on such a ⅛-inch grid. To make a pattern that will produce Charlie in the same size pictured, you must transfer the pattern for Charlie onto a grid whose squares are 1 inch in size, as noted with the pattern.

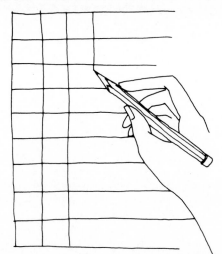

To enlarge the pattern, prepare a grid that has the same number of squares as our illustrated grid for Charlie, but one in which each square measures 1 inch on each side.

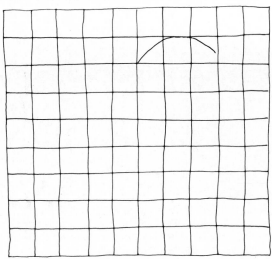

Draw pattern onto your 1-inch grid a square at a time.

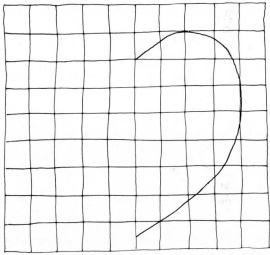

Follow the lines around, checking the book as you go.

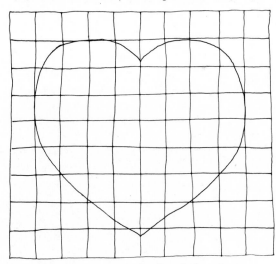

You will find it easy to transfer the whole pattern.

HOOKED RUGS
Latching onto an Heirloom

Lisa Deiches, a graduate of Antioch College, is a young craftswoman deeply involved in the textile crafts. She has been accepted at the Textile Institute in Boras, Sweden, to do graduate research on textile techniques, and, in her own work, has woven rugs and tapestries, spinning her own yarn and dyeing it with natural dyes. Lisa has woven a large number of tapestries for a corporation and has exhibited her work in both Ohio and New York.

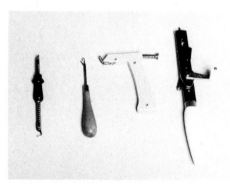

1: The various hooks used in making rugs by hand are (left to right) a punch needle, a latch hook, a latch gun, and a speed hook.

Hooking rugs by hand is an ancient technique of rug-making that has come to us through two very different cultures. Each culture made rugs with a soft, thickly woven surface called the pile. Craftspeople in the Scandinavian countries developed a thick pile rug called *rya*, which means "rug" in Swedish. Perhaps the cold arctic winters inspired the creation of these rugs. The original rya rugs were made on looms with the pile woven in during the weaving process.

Today, rya rugs can be made by knotting the pile by hand onto a woven fabric backing. People in the Middle East and the Orient developed a similar method of making rugs—one that involved tying the pile onto a backing, using what became known as an Oriental knot. From these two rug-making methods have come the various techniques that are used today in rugs hooked by hand.

Hooked rugs are made by forcing loops of yarn or cloth strips through a backing fabric to create a pile surface, which can be either looped or cut. The materials used are generally very coarse and usually economical. Good use was made of this technique in early America: Coarse handmade cloth was available for backing, and cloth strips cut from worn but still valuable clothing or bedding served as the tight pile loops. Designs portrayed notable events or scenes, simple geometric patterns, or adaptations of flora and fauna motifs such as the Shaker representation of a horse (opposite). These sturdy rugs are still economical. Making them requires no large equipment. With only a few special tools, some backing fabric, and suitable fabric or yarn, you are ready to start.

Materials

Although rugs can be hooked by machine today, making them by hand is still a popular craft. Most hooking methods require a frame, backing fabric, yarn or cloth strips in various colors, and one of the many types of hooks. To make a frame, use four strips of wood that, with joints butted together rather than lapped, will give you a rectangle 2 inches longer and wider than the rug to be hooked. Nail these wood pieces together and use 90-degree angle irons on each interior corner to keep the rectangle true and rigid. One-by-twos or two-by-twos are suitable, but even two-by-fours may be used for large rugs. Canvas-painting stretchers, available in many sizes at art supply stores, can be reinforced as above to make a suitable frame. The backing fabric should be a coarse material with a fairly open weave. Burlap usually works well, but for finer work—intricate wall hangings or carefully matched designs—a higher quality fabric such as monk's cloth is the best choice. This can be purchased in widths up to 72 inches, and like the burlap, it can be pieced together to make very large or unusual shapes. This backing is stretched taut and tacked or stapled to the frame. The type of hook used will depend on the design and personal preference. Photograph 1 shows the instruments used for the two basic methods of rug-hooking. The punch needle is used on the back of the fabric backing to force a continuous piece of yarn in and out, causing loops to form on the right side. The speed hook is used in similar fashion and produces the same results as the punch needle, but at a greater speed as the in-and-out motion is accomplished by turning a handle, much as one would operate an egg beater. The latch hook is used to knot short pieces of yarn or cloth strips to a canvas backing, working from the front, while the latch gun simplifies the knot-tying process into one step, and is, therefore, faster than the hook. Each of the following projects makes use of a different hook so the advantages and disadvantages of each can be learned.

Rug yarns of wool, cotton, synthetics, and various blends are suitable for these projects. They are sold at craft shops, variety stores, and by mail order houses, and are designed to wear well underfoot and make long lasting products. Cloth strips cut from partly worn articles or new yardage should be very narrow—about ¼ inch wide—so they work smoothly in the various hooks. Yarn strips can be bought pre-cut, or prepared by hand—small cutting machines are available to facilitate

Made by a member of the Shaker religious community in Pleasant Hill, Kentucky, in the nineteenth century, this museum rug has pile made from rags of homespun wool hooked into a heavy canvas backing. The outer border is a braid made from the same rags of homespun wool. The Shakers were noted for the simple beauty and economy of all their arts.

this. With yarn or cloth strips, count on using about ½ pound per square foot of rug area. Be careful not to mix yarns that will wear unevenly or require different care. Wool must be dry-cleaned and should not be combined with washable cotton.

Design Possibilities

Sculptured effects may be achieved by varying the pile heights in one rug or combining two or more methods of hooking. Using additional needlework methods, such as embroidery with hooking, opens up an exciting range of possible texture and pattern ideas. Emphasis on the important design elements is possible through color, as well as by varying the pile height. The general rule that cool colors—blue, green and purple—recede and warm colors—red, yellow and orange—appear to come forward is useful in planning rug designs. Remember, too, that light tints may seem to float off the floor and dark shades sink into it, if concentrated heavily in one area. Light and dark colors also tend to show soil more readily than do medium tones.

Hooked rugs should be shaken and vacuumed often to stay fresh and clean. If the materials used are washable, then the rug can be washed safely with a mild detergent. Wool rugs require drycleaning, but will remain fresh for a long time if vacuumed regularly. This is true for hooked pillows and wall hangings as well.

The rug design, using one geometric motif in several sizes, was created by moving paper shapes around until a dramatic pattern was achieved.

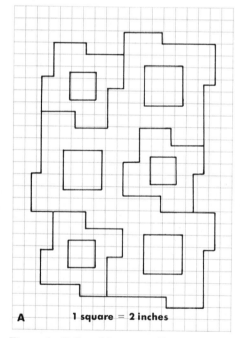

A   1 square = 2 inches

Figure A: Follow this pattern if you would like to duplicate the geometric rug. See page 117 for instructions for enlarging it.

Geometric-pattern rug $ ● ♟ 🐭

The geometric rug shown in the photograph at left was made with a speed hook, probably the best method for working large contemporary designs. This kind of hook can fill in large areas very quickly—this rug was completed in one week. There are several makes of speed hooks; they vary in cost and complexity. The Scandinavian-type hook used here is efficient and inexpensive. Speed hooks are advertised in craft magazines or may be purchased in craft supply shops. The advantage of a speed hook is its speed, of course. It uses a continuous length of yarn. Leftover yarn is appropriate only if the design has small areas of color. For this 32-by-46-inch rug, I used about 6 pounds of yarn, 3½ of red and 2½ of purple.

The geometric pattern of this rug is created with one motif repeated several times in two sizes. I made the plan by cutting out paper shapes and shifting them around until I had a pleasing effect. When pasted to a backing paper, the shapes became the sketch for the rug. Unusual shapes, well suited to hooking, will often suggest themselves with this planning method.

To transfer this design to a backing fabric, enlarge the pattern (Figure A). Cut backing fabric at least 6 inches longer and wider than the design area. The rug shown here, 32 by 46 inches when finished, needs a backing fabric 38 by 52 inches. If the fabric you use is not wide enough, seam two or more pieces together. Let the seams face the underside of the rug. Use colored chalk to plot the general pattern lines, allowing for the 3-inch-wide border. This border will be used for tacking the fabric to the frame, and, later, for hemming the finished rug. When the placement seems right, begin exact measurements of the design parts according to your pattern grid. Draw the final pattern lines in a bold color, using an indelible marking pen (photograph 2). (Water-soluble colors may run when the rug is blocked or cleaned, so be sure you use indelible ink.) For a more comprehensive guide, fill in small or complex areas with color (photograph 3).

The frame should be as large as the rugmaker finds comfortable to use, but the entire pattern does not need to fit within the frame at one time. One area can be stretched on the frame, and, when that hooking is completed, the backing can be shifted to stretch an unhooked area in the frame opening. If you use a small frame, decide which part of the pattern you want to work and place it drawing side up on the frame so that none of that section is over the wood. Staple or tack the cloth to the wood, attaching it at the middle of each frame piece, and stretching the backing slightly. Check the placement again to see that none of the design is resting on wood. Continue stretching the fabric, stapling at 2-inch intervals, working from center of wood toward the corners. Stretch the cloth taut so it sounds like a drum when tapped. This tension allows the hook to pass in and out of the cloth smoothly.

2: Follow a small sketch above, as you draw the pattern directly on the back of the backing fabric with an indelible marking pen.

3: Completely color in any intricate area of the pattern, making color identification easier and forestalling errors as you hook.

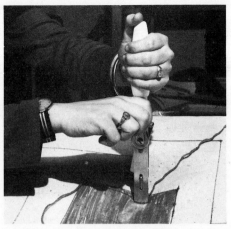

4: To start hooking, first outline the shape to be filled in, then fill it in, working back and forth in rows or in a random pattern.

To begin working the rug, thread the hook according to package directions. Working from the back or drawing side, hook the outline of the shape (photograph 4), keeping the yarn just inside the lines of that area. Then fill the entire shape with loops of yarn arranged in rows or random patterns. The speed hook is adjustable so you can use different pile heights for each project or even within a project for a sculptured effect. Some experimenting is necessary to decide which height or combination of heights you prefer. I made high loops in the red areas and smaller ones in the purple areas to get contrasting textures as well as colors. As you work with any hooking device, check to see that the yarn is feeding into it freely; otherwise, some loops will be too short.

When one area is complete, pull the hook out of the cloth until the point appears, and guide 3 inches of yarn out of the hook. Cut the yarn next to the hook. Continue working, either completing another area of the same color, or threading the hook with the next color. I find it is easier (and time-saving) to continue working areas of the same color. As you develop an area, check the density of the stitches. If they are so close together that they seem to bend the backing away from you, allow more space between rows. If the pile is too dense, the rug will not lie flat; too few loops, on the other hand, will give a bald effect with the backing fabric showing through.

After one section of the rug is complete, you may need to shift the cloth on the frame to stretch an unfinished area. Continue in this way until the entire design is worked. During the hooking process, the backing fabric is often pulled off grain, and the finished rug may need blocking. This will adjust the final shape of the rug slightly and help it relax in its final position, but it will not correct too dense a pile or other defects of workmanship.

To block, chalk the outline of the rug on a large board or workroom floor. Place the rug face up over the outline and tack it in place, using rustproof tacks or staples just outside the last row of loops. Place two or three layers of damp towels over the entire rug, cover it with a piece of plastic and let it stand overnight. Remove the plastic the next day, and the towels the third day. Allow the rug to dry thoroughly in this position and then remove it from the board.

Spray or paint-on latex backing used to keep scatter rugs from slipping can also be used to hold the loops in place. Apply it liberally to the underside of the hooked rug, and it will glue the loops firmly to the backing fabric.

To finish the rug, hem it, using the 3-inch border trimmed down to 1 inch as the hem allowance (photograph 5). Fold this hem allowance under, stitching it down with heavy-duty thread (photograph 6). An alternate method is to use an iron-on tape. In this case, cut the hem allowance down to ¾ inch. Fold it to the rug backing, and hold it in place with the iron-on tape. Follow the package directions for the tape exactly, and protect your iron by using a pressing cloth. Work small areas of the edge, and, if necessary, cut the tape into small sections where the rug silhouette changes direction.

5: Before hemming, trim the backing fabric border to 1 inch, and cut out the corners so the hem will not be bulky when it is turned under.

6: Fold back the 1-inch hem allowance, pin it in place, and stitch it to the back of the rug with heavy-duty thread.

121

The wise and solemn owl becomes a bird of fantasy when worked in pink, yellow and orange.

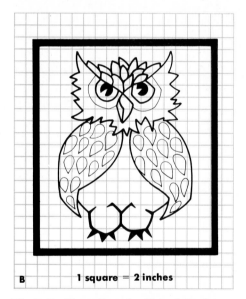

B   1 square = 2 inches

Figure B: The pattern for the owl can be worked in a smaller version for a pillow by reducing the background grid; see page 117.

7: To form loops with the punch hook, just push the threaded needle through the back of the fabric and pull it out again.

Intricate owl rug

A punch hook, while not as fast as a speed hook, is a much more flexible tool. It can be used with many more yarn weights, it makes more varied pile heights, and it is inexpensive. In many ways these advantages make up for the loss of speed. Punch hooks are available in needlework shops and department stores. The punch hook process is basically the same as the speed hook process. The planning, the design transfer, the use of the frame, and the hooking itself are the same as for the geometric rug (page 120). But the punch hook is suited to making a different kind of design. Because it is excellent for outlining and filling intricate areas and provides the greatest degree of control, it is used for detailed designs such as the owl pictured (left). The feathery outline and the fine detailing of the claws and eyes are easily managed with the punch hook. These hooks are inexpensive and you may want to have several, each threaded with a different color and ready to be picked up when needed. This is particularly useful if you are filling in small areas such as animal spots and foliage.

Preparation and Hooking

To make this rug, you will need a 35-by-39-inch piece of backing fabric and rug yarn in the following amounts: 26 ounces of green, 14½ ounces of brown, 13 ounces of yellow, and 6½ ounces each of orange and pink. The design used for such a rug can be adapted from children's books, fabric or wallpaper patterns. With a grid placed over the original design, larger grids can be laid out on the backing cloth and the pattern transferred square by square (see page 117). To copy the owl shown here, use the grid in Figure B. Center the motif on the fabric. Leaving a 3-inch border around the outside of the pattern for a hem allowance, stretch the backing on the frame.

Thread the hook, following package directions and using dark brown yarn, since you will outline the central animal shape first (photograph 7). Make sure the yarn is flowing freely so that loops are being formed on the right side. Using pink, yellow, and orange, or any other colors desired, fill in the body areas. One way to adapt this design to your own decor is to fill in the body areas using three colors that coordinate with a child's room. Do the border after the owl's body, using dark brown yarn, and complete the hooking by working the green background area. Secure the loops with latex following the directions on page 121.

Design Effects With Pile

The final effect of the hooked rug will change with the next step. Decide on the effect you want: uncut loops, cut loops—they will impart a velvety appearance—or a blend of the two textures. Even within one color area, there will be a marked visual difference between cut ends and loops. There is a variation in texture and a dramatic difference in color. Loops catch the light and highlight the rug, giving it an overall lighter color, while cut ends do not catch the light and make the rug seem much darker. This variety in texture gives you a good way to achieve added interest. Cut the loops after the latex backing is applied. Slip one blade of a sharp scissor through a group of loops, and slice upward while pressing the blades closed. This motion helps to fluff the ends and keep the loops uniform. When a section is completely cut, the ends may be slightly uneven. If you do not want this effect, use the scissors like a hedge trimmer to sheer the pile, checking the level frequently by fluffing the pile. Be careful not to trim the pile too closely as the backing fabric may show through.

You may want to experiment with different pile heights for the separate design elements. Working the owl in longer loops and the background in shorter loops, for example, makes the owl stand out from the background. Or perhaps you might work the orange feathers in longer pile and the pink background in shorter pile to give the wings added texture. Adjust the hook and try a small section of each texture before continuing to hook the rug. To finish the rug, hem it, following the directions on page 121.

Love comes to the fore when spelled out in vibrant primary colors.

Design for love

Another type of hook used for making pile rugs is the latch hook. This is a simple tool to operate, and can be mastered with only a little practice. The differences between hooking with a latch hook and the methods previously described are: (1) it is not necessary to stretch the backing onto a frame; (2) the work is done from the front of the rug; and (3) the hook requires the use of pre-cut yarns. The latch hook makes longer pile and therefore opens up a whole new range of design possibilities.

Without a frame, you are free to fill in any area of the backing at any point in the work, and can complete one color throughout the rug before going on to the next. Working from the front of the rug also means that you may tack the canvas to a wall and step back to consider the general effect of the design, making changes as you go along, much as a painter works at his easel. Pre-cut yarns make much longer pile than the punch-hooking techniques, and these yarns are used for the luxurious ryas—the Scandinavian shag-type rugs. These rugs emphasize color more than specific designs, and one excellent way to achieve this effect in sketching a design is to use watercolors on wet paper, applying liberal washes so the paints can run into each other. The combination of pure and blended areas of color will suggest ways to mix yarns in the rug.

The fabric backing for latch-hooked rugs must have a very coarse, open mesh, similar to that used for needlepoint, so rug canvas is used. This has double horizontal and vertical threads for extra strength and the mesh ranges from a coarse 3½ or 4 squares per inch to 18 or more squares per inch in needlepoint canvas. Generally, the coarsest mesh is best for rug work, but in adapting designs to a finer scale for pillows or wall pieces, investigate smaller meshes.

Started as a hobby eight years ago, rug designing is now Bert Zagory's full-time career. His first three designs were chosen by a national magazine; subsequently his work has appeared in many other magazines, books and mail order catalogs. He has designed the majority of the Spinnerin and Valiant rugs. Bert also designs needlepoint rugs and pillows. He designed the owl and the love rugs.

123

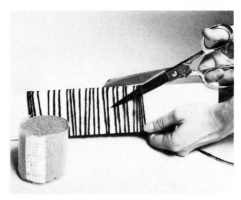

8: For latch-hooking this rug, purchase yarn in pre-cut 2⅝-inch lengths, or cut leftover yarn to this dimension as shown above.

9: To begin working with a latch hook, insert the hook under and through one pair of the double threads of the rug canvas.

10: Fold the yarn under the hook. Attaching the yarn to the latch hook at this stage allows you to make sure the ends will be even.

11: Moving the hand that is holding the yarn slightly away from the hook, catch the yarn into the latch in a smooth motion.

12: Pull the latch hook back through the mesh and out to tighten the knot. Latch knots can not be pulled loose by tugging on the yarn ends.

The design for latch hooking is transferred to the backing in the usual fashion (page 120), except that a wider marking pen is used since the meshes are open and tend to break the drawing lines. Solid areas of color are harder to fill in.

To make the love-pattern rug, you will need a piece of rug canvas 27 by 39 inches (allowing a 1½-inch border around the 24-by-36 inch design), and the following yarn: 16 ounces of yellow, 13 ounces of blue, 11 ounces of red, and 9 ounces of white.

Yarn for latch hooking can be purchased pre-cut to prcisely 2⅝ inches, and packaged in small rolls of one color. This is very convenient, but you may want to economize and cut your own yarn lengths—an excellent way to use scrap yarn from other projects. Decide what length yarn you will use and cut a piece of cardboard to one-half that width (photograph 8). Make the cardboard fairly long so you can wrap a continuous length of yarn around it. Hold the yarn in place as shown and cut it at one edge. To keep the cut pieces neat, gather them into a pompom and bind lightly with a rubber band. (Craftsperson's hint: Another way to do this, and for many people an easier way, is to cut the cardboard as wide as the yarn pieces will be long. Wrap the yarn as before, but secure it with a rubber band running the length of the cardboard and cut the yarn on both edges. In this case, the rubber band used to hold the yarn around the cardboard is used to bind the cut lengths.) The lengths need not be precisely even if the desired effect of the rug is one of bold color. The uneven pile resulting from uneven ends creates a casual appearance.

Using the latch hook requires four motions. The first inserts the hook under the double canvas thread (photograph 9). The second attaches the yarn. (This may be done before or after the hook is inserted into the canvas. Photograph 10 shows the yarn being attached after the hook was inserted. Experiment to discover which method is easier for you.) The third step is to hook the yarn into the latch (photograph 11). This should be done as smoothly as possible. Finally, the latch hook is pulled through the backing and out of the canvas to close the knot (photograph 12). The latch knots can not be loosened by tugging on the yarn ends; this will only tighten the knot. To remove a knot, if necessary, use a needle to loosen it at the center first. (There is a latch gun that speeds this type of hooking process. To use it, follow the package directions.)

For the love-pattern rug, transfer the pattern using the grid in Figure C. Since the design has some complex areas, color in any areas that might be confusing in the hooking process. The pile should be about 1 inch high. If the pile is too long, it will tend to distort the pattern. To get this length, the precut 2⅝-inch yarns are ideal; the knot uses approximately ½ inch of yarn so the pile will be about 1 inch high. The pile must also be kept even to prevent distortion of the design; if you cut your own yarn lengths, make sure they are as even as possible. The design can be worked from top to bottom or done by color area. Experiment to find the most comfortable method for you. When finished, trim any uneven yarn ends.

To finish the rug, you need rug binding (available at department stores); heavy-duty thread; and a sewing needle. First, trim the excess canvas to leave 1 inch along the sides and, by cutting diagonally, ½ inch at the corners (Figure D). Fold the canvas to the rug back and stitch it down (Figure E). Starting at one corner of the rug, stitch the binding all around the outside rug edge (Figure F). Stitch the inside edge of the rug binding to the backing (Figure G) mitering the corners as shown (Figure H).

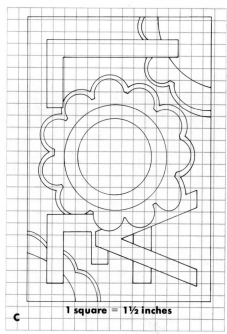

1 square = 1½ inches

Figure C: For instructions on how to enlarge this rug design, see page 117.

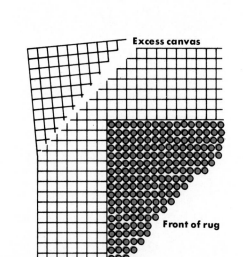

Excess canvas

Front of rug

Figure D: To start a hem, trim excess canvas to 1 inch along sides; cut corners diagonally.

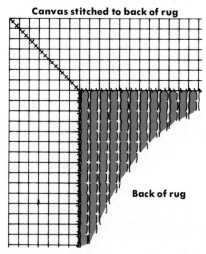

Canvas stitched to back of rug

Back of rug

Figure E: Fold this trimmed excess to back of rug and stitch it down.

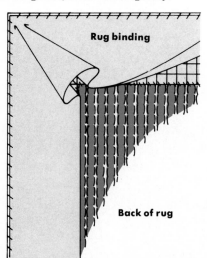

Rug binding

Back of rug

Figure F: Stitch rug binding around the outside edge of the back of the rug.

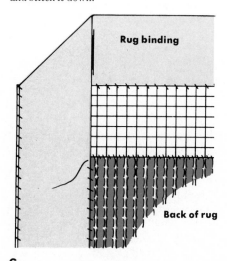

Rug binding

Back of rug

Figure G: Stitch inside edge of rug binding to rug back covering the excess canvas as shown.

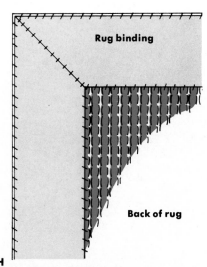

Rug binding

Back of rug

Figure H: Miter corners of binding as shown, having folded the excess binding to the inside.

125

INKLE WEAVING
Belts, Bands and Straps

One of the simplest kinds of loom weaving is the one that creates the inkle—a narrow strip of woven material that can be used as a belt, a strap, a handle or a headband. To form a wider piece of fabric, several inkles can be sewn together. Inkle is a Scottish word that means band, tape or strip. The inkle loom used in the U.S. can indeed be traced back to Scotland, but the history of inkle weaving goes back much farther.

Narrow belt-like braids were introduced into southern Gaul by Egyptian weavers during the Roman Empire. These braids were the forerunners of the woven band and, in their simplest form, could be made without a loom. Subsequently, narrow loom-woven strips were developed in various parts of the world—in Madagascar and other parts of Africa, in South America, and in Latin America. In fact, the belts woven in Guatemala today closely resemble inkle belts.

Inkle weaving is also well recorded in English literature. Shakespeare, Chaucer and Swift all mentioned inkles woven of linen and alluded to the fact that inkle weavers had less status than did weavers of wider cloth. The British inkle looms of those times were adapted from the Scottish, the type of loom originally used to make intricate braids. English and Scottish weavers both worked with sturdy, inexpensive fibers—linen, cotton and wool—and the inkles they made served as the poor man's trimming in place of costly lace and silk.

History has it that a woman named Mary Atwater, author of *Byways in Handweaving* (published in 1968 by Macmillan Publishing Co., Inc.), introduced the inkle loom to the U.S. in the 1930s, and then, with great ingenuity, went on to improve the basic technique. Dissatisfied with the plain-weave instructions sent with the loom, she devised intricate patterns using several colors of thread.

Today, inkles are becoming popular again, though no longer as a poor man's trim. The striking color and texture combinations that can be achieved through inkle weaving have brought inkles to the attention of craftspeople who have never woven before. Learning to weave on an inkle loom makes possible the creation of a satisfying product and serves as a good introduction to yarns, looms and the more complicated forms of weaving.

Inkle looms are available through mail-order loom suppliers, including E. E. Gilmore, 1032 Broadway, Stockton, Cal. 95205; Lily Mills Company, Shelby, N.C. 28150; and School Products Co., Inc., 312 East 23rd St., New York, N.Y. 10010.

Threading the Loom

All weaving is the process of interlocking lengthwise and crosswise threads. In the weaving done on an inkle loom (photograph 1), the pattern of the woven piece depends entirely on how the lengthwise threads are arranged on the loom, since the crosswise threads will show only at the edges. These lengthwise threads, known as the warp, are strung on the loom so they are parallel to each other. The variously colored threads are tied to each other to form one continuous strand around and around the loom, so the tension is equal throughout. The process of putting these threads on the loom is known as warping the loom.

The crosswise threads, which constitute the weft of the fabric, are added as the weaving progresses. To make it easier to pass the weft thread from one side of the loom to the other, it can be wrapped around two of the weaver's fingers to form a figure eight, called a butterfly (photograph 2), or wrapped on a shuttle.

In inkle weaving, there are two sets of lengthwise threads on different planes on the loom, and the weft thread is passed between them, producing what is termed a warp-faced band because the visible pattern is formed solely by warp threads. The weft serves the important function of holding the lengthwise strands together.

Gudrun Mirin is a self-taught weaver. After taking only one course in weaving, she was so taken with the craft that she learned inkle weaving on her own. Her work, both weaving and pottery, has been exhibited and sold in galleries and at craft fairs. President of the Queens Craft League and a member of the board of the New York Handweavers' Guild, Gudrun was born in Austria. She lives in Ithaca, New York.

1: In inkle weaving, heddles made of string are attached to the heddle bar (center), tension is adjusted by a movable tension bar (bottom right), and length is adjusted by a movable peg (arrow).

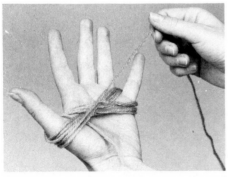

2: Yarn to be used for the weft is wrapped around the thumb and little finger to form a figure-eight shape called a butterfly. This facilitates passing the weft through the warp threads.

Inkle belts are not only functional but can be twisted and sewn together to create unusual wall hangings such as this one the artist has titled "A Twist of Inkles."

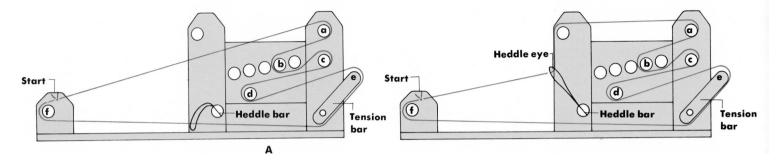

A

Figure A: To warp the loom, thread the yarn alternately through the open space between heddle loops (left) and through the heddles themselves (right). The path from a to f for both warps is the same.

3: The loom is warped (threaded with warp yarn) to make the hat band and tote bag handle pictured on page 130.

Due to the way the loom is threaded (Figure A), the two sets of warp threads—known as the heddle warp and the open warp—can exchange planes as a unit, although only the open warp moves. When the loom is being warped, every other thread is passed through a loop of string called a heddle, one loop for each thread. These become the heddle warp; the alternating threads—the open warp—do not go through string loops. The space between the two sets of warp threads is called a shed.

To fill the loop with warp threads, tie the first thread temporarily to the front bar of the loom. Figure A, left, shows the path taken by an open warp thread. When the first thread gets back to where it started, it can continue around again, or it can be cut and the end tied to a thread of a different color, depending on the pattern planned. The second warp thread goes through a heddle eye; Figure A, right, shows the path taken by such a heddle warp thread. The warp threads continue to alternate between the two paths as they are placed on the loom until the desired width is reached; when all are in place, the last end is tied temporarily to the front bar. When it becomes necessary to move the warp threads around the loom (after about 5 inches of belt are woven), both first and last warp threads are untied from the loom peg and tied to their adjacent warp threads.

One of the central pegs is adjustable, depending on which of a row of holes is used; its position determines the length of the belt that can be made. The loom pictured can produce a belt 6 to 8 feet long. The number of threads placed on the loom depends on the thickness of the thread used and the planned width of the finished belt. Photograph 3 shows warping completed for the hat band and tote bag handle pictured on page 130.

Weaving

When all of the warp threads are in place on the loom, weaving can begin. In this process the weft thread is passed through the open space between the upper and lower sets of warp threads. The threads of the open warp are then shifted with pressure of a finger so the positions are reversed; if the open warp was on top, it is

4: To make the first shed—a space between the two sets of warp threads—push down on the open warps so the heddle warps are on top and the open warps on the bottom.

5: To make the second shed, push up on the open warp threads. The shed is now reversed, with open warp threads on top and the heddle warp threads on the bottom.

6: To weave, put the weft through a shed. This is known as making a shot. Then change the shed for the next shot of the weft, thus weaving the weft thread through the warp threads.

7: To make the weave firm, push each shot of the weft thread down with a ruler or other flat stick, as shown. This procedure is known as beating down.

Glossary

Beating: Tamping down each crosswise (weft) thread after it is inserted and shed changed, to make the fabric firmly woven.

Butterfly: Thread arranged in a figure-eight shape in order that it might easily be passed back and forth through the loom.

Draft: A weaving pattern drawn on graph paper to show the order of various colors of lengthwise (warp) threads.

Heddles: A series of loops made of string and attached to the loom, through which half of the lengthwise threads pass.

Heddle eye: The string loop through which a lengthwise thread passes.

Heddle rod: The projecting bar on the loom that holds the string loops.

Pick-up stick: A flat, thin stick used to lift certain lengthwise threads when special pattern effects are sought.

Selvage: The side edges of a strip of woven cloth.

Shed: The open space between the two sets of lengthwise (warp) threads; as these sets successively exchange top-and-bottom positions, the crosswise (weft) threads pass through the sheds that are created.

Shot: The passage of one crosswise thread through a shed.

Shuttle: A flat wooden paddle for holding the weft (the filling thread) so it can be easily passed through the shed.

Take-up: The shortening of the lengthwise threads that results as they go over and under the crosswise threads.

Tension bar: An adjustable rod that can be loosened so thread is not stretched.

Warp: The lengthwise threads that are strung directly on the loom, through which the crosswise (weft) threads are woven.

Warp-faced: A weaving, as in these projects, in which the lengthwise threads show on the surface; the crosswise threads are visible only along the edges.

Weaving: The interlacing of lengthwise and crosswise threads to form fabric.

Weft: The crosswise threads that are woven through the lengthwise threads on the loom.

moved to the bottom. Photographs 4 and 5 show the two sheds that can be formed successively by raising and lowering the open warp.

Weaving on the inkle loom is the process of passing the weft thread through a shed (called making a shot, photograph 6), changing the shed, tamping down the weft to make it firm (photograph 7), then passing the weft thread back through the new shed. A small ruler (as shown), a tongue depressor, or a beater made specifically for this purpose can be used to press the weft into place, a process called "beating down." The weaving process then continues—make a shot, change the shed, beat down, make a shot, change the shed, beat down . . .

Designing Inkles

One of the reasons why inkle weaving is growing in popularity is that the design of the inkle is established as soon as the loom is threaded. Weaving is a continuous process of filling the threaded loom with weft. For a solid-color inkle, the loom is filled with one color. If a pattern is desired, the loom must be carefully threaded, and a graph-paper pattern, called a draft, is the easiest way to note the number of colors and their order. This is done as shown in Figure B, page 130.

To make lengthwise stripes, the colors are placed alternately on the loom. If a stripe one thread wide is desired, two threads of the same color must be used side by side—one through a heddle loop and the other through the open space. This is done because only the threads on the top are visible at any one shot of the weft. The change of shed for the next shot of the weft brings the bottom warp threads to the top, so for a continuous lengthwise stripe, both one open warp thread and its adjacent heddle warp thread must be in the same color. For wider stripes, any multiple of two will work.

To make crosswise stripes, on the other hand, contrasting colors are used for the open warp and the heddle warp. When the open warp threads form the top of the shed, only that color will be visible. On the next shed, when the heddle threads are on top, that color will form a contrasting stripe, thus producing a pattern of crosswise stripes in alternating colors. Figure D (page 131) shows a pattern for crosswise stripes; the watch band made from this pattern is on page 131.

The only place where the weft thread shows is at the edges. The weft is shot through the sheds from either side; if you start the weft on the right and pass through to the left (photograph 6), the next shot will be from left to right. The small loops of weft that show from one shot to another form a woven edge called selvage. In order to make this selvage edge an integral part of the weaving, use the same color thread for the weft as the outermost warp threads. As you gain experience in weaving and can make selvages that are even and of an equal tension, you might use leftover yarn in a coordinated color for the weft.

The thickness of the weft thread determines the speed of the weaving: The thicker the weft thread, the faster the weaving goes. Too thick a weft, however, will result in a loose, uneven belt. When working with a thin yarn such as No. 5 pearl cotton, I use a double strand for the weft to accentuate the design in the warp.

An inkle belt used as a hat band and bag handle is an attractive way to coordinate a hat and bag.

This detail shows the design created when the loom is warped following the pattern in Figure B.

8: To remove the finished belt, cut across the warp threads, leaving several inches for fringe.

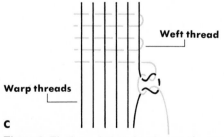

Weft thread

Warp threads

C

Figure C: Tie the weft thread to the outside warp thread to secure the weaving at both the beginning and the end of the weaving.

Hat band and bag handle ¢ ⌧ ♦ 🐘

The hat band and matching bag handle at left were made with No. 5 pearl cotton thread in 5 colors. You will need a total of 4 ounces of thread and a sewing needle.

Measure the crown of the hat and decide the length of the handle you want, allowing 1 foot extra for tying the inkle on the hat, making the fringe, and sewing on the handle. I needed a belt about 6 feet long, so I warped the loom with the adjustable peg in the position shown (photograph 3, page 128). To make the band 1¾ inches wide, warp the loom following the pattern, called a draft, in Figure B. These graph patterns are a convenient and concise way of showing how to warp a loom. Reading from left to right, the first thread is maroon and it is threaded through the open warp. The path of an open warp was shown in Figure A, page 128. The next thread is also maroon and it is a heddle warp, also in Figure A. The

middle repeat from right to left——

Heddle	M	M	M	M	P	B	B	B	B	L	L	L	L	L	L	L	L	L	L	G
Open	M	M	M	M	P	B	B	B	B	G	G	G	G	G	G	G	G	G	G	G

B Key: M = maroon P = purple B = blue G = gold L = light blue

Figure B: Warping the loom according to this pattern will produce the design pictured (left).

threads are warped alternately through the open space and through a heddle. This creates the two sets of warp threads between which the weft passes in the process of weaving. To continue warping, follow the draft. Each lettered block indicates one thread: The letter tells what color and the placement of the letter tells whether it is warped open (bottom line) or through a heddle (top line). After 8 maroon threads are warped, a purple thread is attached. To do this, cut the maroon thread, leaving enough to tie to the purple thread, just in front of the front bar (photograph 3). Tie the purple to the maroon; all new colors are tied on this way to form a continuous warp. The knots can be cut off together when the weaving is completed.

To make the draft—the graph-paper pattern—more concise, any belt that is symmetrical from left to right can be shown with only half a draft. The first half is written out and the second half is a repeat of the first, but worked in reverse. When you get to the last gold thread at the far right of Figure B, for example, you will be at the center of the belt. To warp the second half, follow the colors backwards (from right to left), but ignore the placement, simply alternating open and heddle warps. The last thread warped according to the pattern was a gold through the open space. To warp the second half, repeat the gold but since the last thread was through the open space, this gold must be threaded through the heddle. The next thread (second from right) is also gold and goes through the open space. A glance at your loom will tell you whether the next thread is open or heddle, and the pattern indicates which color is used. The pattern ends with 3 gold threads; when you repeat it backwards, you add 3 gold for a total of 6. Then alternate the gold and light blue, followed by 8 blue, 2 purple, and 8 maroon. The draft shows 43 threads; the completed warp will have 86. To make the stripes appear thicker, I used 2 strands of maroon (the color of the outer warp threads) for the weft.

To weave, raise the warp to form a shed (photograph 4), insert the weft (photograph 6), change the shed, and beat down (photograph 7). Continue weaving this way until the shed is so small that it is difficult to pass the weft through. Loosen the tension bar and rotate the woven area under the first peg; then tighten the tension bar and continue weaving. Repeat this procedure each time the shed becomes too small. To remove the finished belt, hold the warp threads and cut across as shown in photograph 8. The weaving will unravel if the weft threads are not secured, so tie a knot at the edge of the weaving (Figure C), both at the beginning and end of weft. Trim the fringe to approximately 2 inches.

For the hat band, tie the belt around the crown of the hat, knot it, and cut off the excess. Unravel 2 inches of weave of the cut end to match the fringe on the other end, and knot the weft. Use the remaining belt for the bag handle, folding one end around one ring of the tote bag and hemming it under. Adjust the length of the strap until it is comfortable for you, then secure the other end.

A narrow inkle band and a small buckle make a durable and attractive watch band.

A vase for dried flowers is made from a length of inkle belt and a juice can.

Watchband and vase ¢ ⊠ 🚶 🏃

The watchband and vase cover pictured above were made from No. 5 pearl cotton thread. The navy and raspberry stripes are bordered in light blue; and a double strand of the same color is used for the weft. You will need 1 ounce each of navy and raspberry, less than 1 ounce of light blue, a small buckle (available at jewelry or department stores), a sewing needle, a 6-ounce juice can and white household glue. Since the inkle belt is very narrow, the complete pattern for warping the loom is shown in Figure D. I needed less than 1 foot of inkle for the watchband and, thinking it would be a shame to waste the extra warp threads, I wove a 6-foot length and used the excess belt to make a vase cover.

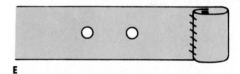

Figure E: To finish the watch band, fold the end under so the warp threads are covered, as shown, and stitch down.

Heddle	B	N		N		N		N		N		N		N		N		N		N		N		N	end →
Open	B	N	N	R	R	R	R	R	R	R	R	R	R	R	R	R	R	R	R	N	N	B			

D   Key: B = light blue   N = navy   R = raspberry

Figure D: This pattern is used to warp the loom for a narrow band with crosswise stripes.

To warp the loom, follow the pattern, reading from left to right. Each lettered block indicates one thread. There are 36 threads indicated which, placed on the loom, make a ⅝-inch-wide band. To determine the width inkle you need, measure the strap opening on your watch. Push the warp threads close together (but not overlapping) to determine the width the inkle will be after weaving, and warp as many threads as you need for the strap opening on the watch.

Weave the belt following the directions on page 128. Remove the belt from the loom, and knot the weft. Measure your wrist, allowing 3 inches extra for hemming. Divide this measurement in half (for the two parts of the strap), and cut two pieces of inkle to this half measurement. Slipping one end through the opening on the watch, hem the belt on the reverse side. Repeat for the other strap, then slip one loose end through the buckle, and hem it under, securing it to the buckle. At this point, try the watch on to determine the placement of the holes for the buckle. Measure for two holes so the watchband is adjustable. Fold the end of the band as shown in Figure E, and hem. To make the holes, simply move the weaving aside until you can push the needle through from one side to the other. Using a needle threaded with one of the colors of the belt, outline a hole with small stitches (Figure F). Repeat for the second hole.

To make the small vase with the leftover inkle belt, I used a 6-ounce juice can. Measure the circumference of the can and, allowing ¾ inch for overlap, cut six pieces of inkle to this length. Use white household glue to attach the inkle belt lengths to the can, folding the cut ends under. Continue gluing all six rows, overlapping the ends at the same place, and let dry for 2 hours. To keep the ends secure, stitch the folded ends under, keeping this seam in the back of the can.

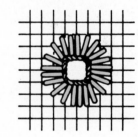

F

Figure F: The belt holes are made by separating the threads to form a hole, which is bound with a buttonhole stitch (see Embroidery Craftnotes, page 90).

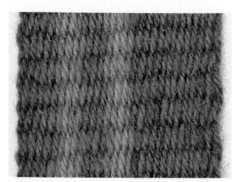

A detail shows the design that results from warping the loom following Figure H, top.

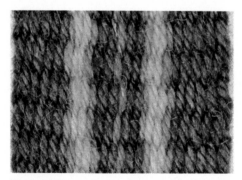

This is the belt woven following the second from the top pattern in Figure H.

The third pattern in Figure H produces the design shown here.

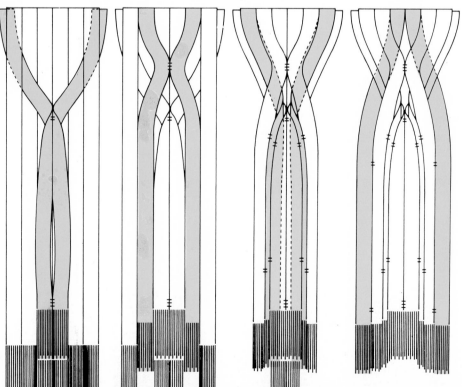

Warping for this inkle belt is shown in the bottom pattern in Figure H.

A twist of inkles

The wall hanging (page 127) is made from four inkle belts, which are twisted together as shown in Figure G. The pattern calls for stripes of different widths made in several shades of brown and gold. I used 3-ply wool yarn and hand-dyed it, using commercial acid dyes. The stripes are made by warping an even number of threads, as shown in Figure H. You can change the width of the stripes simply by warping any even number. You will need a total of 20 ounces of yarn and a ¼-inch dowel 14 inches long to make the hanging.

Warp the loom, following the patterns in Figure H or varying the design if you so desire. Use one strand of the outside warp color for the weft, and make each belt 8 feet long, following the directions on page 128. Knot the weft to prevent unravelling, and leave the fringe slightly uneven for a casual effect.

To make the wall hanging, cut each belt in half and stitch the cut end of each piece over the dowel so that it is completely covered. (I arranged the belt halves symmetrically, starting in the center and working out toward each end, and overlapped the third and outermost belt pieces slightly.) To arrange the belts, start with the outermost belts, stitching their inner edges together about 1 foot down from the dowel (Figure G, far left). Turn the belt pieces over so the back faces out and stitch them together just above the fringe. To sew inkle belts together, use the same color thread as the outer warp color and pick up the piece of weft that shows along the edge. This way the stitches are hidden in the weaving. Now join the belts that lie next to the center belts, bringing the inside edges together about 7 inches down from the dowel and stitching as before (Figure G, center left). Let the ends hang loose until the next two belts are joined. The third belt (Figure G, center right) is next. Bring the pieces to the center under the stitching on the second belt, turn the belt so the back faces front, and stitch the pieces to both the second and fourth belts. Lastly, bring the innermost belt pieces to the outside and stitch to the second belt (Figure G, far right). Trim the fringe if you want an even edge; I prefer the casual look of uneven fringe.

Figure G: The wall hanging shown on page 127 is put together by arranging each of the four belts as shown below. Work from left to right, positioning and stitching the belts as indicated.

G

1 Heddle	C	C	C	C	P	P	P	P	P	P	P	R	R	R	C	← middle repeat from right to left															
1 Open	C	C	C	C	P	P	P	P	P	P	P	R	R	R	C																
2 Heddle	C	C	C	C	R	G	G	R	C	C	C	R	G	G	R	C	C	C	C	C	C	C	C	C	C	C	C	C	C	end →
2 Open	C	C	C	C	R	G	G	R	C	C	C	R	G	G	R	C	C	C	C	C	C	C	C	C	C	C	C	C	C	
3 Heddle	B	B	B	B	B	G	Y	Y	G	B	B	B	← middle repeat from right to left																	
3 Open	B	B	B	B	B	G	Y	Y	G	B	B	B	R																	
4 Heddle	D	D	D	D	D	D	D	D	D	D	D	D	D	D	C	C	C	C	C	G	G	G	G	D	← end					
4 Open	D	D	D	D	D	D	D	D	D	D	D	D	D	C	C	C	C	C	G	G	G	D								

Key: Y = yellow   G = gold   C = cinnamon   R = rust   P = pumpkin   B = brown   D = dark brown

H

Figure H: Follow these patterns to warp the loom for the four belts used in the wall hanging.

A pick-up belt

¢ ⬛ 🧍 🧵

Inkle belt design possibilities are greatly increased with the use of a pick-up technique. This is easily learned but is slower than plain weave. To make the belt shown below, warp the loom following the pattern in Figure I. You will need 4 ounces of 4-ply wool (2 ounces of each color). Pick-up patterns are plotted on graph paper (as shown in Figure J). Each square represents one pair of warp threads. The pattern is read from the bottom up and represents one complete motif. In this pattern, 8 rows form the stylized flower which is repeated along the belt.

Heddle	G	G	R	R	R	R	R	R	R	R	R	R	R			middle repeat from right to left
Open	G	G	R	R	R	R	R	G	G	G	G	G	G	R		

I   **Key: G = gold   R = red**

Figure I: Warp the loom according to this pattern to make the flower-motif belt below.

In plain weave, you open each shed and weave completely across the row; there is no manipulation of threads. If weaved this way, the belt would be alternating red and gold horizontal stripes separated by a center vertical red stripe. In the pick-up technique, you pick up certain warp threads with your fingers, a knitting needle, or a smooth stick called a pick-up stick to form a pattern. The pattern alternates a row of plain weave with a pick-up row. Weave one row as usual, change the shed, beat down, then pick up the indicated warp threads and hold all of these threads on top. Put weft through this newly-created shed, change shed, and beat down. Repeat these steps, picking up the warp threads as indicated in Figure J.

Since one warp thread is part of the top warp several weaves in a row—it is on top, then it is picked up, then it is on top in the usual weave—the pattern also takes on a new dimension of texture, as the lifted warp threads create a raised effect.

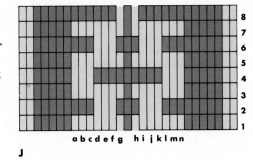

A flower motif is created by following the pick-up pattern in Figure J.

a b c d e f g   h i j k l m n

J

Figure J: The pick-up pattern for the flower motif is a repeat of these 8 rows.
Row 1: weave as usual.
Row 2: pick up threads d-e-f-i-j-k.
Row 3: weave as usual.
Row 4: pick up threads a-b-c-l-m-n.
Row 5: weave as usual.
Row 6: pick up d-e-f-i-j-k.
Row 7: weave as usual.
Row 8: pick up g-h.

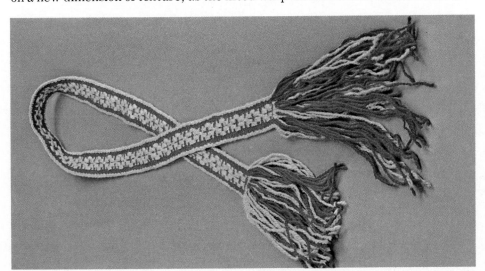

A pick-up pattern is repeated along the entire length of the belt to form a chain of flowers.

133

MACRAMÉ
All Tied Up In Knots

Sue Preston (left) and daughters Laura (center) and Rachel (right) are known in craft circles as The Prestons. They create, each in her own style, beautiful and functional pieces of macramé that have been exhibited at craft shows, galleries and shops. Sue Preston teaches macramé and is publicity director for an annual crafts show at Bear Mountain, New York. Laura, an illustrator, hopes to collaborate on children's books with her father. Rachel, a graduate of Duke University, divides her time between the Preston home in Blauvelt, New York, and her home in Durham, North Carolina.

Few crafts have attracted such a diverse following as macramé. Salty old sailors, proper Victorian ladies, and teen-agers have all taken to this ancient art of knotting with equal enthusiasm and often quite different results.

One of the marvelous things about macramé is exactly this versatility. Macramé can be whatever you want it to be—strictly functional, pure fantasy, or a little of both. It can take shape as a decorative trimming, as a textured fabric, or as a three-dimensional sculptural form; the knots can be tied with anything from tough, earthy-color ropes to peacock-hued sewing threads. You can add feathers or beads or leather to macramé, or you can simply add your imagination.

Another nice thing about macramé is that although it often looks complicated, it is really quite easy to learn. You do need lots of patience and an eye for detail, but the knotting itself is not difficult to master. Macramé consists of a few basic knots plus many fancy knots, but you needn't learn them all; you will be surprised by how much you can do with just a few of the basic knots.

Materials and Tools

Macramé knots are worked with cords that are flexible enough to be knotted, yet not so elastic that they lose their shape. Some suitable cords of varying thicknesses and weights are listed in the column at the right. They can be found around the house; in hardware stores, yarn and craft shops, housewares and upholstery departments, and mail-order catalogs; and at weaving suppliers, notions and stationery counters.

Cords that are generally not suitable include flat leather lacings that are hard to control, nylon cords that tend to slip, and knitting worsted yarns that are too fuzzy and stretchy for satisfactory knotting.

Most of the cords you will buy are white, off-white, or natural color; some can be dyed successfully at home with fabric dyes. For an even color, dye the cords before knotting and always test a sample before you start. To fix the color, add salt when you dye rayon, cotton or linen cord and add vinegar when you dye silk or wool. For an antique look in white cords, try steeping them in very strong tea or coffee. Remember that any dye will look darker when wet.

Your basic tools are your own two hands. You will also need a simple knotting board to work on—this can be a rectangle of rigid plastic foam, a light-color cork bulletin board, a polyurethane-foam pillow form, a piece of insulation board, or corrugated cardboard ½ to 1 inch thick. The board can be marked with a grid if you feel that such a guide is helpful.

Gather together your cords, the knotting board, scissors, a tape measure or yardstick, T-pins to hold the knots, rubber bands or yarn bobbins to keep the excess cords out of the way, liquid glue to prevent fraying, and you are all set.

Some suitable cords
Natural or dyed jute
Sisal
Seine twine
Butcher's twine
Clothesline
Cotton cable or shear cord
Polished cotton navy cord
Rayon twist or flag cord
Rattail rayon
Linen rug warp
Venetian-blind traverse cord
Upholstery welting
Pearl cotton
Crochet cotton
Non-stretch yarns
Dental floss
Cotton or silk sewing threads
String

A four-panel macramé screen serves as a movable space divider and gives a sense of privacy, yet it has an open, airy look. Two panels are made of square knots with a central diamond motif; the other two are a repeat of an open diamond pattern. For directions, turn to page 142.

Reverse lark's head knot

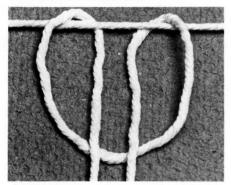

Double the cord and bring the loop end up under the mounting cord and to the front. Bring the ends through the loop; tighten.

Square knot

This macramé knot is not the familiar Boy Scout square knot; it is always worked with four cords. First, the right cord is brought under the two center cords and over the left cord; the left cord is placed over the center cords and under the right cord.

Next, the first half of the knot is tightened, then the left cord is brought under the center cords and over the right cord; the right cord goes over the center cords and under the left cord.

Finally, the second half of the knot is tightened. Each half is called a half knot; a chain of half knots makes a twist.

Alternating square knots

The first row is worked with all the cords. The second row skips the first two cords, works a square knot with the next four cords and continues across, ending with two unworked cords. The third row repeats the first row, starting at the extreme left and working with all the cords.

The granny knot

This, in macramé terms, is a square knot without the two center cords.

The bobble

Make a chain (a sennit) of square knots.

Then bring the two center cords up and back down through the top of the chain.

Horizontal double half hitch (cording)

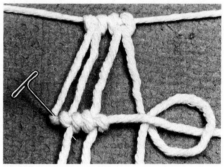

First, the anchor cord is placed straight across the working cords. Each working cord is brought under and looped over the anchor cord.

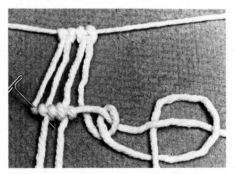

Next, the same working cord is brought over and looped under the anchor cord, to the right of the first half of the knot.

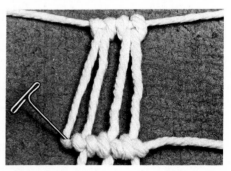

Finally, both halves of the knot are tightened over the anchor cord.

KNOTS

X of diagonal double half hitches

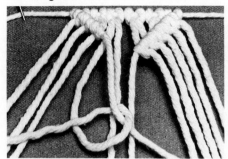

First, the cords on each side are knotted on the diagonal with a double half hitch. The outside cords are the carrying cords.

Next, the left carrying cord is double half hitched to the right carrying cord.

Then, two more rows of cording are worked below the first two. The row on the left stops at the center; the right-hand row continues across to the left edge.

Finally, on the bottom half of the X, the second row on the left becomes the first row on the right. The X is shown here with a diamond of alternating square knots and the beginning of a second X below.

The berry knot

First, make two square knots under the rows of diagonal cording.

Here the first row of the berry knot is shown. Cords on the right are carrying cords only; cords on the left are working cords only.

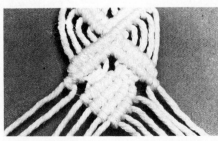

Here, four rows of cording for the berry knot are shown before they are tightened.

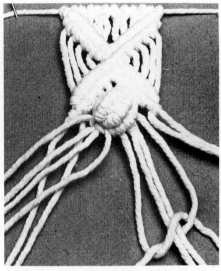

Finally, gather up the cording into a rounded shape and secure underneath with two square knots.

Alternate half hitch chain

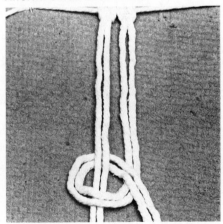

First, loop the two right cords around the two left cords.

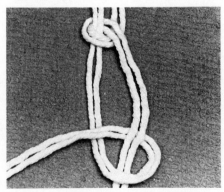

Then loop the two left cords around the two right cords. Tighten the loops.

Father, mother and teen-agers can all wear a diamond-pattern belt like this with their jeans. The diamonds are alternating square knots outlined with diagonal double half hitches.

Another belt you can make combines square knots, diagonal double half hitches, berries (center), bobbles (top and bottom), and half knot twists.

Adjustable belt ¢ ● 👤 🏺

This diamond-pattern belt has a casual, tailored look that appeals to almost everyone. The buckle's hook fits between knots so eyelets are unnecessary.

Size: 36 inches long (adjustable) and 1¾ inches wide.

Materials: 4 ounces of linen rug warp. Buckle with a hook.

Knots: Reverse lark's head knot, alternating square knots, diagonal double half hitch, alternating half hitch chains (see Craftnotes, pages 136 and 137).

Belt: Cut 12 cords as follows: one cord 18 feet long, two cords 23 feet long, and nine cords 28 feet long. When estimating the length of the cords needed for any project, plan on each cord being about eight times as long as the finished length. Because the cords are doubled over the mounting cord, each end will be about four times the finished length. Some knots take more cord than others so it is a good idea to work a sample. Knot one pattern repeat to see how much cord is needed and multiply that amount by the number of repeats in the project. Always add a little for good measure; it is easier to trim the ends than to splice two cords near the end.

Center and pin the 18-foot-long cord horizontally on the knotting board with the center section about 1¾ inches long. This will be the mounting cord that holds the other cords and the two long ends will be cords No. 1 and No. 24 at the extreme sides (what will be the top and bottom edges of the belt).

Mount the nine 28-foot-long cords on the mounting cord, between the two ends, using reverse lark's head knots (Craftnotes, page 136). You will have 18 working ends, each about 14 feet long. The two remaining cords, each 23 feet long, will be mounted between the two outside ends and the center group and will be numbered 2, 3, 22 and 23. Mount them with reverse lark's head knots, leaving uneven ends—the No. 2 and No. 23 ends should be 9 feet long, No. 3 and No. 22 should be 14 feet long. The four outermost ends, Nos. 1, 2, 23 and 24, will be the carrying cords for the diagonal double half hitches that form the Xs in the pattern.

Tie all the working cords in butterfly bundles to keep them from tangling. To tie a butterfly, wrap the cord around your thumb and little finger in a figure-eight, then secure it with a rubber band. Start at a comfortable distance from the mounting cord, rather than at the end of the cord, to make it easy to pull the cord out. In order to keep track of the carrying cords, you can use four rubber bands of different colors to hold the butterflies on cords 1, 2, 23 and 24.

Working with all 24 cords, work 3 inches of alternating square knots. The alternating rows will have six and five knots each. End with a row of six knots. This section of the belt will be attached to the buckle. There are several ways you can attach it; see photographs 1 and 2.

On the following five rows, work five square knots, then four, three, two, and lastly, one, forming a V-shape in the center of the belt.

1: A macramé belt can be worked directly onto a metal buckle or a leather strip, using that as the mounting cord. Heavy-duty snaps make a belt wearable with several different buckles.

2: Lacing is the simplest way to attach a macramé belt to a buckle. Pull one end through the buckle and fold it over, then lace a double length of cord through both layers and tie it with a granny knot.

Next, work a diagonal row of double half hitches (also called cording or clove hitches) down one side to the center of this V shape. Use the outermost cord as your carrying cord, the cord over which the knots are formed. Repeat the diagonal double half hitches down the other side, using the outermost cord on that side as the carrying cord. Double half hitch No. 1 onto No. 24. Repeat the two rows of diagonal double hitches, this time using the next cords, Nos. 2 and 23, as the carrying cords. Double half hitch No. 1 onto No. 23, then hitch No. 24 onto No. 2 and No. 2 onto No. 23. This completes the top of the X.

Now work the alternate half hitch chains that fill in the sides between the arms of the Xs. Pick up the four outside cords on one side and, with two cords worked as one, make a chain of eight half hitches. Using the next four cords, work a chain of four half hitches. Repeat the chains on the other side, starting at the outside and working toward the center. (The remaining cords on each side of the X will not be worked.)

You will now work the bottom half of the X in cording or diagonal double half hitches. With No. 2 as the carrying cord, double half hitch down to the right. Next, with No. 23 as the carrying cord, double half hitch down to the left, starting with the No. 24 cord. (The colored rubber bands will help you find the right cords here.) The bottom row on the upper left arm of the X will become the top row on the lower right arm and the bottom row of the upper right arm will become the top row on the lower left.

Work the two bottom rows of diagonal double half hitches with No. 1 as the carrying cord for the left side and No. 24 as the carrying cord for the right side.

Fill in the diamond with alternating square knots, starting with one knot under the crossing of the X, working to a full row of six knots at the center of the diamond, then back down to one knot at the bottom point.

Outline the diamond with cording as before. Repeat this diamond pattern with cording and alternate half hitch chains until the belt is about 6 inches from the finished length. After the bottom half of the last X, finish by making a section of alternating square knots ending in a V-shape point and add four more rows of cording.

Use a tapestry needle to pull the cords through the knots on the reverse side and cut them close. Dab white fabric glue over the ends to prevent fraying.

For a simpler X with arms that cross exactly in the center: Work the two rows of diagonal double half hitches on one side, first with the outside cord and then with the next cord; double half hitch the two carrying cords. Switch to the other side and work both rows, first with the outside cord and then with the next cord. Double half hitch the two carrying cords on that side and then join the two sides with a double half hitch of the two inner carrying cords. To work the bottom half of the X, count to the center and pick up the two center cords as the carrying cords. The cord on the left goes to the left, the cord on the right goes to the right. For the second row, pick up the cords next to the center cords and work as before.

A dress yoke is an unusual way to show off your macramé skills. Many pleasing color variations are possible.

This is a detail of one corner of the yoke. The front and back yokes and the shoulder straps are worked in one continuous piece.

Figure A: The pattern is for the front yoke and half of the shoulder straps; flop the pattern over for the other half of the straps and the back yoke. The pattern shown, when enlarged on a half-inch grid, is for a large size. A small size would have four sections of natural cords in the center. A medium size would have five sections of natural cords in the center.

Dress yoke and sash $ ● ♀ 🎎

A muslin peasant dress becomes something special when you add a macramé yoke and sash done in a natural color spiced with yellow and orange.

Dress sizes: Small, medium or large. Directions are given for the large size; see Figures A and B for directions for converting to small or medium.

Materials: Dress takes about 3½ yards of cotton muslin and ½ yard of narrow elastic. If you wish to make a print dress with a macramé yoke of one color, you can use an Indian-print cotton bedspread or any lightweight fabric. Yoke and sash together take approximately 4 ounces of linen rug warp (natural) and 2 ounces each of yellow and orange pearl cotton.

Knots: Horizontal and diagonal double half hitches (see pages 136 and 137).

Cutting: For the yoke, cut the cords as follows:

Natural	Orange	Yellow
16 cords 100 inches long	8 cords 100 inches long	8 cords 100 inches long
48 cords 28 inches long	24 cords 28 inches long	24 cords 28 inches long
2 cords 30 inches long		
2 mounting cords 18 inches long		
1 mounting cord long enough to tie around your board		

Mounting: Mount all 100-inch-long cords and half of the 28-inch-long cords of each color on one mounting cord which you have tied around and pinned to your knotting board (see Figure A). (Because the cotton cord is half as thick as the linen cord, you need two ends of cotton to equal one end of linen.)

For each side piece that starts in the front yoke, goes into a shoulder strap and ends in the back yoke, use 8 natural cords, 4 yellow cords and 4 orange cords, each 100 inches long. For the center of each yoke, use 24 natural cords, 12 yellow cords and 12 orange cords, each 28 inches long. Mount the side cords so that each end is 50 inches long; mount the center cords so that each end is 14 inches long, except for the linen carrying cords that are mounted unevenly as shown in Figure A. (The carrying cords are indicated by the dash lines.) Mount only the front yoke center to start; mount the center of the back yoke when the shoulder straps reach that point.

Introduce one of the 30-inch linen cords directly below the mounting cord and work two rows of horizontal double half hitches (cording) with this as the carrying cord. Work ends of the carrying cord through knots on the reverse side.

Work the rest of the front yoke in diagonal double half hitches, using Figure A as a guide for the direction of the carrying cords. When the long cords reach the edge, they turn back into the work and continue to zigzag throughout the entire piece. Let the cords curve between the rows of cording, rather than pull them tight; some will even overlap. In the beginning you might want to pin them to get the proper spacing, but with practice it will come easily.

When you reach the shoulder straps, mount an 18-inch-long cord to the carrying cords which reach the corners and work two rows of cording over this cord. Work ends through knots on the reverse side and cut close.

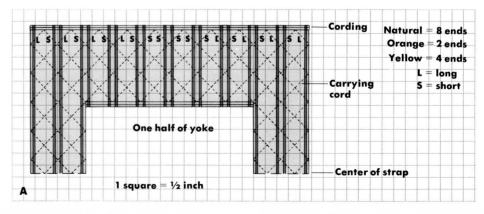

One half of yoke

Cording
Carrying cord
Center of strap

Natural = 8 ends
Orange = 2 ends
Yellow = 4 ends
L = long
S = short

1 square = ½ inch

A

Continue to work the shoulder straps until they are the desired length. The average total length of the yokes and straps is 15 inches. At the beginning of the back yoke, attach another 18-inch long cord to the carrying cords at the corners of the shoulder straps as you did at the finish of the front yoke. Again, work two rows of cording over this cord, then continue across the entire width of the piece with diagonal double half hitches. Finish with two more rows of cording worked over a newly-introduced 30-inch cord. Work ends through knots on the reverse side.

If you make a one-color yoke, you can vary the macramé design by putting beads, berry knots or bobble knots inside the diamonds.

The Dress

To make the dress itself, enlarge the patterns in Figure B, adjusting the length to suit you. Place the sleeve pattern on a lengthwise fold and cut two. Place the pattern for the body of the dress on a fold and cut it out; cut two, since the front and back are identical.

Sew two rows of gathering stitches at the top of the dress front and dress back and at the top of the sleeves, ½ inch and ⅝ inch from the edges.

Sew the side seams of the dress and the sleeve seams with double seams such as those on blue jeans. To do this, first sew the seam with the right side of the fabric out, then turn so that the wrong side is out and the seam is inside. Stitch the length of the seam again, enclosing the raw edges of the seam inside. Open the fabric, press the seam flat, and top-stitch two rows about ½ inch apart on the right side over the double seam.

Next, gather the sleeves and with the right sides together, pin the sides of the sleeves to the curved armhole sections of the dress. Sew, being sure that the gathering stitches are inside the seam allowance. The center sections of the sleeves will not be sewn to the dress; they will be joined to the shoulder straps of the yoke. To finish these seams neatly, trim the seam allowance of the sleeve just above the gathering stitches, turn the edge of the dress seam allowance under and stitch over the seam, encasing the edges. Or, bind the edges with double-fold bias tape.

Make shallow hems on the sleeves, leaving a small opening on each, and insert narrow elastic to fit comfortably around your wrists.

At this point, try the dress on and have a friend pin the yoke in place, wrong side of the yoke on the right side of the fabric. Put the bottom rows of cording over the rows of gathering stitches at the top of the dress and cover the gathers on the sleeves with the edges of the shoulder straps. Hand-sew the yoke to the dress with strong, invisible stitches. Trim the seams that still show on the inside and cover with bias tape.

The dress as shown can be washed by hand in cold water. If other fabrics and cords are combined, keep them compatible in their care requirements.

The Sash

The sash that matches the yoke is worked much the same as one shoulder strap. Cut a linen mounting cord about 12 inches long. Cut 8 cords each of yellow and orange, each about 18 feet long. (When working with the colored cords, use two cords as one, just as you did for the yoke.) Cut 16 cords of natural linen, each about 24 feet long.

Make overhand knots at the ends of the mounting cord and pin it to your knotting board. An overhand knot is a simple knot you use all the time. Bring the top end of the cord down and make a loop; bring the end through the loop and tighten. Using the overhand knot and leaving 7 inches for fringe, mount the working cords in the center of the mounting cord, following the pattern for the strap in Figure A. There will be 8 cords in each natural section.

Work two rows of cording or horizontal double half hitches, using the two yellow cords at one side together as the carrying cord. Work in diagonal double half hitches to form the X-and-diamond pattern for the desired length of the sash— about 5 feet. End with two rows of cording (add a 12-inch linen cord inside the second row to match the mounting cord at the other end) and leave 7 inches for fringe. Untie the overhand knots at the ends of the mounting cord and let the ends become part of the fringe.

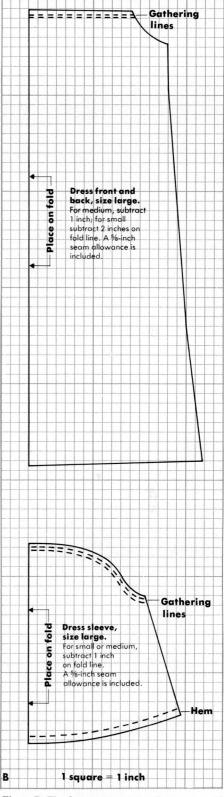

Gathering lines

Place on fold

Dress front and back, size large.
For medium, subtract 1 inch; for small subtract 2 inches on fold line. A ⅝-inch seam allowance is included.

Place on fold

Gathering lines

Dress sleeve, size large.
For small or medium, subtract 1 inch on fold line. A ⅝-inch seam allowance is included.

Hem

B   1 square = 1 inch

Figure B: The dress patterns are shown on a grid in which one square equals 1 inch. Make a grid of 1-inch squares on tracing paper. On this larger grid, mark off the same number of squares as shown on the pattern grid and transfer the outline of the pattern, one square at a time. You will find it easy to copy the pattern in small segments.

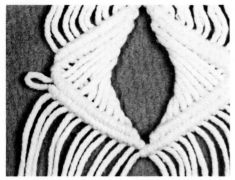

3: Loops on the outside edges of each panel, spaced about 4½ inches apart, will be used to attach the panels to the frame of the screen.

4: To create the open diamond pattern with diagonal double half hitches, the cord being knotted is brought underneath the other working cords before it is hitched to the carrying cord.

5: The last two carrying cords of the open diamond are hitched in the center of the pattern to bring the two sides together.

Room-divider screen

Your patience will be well rewarded when a screen like the one pictured on page 134 takes its place in your living room and inspires compliments from your guests.

Size: Screen as shown has four panels of macramé, each about 17 by 64½ inches. The design can be adapted to fit any screen frame (I found this one at a flea market).

Materials: Sixteen 140-yard boxes of No. 50 cotton cable cord; staples or brads; four-panel hinged screen frame or the materials to build one.

Knots: Alternating square knots, diagonal double half hitch (see Craftnotes).

A test swatch: It is most important to keep the tension of the knots loose enough so the macramé will fit the screen frame. Work 3 inches of alternating square knots with 12 ends each 16 inches long. If your knotting tension is average, you will have about 4 inches left. If you have more or less, adjust the amount of cord needed. Also, measure the width of your test swatch (12 ends across). If you need to add cords to fit the width of the screen, always add them in multiples of four.

Square Knot Panels

For each square knot panel (first and third in the photograph on page 134) cut 46 cords, each 48 feet long. Cut a mounting cord to fit across the top of the screen. (You can work right on the screen frame, on a dowel that will be inserted into the screen, or on a large sheet of insulation board or cork.) Mount the 46 cords with reverse lark's head knots so that there are 92 ends, each 24 feet long.

Work one row of cording (horizontal double half hitches) at the top of the panel. Work alternating square knots for 4½ inches, ending with a row of 23 knots. Here, and every 4½ inches, leave a loop on each side as shown in photograph 3. Simply put a T-pin at the outside edge and loop the outer cord around the pin. This loop will be attached to the side of the screen frame when the panel is completed.

On the next row, start the diamond pattern by working 22 knots, 11 on each side, and *not* working the four cords in the exact center of the row. Continue decreasing the number of knots until you have a row with 7 knots on each side and 36 unworked cords in the center. This will be the widest part of the diamond. On the next row, work 8 knots on each side, and continue increasing the number of knots until the bottom half of the diamond is completed. The diamonds will be about 4½ inches long with 4½ inches of square knots between, depending on the tension of your work.

When you reach the bottom of the panel, work two rows of cording and pull any loose ends through the last row. Gather the centers of both sides of the diamonds with a short cord and tie in back with granny knots (see Craftnotes, page 136). Use staples or brads to attach the panel to the frame, through the loops on the sides and through the rows of cording at the top and bottom. Cover the edges with strips of wood molding, about ¼ inch wide, if the back of the screen will be seen.

Open Diamond Panels

Each second and fourth panel has alternating rows of four diamonds and three diamonds; each diamond has 24 ends, 12 on each side. Therefore, you will need to cut 48 cords, each about 42 feet long.

Mount the cords with reverse lark's head knots and work one row of cording at the top, as you did for the square knot panels. The diamond pattern is worked in diagonal double half hitches and each diamond is about 4½ inches long. Start each diamond with 12 ends on each side. Work 2 rows of diagonal half hitches on each side, using the four inner cords as carrying cords (first 12 and 13, then 11 and 14). At the end of the second row, double half hitch the first carrying cord on each side to the second carrying cord on that same side (12 onto 11 and 13 onto 14). On the bottom half of the diamond, the cord being knotted is brought *underneath* the other working cords (photograph 4). Start the bottom half with the last-used carrying cords first (11 on the left, 14 on the right) and start knotting from the center out to the sides. (On the left, the order will be 10, 9, 8, and so on.) When the open diamond is completed, hitch the last two carrying cords, 12 and 13, in the center of the pattern (photograph 5). Make attachment loops and finish with cording.

Willow tree sculpture

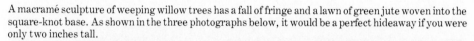

These weeping willows are pure whimsy; three colors of jute and the square knot are all you need to make your own macramé sculpture (see Craftnotes, page 136).

Size: The base is about 9½ inches long (without fringe) and 5 inches wide. The tallest tree is 8 inches high.

Materials: Three 4-ounce cones of jute, one each of natural, green and brown.

Base: Cut 12 cords of natural jute, each 5 feet long. Mount them on a mounting cord with reverse lark's head knots so that there are 24 ends, each 2½ feet long. Work in alternating square knots (6 knots and 5 knots per row) for 6 rows. On the next row, begin adding cords for the natural-color tree as shown in Figure C, page 144. The numbers indicate the number of ends (2 ends to a cord). To add one cord, simply include it in the center of the square knot. To add 2 cords, add the second cord between the knot being formed and the one above. The extra cords should be

Deborah Susswein has a flair for the unusual that comes across in her macramé sculptures. Debbie is a member of "A Show of Hands," a craft cooperative in New York City, where her work has been exhibited in a one-woman show. She plans to work in the field of art therapy, helping both children and adults.

A macramé sculpture of weeping willow trees has a fall of fringe and a lawn of green jute woven into the square-knot base. As shown in the three photographs below, it would be a perfect hideaway if you were only two inches tall.

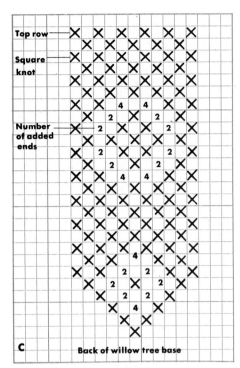

Figure C: The base of the tree sculpture pictured on page 143 is made of alternating square knots (indicated by the Xs). Ends are added in the numbers indicated and these extra cords are knotted in a spiral to form the tree trunks. The pattern shows one way to place and shape the trees; feel free to make them as individual as you like.

6: The pointed end of the base ends in fringe. The dark spots are the brown cords added to the natural-color base.

5 feet long. Continue working the base, adding extra cords as indicated. For the two-tone tree in front, stagger the colors any way you like for the light-and-dark effect. On the third row of this tree, start decreasing the number of knots in the base to form the V-shaped point. When the base is completed, the leftover cords will form the fall of fringe. (Photograph 6, this page, shows the back of the base.)

Trees: To form the hollow tubular trunks, work square knots in a spiral with the cords you added to the base. Continue the spiral, always using the next four cords for the next knot, regardless of their colors. Where you want a fork in the trees, divide the cords and work in two separate spirals. Leave long ends and unravel them to make the weeping willow branches.

Lawn: Cut short ends of green jute and weave through the knots in a random pattern for the grass. Remove the mounting cord and knot medium-long lengths of green jute to the loops for the grassy fringe.

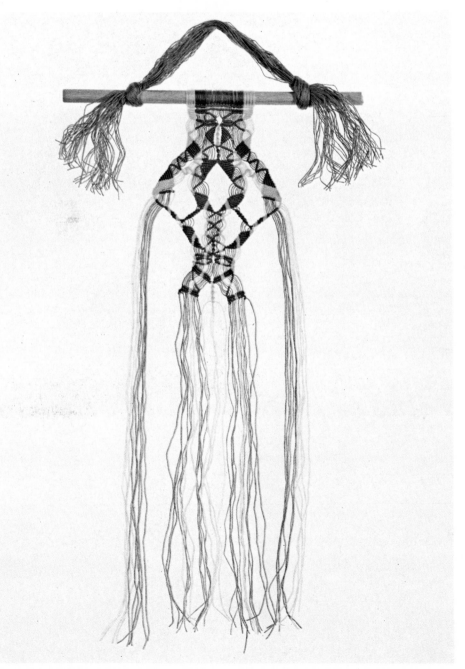

Micromé is macramé in miniature, worked with cotton sewing threads. This hanging is only 7½ inches long to the bottom of the fringe.

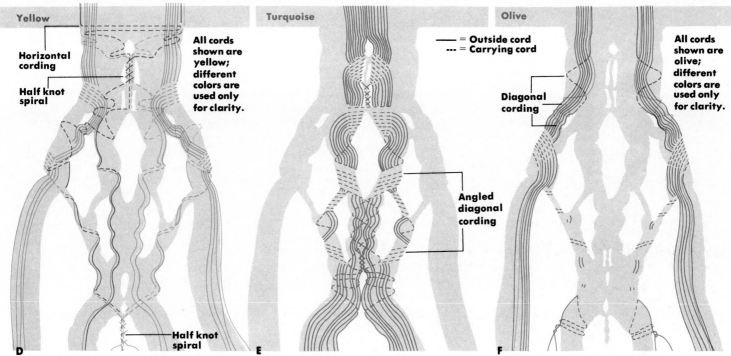

Yellow

Horizontal
cording

Half knot
spiral

All cords
shown are
yellow;
different
colors are
used only
for clarity.

Half knot
spiral

D

Figure D: Place the yellow carrying threads as
shown in relation to the working threads.

Turquoise

—— = Outside cord
--- = Carrying cord

Angled
diagonal
cording

E

Figure E: Place the turquoise carrying threads
as shown in relation to the working threads.

Olive

Diagonal
cording

All cords
shown are
olive;
different
colors are
used only
for clarity.

F

Figure F: Place the olive carrying threads as
shown in relation to the working threads.

Micromé hanging

¢

Micromé is my word for macramé done on a very small scale with sewing threads. It
takes nimble fingers and lots of patience, but the finished project is a small gem to
be treasured.

Size: From the dowel to the tip of the fringe is 7½ inches.

Materials: Three 125-yard spools of cotton sewing thread in yellow, turquoise
and olive; a wooden dowel, ¼ inch in diameter and 4 inches long.

Knots: Diagonal and horizontal double half hitches, half knot chains (see Craftnotes, pages 136 and 137).

Hanging: Cut 25 threads—9 turquoise, 8 olive and 8 yellow, each about 14 feet
long. Tape the dowel to the knotting board and mount the threads in the center of
the dowel in this order: 4 yellow, 4 olive, 9 turquoise, 4 olive, 4 yellow. There will be
50 ends. Because you are working with thin threads that tangle easily, butterfly
bundles are impractical. Instead, wind each end around the center of a small piece
of folded paper, and thread it through a small slit at one end (Figure G).

Work two rows of horizontal double half hitches with the end yellow thread on
the left as the carrying thread. Continue to work in horizontal and diagonal double
half hitches, following Figures D, E and F for the placement of the carrying
threads. Be sure to keep the knots tight. You may use fine needles or silk pins in
place of T-pins to hold the work in progress. The yellow and turquoise chains, or
sennits, of half knots twist to the right so you tie only the second half of a square
knot (right thread under, left thread over the two center threads).

Follow the color photograph on the opposite page for the overall color arrangement, but if Figures D, E and F are not followed, the overall color pattern will
change. Trim the ends, tie a thick bundle of leftover turquoise threads about 7
inches long to the dowel with overhand knots, and hang the micromé in front of a
light to show it to best advantage.

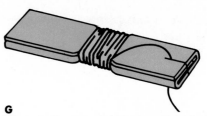

G

Figure G: Tiny paper bobbins keep the ends of the
threads untangled as you work micromé.

LACE
Bobbins or Needles

Brigita Fuhrmann is a lace-maker who uses traditional techniques to express her contemporary ideas. She studied textiles in her native country, Czechoslovakia, and in the U.S., including a year at the Rhode Island School of Design. Brigita directs seminars on lace making and her designs have been exhibited in craft shows and featured in several books. She and her family live in Reading, Mass. Brigita is a member of the Boston Weavers' Guild.

Lace making, with its intricate structures balanced by a freedom of form, is one of the most expressive of all the textile crafts, and certainly one of the most traditional. However, there is growing interest in contemporary lace making that uses modern materials and takes unconventional shapes. So if you think only of bridal gowns and Elizabethan ruffs when you think of lace, consider this: Lace is also a wall hanging, a yarn sash or a modern art necklace, all of which you can learn to make. In a broad sense, the term *lace* embraces any openwork achieved by a textile technique. Such textile techniques as weaving, crochet and knitting can produce openwork as well as solid fabrics. But other techniques from their very beginnings have been used to create *only* openwork, with pattern achieved by threads that are an integral part of the structure. Two of these are needle lace and bobbin lace; therefore, they have been singled out as true laces.

The laces made by these two techniques might on first sight be mistaken for each other. Yet in spite of this design interchangeability, needle lace and bobbin lace differ considerably in their execution. Bobbin lace is a multiple-thread textile worked by twisting and crossing (not knotting) many strands of yarn or thread. It is related to macrame and sprang; the finished lace is soft and pliant. Needle lace is a single-thread textile worked by looping, twisting and knotting one continuous thread around itself with the help of a needle. This technique originated with, and is closely related to, embroidery and is also related to tatting and netting. Needle laces are somewhat stiff and crisp. Making bobbin lace is more like weaving; making needle lace is more like sewing.

This is a detail from a seventeenth-century Dutch painting by Nicolas Maes, "Woman Making Lace."

Bobbin Lace

Bobbin lace is not limited to any fixed number of threads or any regular shape, so it is free to advance in any direction while it is being made. The multiple threads are wound on hand-held bobbins and the work is attached to a pillow with pins. Bobbin lace is sometimes called pillow lace because of this work surface.

A village church done in needle lace, using a technique similar to embroidery, makes a charming window hanging. Instructions and a pattern are on pages 155 and 157.

1: Bobbin lace is sometimes called pillow lace because the work is done on pillows. Sizes and stands vary, but the basic shapes are the bolster and the flat cookie (right center).

2: Pillows for lace making must be stuffed firmly with sawdust, hay or straw. A bolster can be improvised by wrapping several layers of a terry towel around a metal can.

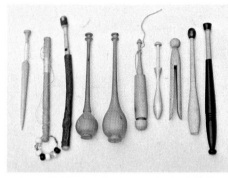

3: Lace making bobbins range from roundhead clothespins and whittled twigs to imported wood bobbins with covers over the shanks and antique bobbins with beaded spangles that dangle from the handles.

4: After the bobbin is filled, the thread is secured with a simple hitch near the head. Turn the bobbin in the direction opposite that of the winding to release the thread while at the same time maintaining the hitch knot.

Pillows and Pins

Pillows most widely used are the bolster (the French mini-bolster being one variation) and the flat cookie pillow. The pillows can be held between your knees, set on a table or easel, or cradled in a floor stand or small wooden box (photograph 1). A flat pillow should be inclined at a 45-degree angle to make use of the tension that the bobbins give the threads.

A bolster pillow of any size can be made by sewing a fabric cylinder with flat endpieces and stuffing it solid with sawdust, hay or straw. As an alternative, you can wrap an oatmeal box, coffee can or shortening can with a length of terry cloth, woolen blanket, quilted fabric or other material that is easily penetrated by pins and holds them well (photograph 2). Be sure the covering is thick enough so the pins will not touch the hard core. A bolster pillow is the best kind to use for making lace tapes or continuous yardage. As the work progresses, the pillow is rotated to expose new work area.

To make a flat cookie pillow, simply cover a round piece of ¼-inch plywood with fabric and stuff with sawdust, hay or straw to achieve a rounded-top shape. Cut the fabric cover larger than the plywood to allow stuffing, and stuff it firmly enough so a pin stuck in the pillow will not be pulled out by the tension of the threads. The flat pillow is useful in making flat, shaped pieces such as collars and cuffs because it can be turned and the lace worked on from any side.

The pins should be long and made of brass or stainless steel so they do not stain the lace with rust marks. They should be strong enough to support the weight of bobbins. For fine lace, you can use brass dressmaker pins; for lace made of yarn or cord, use hat pins, glass-head florist pins or T-head pins. You will need to be careful with any headed pin so you avoid catching the lace on the head. Put each pin into the pillow at a right angle or angled slightly away from the work to give the pin strength and to keep it out of the way of the progressing lace.

The Bobbins

The lace bobbins are spools shaped to be held comfortably in the hands and to be wound with lengths of yarn or thread. The basic parts are the handle, the shank where the yarn is wound, and the head which prevents the wound yarn from slipping off. Bobbins can be purchased at shops specializing in lace making supplies (see page 149 for the names and addresses of two such shops). Or you can make your own from lightweight materials such as whittled twigs, old-fashioned roundhead clothespins, dowels or wooden furniture turnings (photograph 3). My husband has turned several wooden bobbins for me on his lathe. But the bobbins I use most came from Europe and have covers over the shanks to keep the wound thread clean. The musical clatter of the bobbins is a pleasant accompaniment as I work. If you make bobbins from dowels, choose dowels about ⅜-inch in diameter and cut them into 6- or 7-inch lengths. Cut a groove completely around one tip of each, about ½-inch from the end, to create a head for the bobbin.

To wind the yarn on a bobbin, start at the bottom of the shank, and with the bobbin held upright, wind counterclockwise around the shank. After the bobbin is filled, secure the yarn with a simple hitch as shown in photograph 4. As you work, twist the bobbin away from the direction of the winding to release the yarn a little at a time from the bobbin while maintaining the hitch knot. You can either wind each bobbin separately and tie two together with an overhand knot to form a pair, or cut a length of yarn sufficient to fill two bobbins and wind either end on a separate bobbin. If you run out of yarn on a bobbin while working, attach new yarn to old with a reef (square) knot. Because any knot will be on the top face of the lace, this will become your wrong side. However, except for the knots, the two faces will be exactly alike.

Parchment Patterns

The stitches of bobbin lace are first drafted on graph paper and this draft is then transferred to a parchment or card stock the weight of an index card in a color contrasting with the yarn or thread. To make the transfer, hold the draft over the parchment and use a needle to prick through the design points which indicate where the pins will go. Outlines of the shape, texture indications, stitch types and the direction of the work can be indicated on the parchment (as well as on the draft) with non-smear ink. The pricked parchment, called the card, is then placed on the pillow and the lace is worked directly on top of it (photograph 5).

Threads, Yarns and Cords

Traditional lace is made with only fine linen or cotton thread, but contemporary lace doesn't stop there. All types of yarn, macrame cords and twines, metallic threads and fibers—whatever suits your purpose—can be used. Yarns and other soft materials tend to emphasize overall shape and color, while threads and harder cords play up the stitches and the techniques. Linen and cotton threads are graded in numbers, the higher numbers indicating the finer threads.

Suppliers

You can order lace making supplies and books from these shops (catalogs are available): Some Place, 2990 Adeline Street, Berkeley, Calif. 94703 or Robin & Russ Handweavers, 533 North Adams Street, McMinnville, Ore. 97128.

Basic Movements

The stitches of intricate looking bobbin lace are all variations of two basic movements, the cross and the twist. Hang two pairs of bobbins over two pins stuck in your pillow close to each other on a horizontal line (one pair hangs from each pin). Hold and manipulate one pair of bobbins in each hand. With few exceptions, all movements are made simultaneously with two bobbins. The pairs of bobbins are numbered 1, 2, 3 and so on from left to right. Each time a pair changes its position, the instructions will refer to it by the number of its *new* position in relation to the other pairs, rather than by its original number.

Cross the right bobbin of the first pair over the left bobbin of the second pair (photograph 6). The two inner bobbins will exchange hands. This is a cross.

Twist the right bobbin of the first pair over the left bobbin of the same pair and twist the bobbins of the second pair in the same manner (photograph 7). The two twists should be done simultaneously using both hands. This is a twist.

The cross is made left over right; the twist is made right over left. This may sound confusing now, but since these two movements are repeated in all the different stitches and grounds, they will soon become second nature.

The combination of the cross and the twist is referred to as a half stitch. If you repeat the cross-twist again, the pairs will change positions completely, and you will have made a whole stitch. Repeating the cross-twist over and over employing the two pairs of bobbins will make a plait or braid.

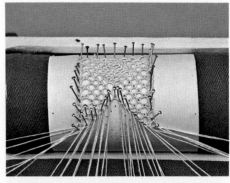

5: Bobbin lace is worked over a sheet of parchment that is pricked with a pattern of pinholes at the design points. As the lace is worked, pins are inserted in these holes to hold the threads in the proper formation.

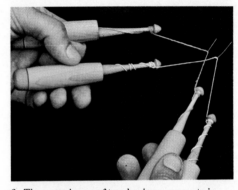

6: The cross is one of two basic movements in bobbin lace. With one pair of bobbins in each hand, cross the right bobbin of the first pair (yellow) over the left bobbin of the second pair (white). A cross is always made left over right.

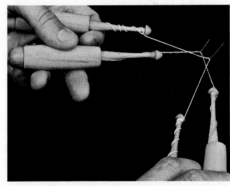

7: The twist, the other basic movement, is always made right over left. (Bobbin pairs are numbered from the left, according to their new positions.) Twist the right bobbin of each pair over the left bobbin of that same pair.

Sampler of Grounds

A lace ground is the mesh or netting that forms the background or fills in between design elements. It is usually a uniform, repetitive pattern of a stitch using multiple bobbin pairs. Make a sampler of the grounds used in the following bobbin lace projects in order to become accustomed to the movements and to have a handy reference piece.

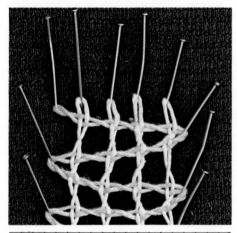

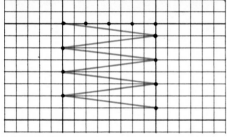

8: A sample of the whole stitch ground, and its draft zigzag line shows direction of leader pair.

▲ Whole Stitch Ground

The 5 dots in a horizontal row across the top of this draft indicate a row of 5 pins to be inserted into the pillow over which 5 pairs of bobbins will be hung. The zigzag line is drawn to follow the direction of the leader pair (the first pair of bobbins at the extreme left side). The vertical columns of dots indicate the edge pins which will hold the leader pair in place at its turning points. Transfer all the dots to the pricking card as shown. The pairs of bobbins are numbered from left to right as 1 to 5. *1st row:* Cross-twist, cross-twist 1 and 2. Cross-twist, cross-twist 2 and 3. Cross-twist, cross-twist 3 and 4. Cross-twist, cross-twist 4 and 5. The leader pair of bobbins which was on the left side should now be on the extreme right side after weaving through the

other four pairs. Twist this leader pair twice and put a pin in the pricked hole under the twisted pair. *2nd row:* Starting at the right side, cross-twist, cross-twist 4 and 5; cross-twist, cross-twist 3 and 4; cross-twist, cross-twist 2 and 3; cross-twist, cross-twist 1 and 2. The leader pair should be back at the left side. Again, twist this pair twice and pin. Repeat these two rows for the whole stitch ground. Notice that the cross is always made toward the right and the twist is always made toward the left, regardless of the direction of the leader pair. These two basic movements never vary in their direction.

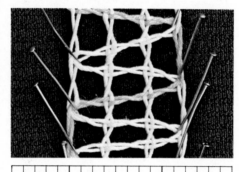

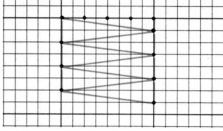

9: A sample of the whole stitch ground with a foot edge, and its draft.

▲ Whole Stitch Ground with Foot Edge

The same pricking used for the whole stitch ground is used to create a whole stitch ground with a straight, strong edge called a foot. The foot edge is indicated on the draft by short bars connecting the vertical dots. *1st row:* Work the first row of the whole stitch ground ending with cross-twist, cross-twist 4 and 5. Put the pin under both pairs. *2nd row,* starting from the right: Cross-twist, cross-twist 3 and 4; cross-twist, cross-twist 2 and 3; cross-twist, cross-twist 1 and 2; put the pin under both pairs 1 and 2. *3rd row:* Cross-twist, cross-twist 2 and 3, and continue as 1st row. Repeat the 2nd and 3rd rows.

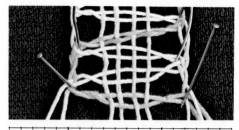

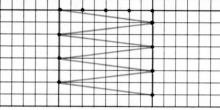

10: A sample of the linen stitch ground with a foot edge, and its draft.

▲ Linen Stitch Ground with Foot Edge

The same 5 pairs of bobbins and the same pricking are used for the linen stitch ground with foot edge as for the whole stitch with foot edge. *1st row:* Cross-twist, cross-twist 1 and 2; cross-twist, cross 2 and 3; cross-twist, cross 3 and 4; twist 4; cross-twist, cross-twist 4 and 5; put pin under 4 and 5. *2nd row:* Cross-twist, cross 3 and 4; cross-twist, cross 2 and 3; twist 2; cross-twist, cross-twist 1 and 2; put pin under 1 and 2. Repeat these two rows. Notice that leaving out the last twist of the whole stitch in the center of each row changes the character of the stitch considerably, making it resemble woven linen; hence the name linen stitch.

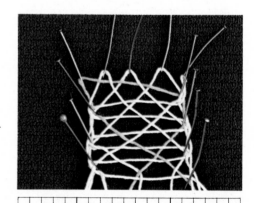

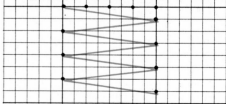

11: A sample of the half stitch ground, and its draft. Draft is same as for whole stitch ground.

Half Stitch Ground (photograph 11)

This ground has the same draft and pricking as the whole stitch ground, yet it looks completely different in its structure. As the name implies, it is a half of the whole stitch. Again, use 5 pairs of bobbins. *1st row:* Cross-twist 1 and 2; cross-twist 2 and 3; cross-twist 3 and 4; cross-twist 4 and 5; twist-twist 5. Put pin under 5. *2nd row:* Cross-twist 4 and 5; cross-twist 3 and 4; cross-twist 2 and 3; cross-twist 1 and 2; twist-twist 1; put pin under 1. Repeat these two rows.

Torchon Ground ▶

The whole stitch, half stitch and linen stitch use one or two bobbins for the leaders and basically their structure is on a right angle; the draft for the torchon ground is on a diagonal and all the pairs are equally employed with no one pair called the leader. This draft resembles a smocking pattern.

Draw rows of 4 and 3 dots in an alternating pattern as shown at right. For each alternating row, the stitches are staggered so that each new stitch is formed by splitting adjacent pairs of the two stitches above. Transfer all the dots throughout the design onto the pricking

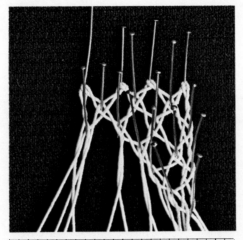

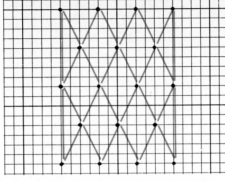

12: A sample of the torchon ground and its draft. Notice that there is no leader pair.

card. Put pins in the top 4 pinholes and hang 2 pairs of bobbins on each pin (8 pairs altogether). *1st row:* Cross-twist 2 and 3; put pin into the left hole of the row below, separating 2 and 3; cross-twist 2 and 3, enclosing the pin in the middle of the stitch; cross-twist 4 and 5; put pin into the center hole of the row below, separating 4 and 5; cross-twist 4 and 5, enclosing the pin in the middle of the stitch; cross-twist 6 and 7; put pin into the right hole of the row below, separating 6 and 7; cross-twist 6 and 7, enclosing pin in the middle of the stitch. In this row, pairs 1 and 8 are not worked. In the next row, they have to be twisted twice before being employed. *2nd row:* Twist-twist 1; cross-twist 1 and 2; pin to separate; cross-twist 1 and 2, enclosing pin; cross-twist 3 and 4; pin to separate; cross-twist 3 and 4, enclosing pin; cross-twist 5 and 6; pin to separate; cross-twist 5 and 6, enclosing pin; twist-twist 8; cross-twist 7 and 8; pin to separate; cross-twist 7 and 8, enclosing pin. Repeat these two rows. In this way, the torchon ground is worked horizontally. You can also work it diagonally (see instructions for bobbin lace sash below).

Bobbin lace sash ¢ ⊙ 🚶 🧺

This wide yarn sash is a combination of torchon ground and half-stitch diamonds. It can also be made in a linen thread (photograph, page 152) and because they are the same thickness, the same draft and pricking can be used for either.

Materials: Cylindrical bolster pillow. Knitting worsted yarn, one 4-ounce skein, or linen thread No. 30/12. 18 pairs of large bobbins (such as round head clothespins) on which a length of yarn at least double the desired length of the sash can be wound. Pricker or needle. Parchment pattern. Pins.
Size: Red sash as shown is 61 inches long, 4 inches wide, and has 24 pattern repeats.
Draft and pricking: The draft (Figure B, page 152) shows the design points where the pins will be inserted and the half-stitch diamonds are indicated by the zigzag lines. On the pricking, the pinholes forming the outlines of the diamonds will seem to be part of the torchon ground; you may find it easier to follow if you transfer the zigzag lines of the leader onto the pricking with

non-smear ink. Prick 2 cards, each with 2 or 3 repeats of the design, and leapfrog them to get a continuous pattern.
Sash: Wind 36 bobbins separately and tie 9 bunches of 4 bobbins together with overhand knots, leaving 3 or 4 inches of ends free to form the fringe. Attach pricked card to pillow. Pin through each overhand knot into the 9 pinholes on the top horizontal row of the card. (There will be 2 pairs on each pin.) The best way to work this design is to complete the torchon ground on the diagonal along the top half of the diamond, work the whole diamond in half stitch, then work the torchon ground along the bottom half of the first diamond and continue to the top half of the next diamond. Refer to your sampler and the directions for torchon ground and half stitch above.

A wide bobbin lace sash worked in bright red wool yarn shows how contemporary lace can be.

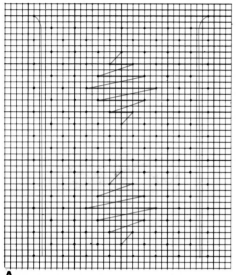

A

Figure A: This small draft reduces the width of the sash pattern from 4 to 1½ inches. Smaller bobbins and much finer thread, linen No. 30/3, are recommended. The length is variable; left short, the lace can be a bookmark; long, it can be an insert for a dress or for household linen.

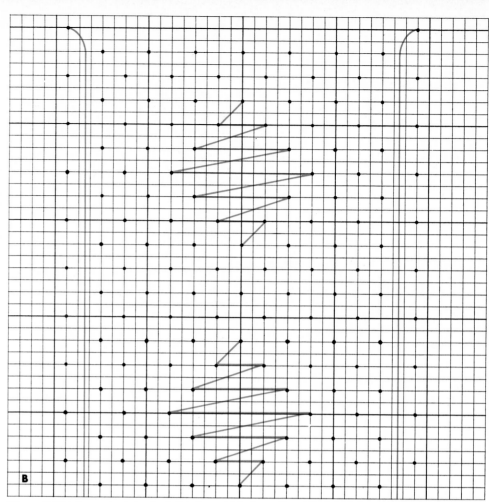

B

Figure B: This is an actual size draft (4 inches wide) of a section of the bobbin lace sash to be worked in wool yarn or linen thread. Reuse this draft until the sash is the desired length.

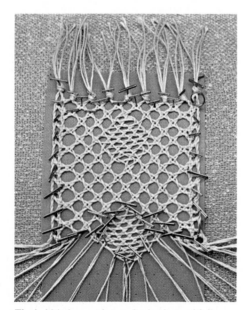

The bobbin lace sash can also be done with linen thread for another non-traditional look.

C = Cross; T = Twist
Start (left side of ground): C-T, C-T 2 and 3; T-T 1; C-T, C-T 1 and 2; pin under 1 and 2; C-T, C-T 2 and 3; C-T 4 and 5; pin, separating 4 and 5; C-T 4 and 5, enclosing pin; C-T 3 and 4; pin; C-T 3 and 4; C-T, C-T 2 and 3; T-T 1; C-T, C-T 1 and 2; pin under 1 and 2; C-T, C-T 2 and 3. Continue on the diagonal, each time employing one further pair and ending on the left side, with the foot edge. Observe that pair No. 2 goes straight down; this is the extra pair that strengthens the edge and is indicated by the vertical straight line on the draft.
Right side of ground: Work same as left side, starting with C-T, C-T 16 and 17; T-T 18; C-T, C-T 17 and 18; pin under 17 and 18; C-T, C-T 16 and 17; C-T 14 and 15; pin, separating 14 and 15; C-T 14 and 15, enclosing pin; C-T 15 and 16; pin; C-T 15 and 16; C-T, C-T 16 and 17; T-T 18; C-T, C-T 17 and 18; pin under 17 and 18; C-T, C-T 16 and 17. (Pair No. 17 goes straight down to strengthen the edge.)
The half-stitch diamond is worked from the topmost point: C-T 9 and 10; pin; C-T 9 and 10; C-T 8 and 9; pin under 8 and 9; C-T 9 and 10; C-T 10 and 11; pin

under 10 and 11; C-T 9 and 10; C-T 8 and 9; C-T 7 and 8; pin under 7 and 8; C-T 8 and 9; C-T 9 and 10; C-T 10 and 11; C-T 11 and 12; pin under 11 and 12; C-T 10 and 11; C-T 9 and 10; C-T 8 and 9; C-T 7 and 8; C-T, C-T 6 and 7; pin under 6 and 7; C-T 7 and 8; C-T, C-T 8 and 9; C-T 9 and 10; C-T 10 and 11; C-T 11 and 12; C-T, C-T 12 and 13; pin under 12 and 13; C-T 11 and 12; C-T 10 and 11; C-T 9 and 10; C-T 8 and 9; C-T 7 and 8; pin under 7 and 8; C-T 8 and 9; C-T 9 and 10; C-T 10 and 11; C-T 11 and 12; pin under 11 and 12; C-T 10 and 11; C-T 9 and 10; C-T 8 and 9; pin under 8 and 9; C-T 9 and 10; pin; C-T 9 and 10. Continue working the torchon ground to the outline of the next diamond. When two repeats are finished, remove the pins near the top and roll the finished work onto itself. Do this as you go along the length of the sash. Finish the last repeat on a horizontal line, with one row of torchon ground stitches below the bottom point of the last diamond. Unwind the remaining yarn from the bobbins and tie 9 bunches of 4 strands each with overhand knots for fringe. Trim ends.

Bobbin lace collar and cuffs ¢ ● ⅄ 🐚

This collar-and-cuffs set was designed to fit a particular dress, but the curved-tape design is adaptable to other sizes and shapes. If the patterns given on page 154 won't fit your dress, use pieces from a sewing pattern or design your own.

A bobbin lace collar and cuffs adorn a dress worn by Nancy Bellantone, Brigita's neighbor. This dress is an original design by Nancy's mother, but you can adapt the lace pattern to fit any style of neckline and sleeves.

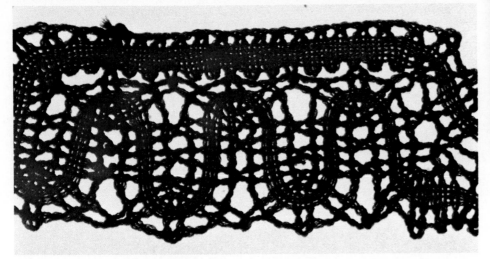

A close-up view of one half of the collar details the curves of the lace tape and the sewings that join it together. The straight edge is sewn to the inside of the dress neckline.

Materials: Flat cookie pillow (so that work can be turned around). Knitting worsted yarn, one 4-ounce skein. 5 pairs of large bobbins, such as roundhead clothespins. No. 9 metal crochet hook. Pricker or needle. Parchment for pattern. Pins.
Size: Each half of the collar is about 10 inches long on the inner edge. Each cuff is about 9 inches long. Can be adapted to fit any neckline and sleeve.
Stitches: Whole stitch and linen stitch. This lace is worked in a narrow tape and involves turning and attaching sections

of the tape together.
Variation: This design can also be used as an edging for a round doily (detail photograph this page and Figure C). The tape is much narrower and is worked with No. 50 cotton sewing thread. Directions are exactly the same as those for the cuff.
Draft and pricking: Graph paper cannot be used for this draft since this lace does not follow a straight line. Actually, designing the curving of the tape is very easy. If you choose to follow shapes other than those given in Figure D,

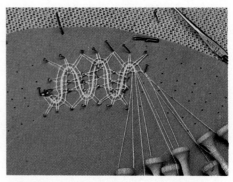

This delicate thread edging for a round doily shows how versatile lace can be; the scalloped lace is the same as the pattern for the yarn collar and cuffs, but on a smaller scale (Figure C).

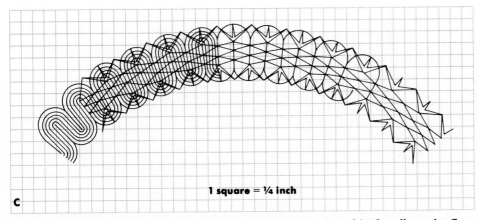

1 square = ¼ inch

C

Figure C: A draft for a scalloped doily edging is same pattern as is used in the collar and cuffs. One-quarter of the complete circle is shown. For how to enlarge this pattern, see page 117.

this page, try to keep the tape a uniform width throughout for best results. You may find it helpful to transfer the design outlines and directional lines from the draft onto the pricking card with non-smear ink.

Cuff: Attach the pricked card to the pillow. In the center of the straight edge, put 5 pins an equal distance apart on one zigzag line which slants as in Figure D. Turn the pillow so that the scalloped edge is on the right and the straight edge is on the left. This will cause the line of pins to slope down to the right. Hang one pair of bobbins on each pin.

C = Cross; T = Twist

1st row (starting at the left): C-T, C-T 1 and 2; C-T, C 2 and 3; C-T, C 3 and 4; C-T, C 4 and 5; T-T 5; pin under 5.
2nd row: C-T, C 4 and 5; C-T, C 3 and 4; C-T, C2 and 3; T2; C-T, C-T 1 and 2; pin under 1 and 2.
3rd row: C-T, C 2 and 3; C-T, C-T 3 and 4; C-T, C 4 and 5; T-T 5; pin under 5.
Repeat 2nd and 3rd rows to the corner. As the work rounds the corner, the width of the tape increases and it turns right. When you reach the pinhole at point A, work *1st corner row* (left to right): C-T, C 2 and 3; C-T, C 3 and 4; C-T, C-T 4 and 5; no pin. *2nd corner row* (right to left): C-T, C 3 and 4; C-T, C 2 and 3; T 2; C-T, C-T 1 and 2; T-T 1; pin

Figure D: Below are the patterns for the bobbin-lace collar and cuffs that are pictured on page 153. For how to enlarge the pattern, see Craftnotes, page 117.

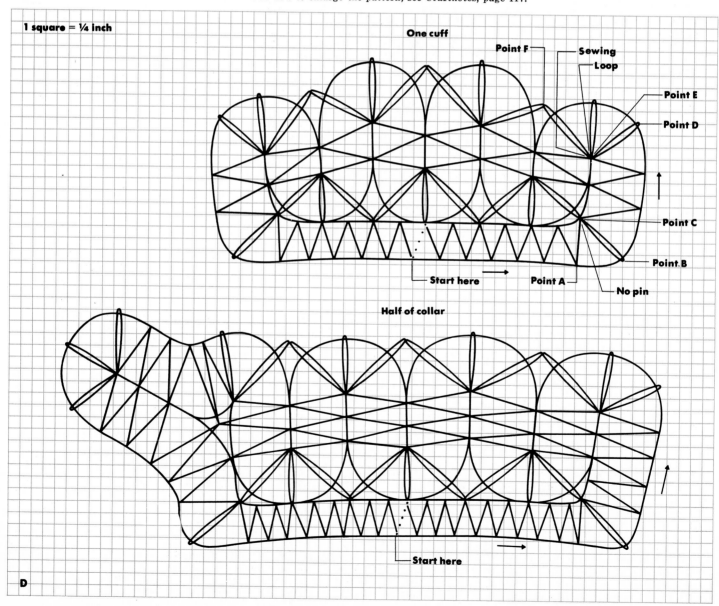

D

under 1. The pin should be inserted in the pinhole at point B. *3rd corner row* (left to right): C-T, C-T 1 and 2; C-T, C 2 and 3; C-T, C 3 and 4; T 4; C-T, C-T 4 and 5; T-T 5; pin under 5. This pin should be inserted in the pinhole at point C. By avoiding this pinhole in the 1st row, the tape turned the corner and is now proceeding toward the scalloped edge with the rest of the cuff on the right.

1st side row (right to left): C-T, C-T 4 and 5; C-T, C 3 and 4; C-T, C 2 and 3; T 2; C-T, C-T 1 and 2; T-T 1; pin under 1.

2nd side row (left to right): C-T, C-T 1 and 2; C-T, C 2 and 3; C-T, C 3 and 4; T 4; C-T, C-T 4 and 5; T-T 5.

Repeat these 2 side rows once more.

Repeat 1st row again, reaching point D.

Next row: (left to right): Continuing in linen stitch, finish by looping pair 1 around a pin inserted in the pinhole at point E.

Next row (right to left): Continue in linen stitch, ending with foot edge.

Next row (left to right): Continue in same stitch, looping end pair around the pin at point E.

Next row (right to left): Continue in linen stitch, ending at point F.

Next row (left to right): Continue to point E; remove pin holding the loops at point E. With crochet hook, enter the released loop from the top, catch one of the strands of pair 5 and pull it through, forming a large loop. Push the other bobbin of pair 5 through this loop, handle first (photograph 13). Remove the hook and tighten the loop. This is called a sewing and it connects the tapes together. Continue to work in linen stitch and at each turn in the design, twice form the foot edge without inserting a pin and sew the loops which share a pin as before. Where there are 3 loops sharing the same pin, two loops go around the pin and the third connects them with a sewing. When the work comes back to the beginning, sew the pairs into the loops which are at the starting points, then tie each pair in a reef (square) knot and cut as short as 1/8 inch. (This is also the way to join the edging on the round doily as shown in Figure C and photograph, page 153.)

Other cuff: Make a mirror-image copy of the pattern and work as the first cuff.

Collar: The directions for the cuff also pertain to the collar, differing only in size and number of scallops. This can easily be read from the draft.

13: The technique for joining two sections of lace together as the lace is being worked is called a sewing. This is done with the help of a crochet hook and a lace bobbin.

Needle lace window hanging ¢ ⌧ 👫 🦩

The needle lace technique, which is very similar to embroidery, is simple and easy to learn. In fact, you may already be familiar with some of the stitches if you do any type of embroidery. Needle lace is portable and in the eighteenth century, European men used to take their needle lace work with them when they attended parties at the royal court.

The only tools needed are a small sharp needle and a larger blunt-point needle. The lace is worked on a sheet of construction paper (for stiffness) which is basted onto fabric (to keep the paper from tearing). In the past, black paper was used as a sharp contrast to the traditional white linen thread. Now, any color paper that contrasts with your choice of yarn or thread is suitable. A piece of old sheet is fine for the fabric backing.

Basic Stitches

There are innumerable stitches of needle lace, all variations of the buttonhole stitch and the filet knot.

First, a thread must be couched to the paper background to outline the desired shape. The thickness of this thread depends on how thick you want the outline. For the sample stitches, a thread thicker than the work thread is used. This shape is then filled in with a chosen stitch. The two faces will look almost exactly alike, but the top face will be the right side.

For the sampler of stitches on page 156, I have chosen square shapes because they are the simplest. In a square, the number of stitches in each row should be the same. When filling irregular shapes, the number of stitches per row will vary, decreasing as the shape narrows, increasing as it widens. Following in the Craftnotes are the needle lace stitches that are used in this and the next project.

CRAFTNOTES: NEEDLE LACE STITCHES

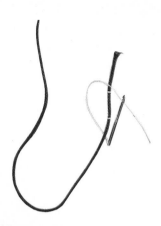

Couching
Outline the lace shape on the fabric-backed paper with pinholes about ¼ inch apart. With a sharp needle and sewing thread, sew the outline thread to the paper, bringing the needle up and taking it back through the same hole. Continue around until the ends of the outline thread overlap.

Twisted buttonhole stitch
This is another variation of the buttonhole stitch. The loop is formed to the right of the needle, then twisted once around the needle. This results in twisted bars between the rows and a squared-off appearance in the stitches.

Filet knot
Form a complete loop to the right of the needle, then slip the needle down under the top thread and through the loop. Insert a pin into the loop to control the size and draw the knot tight. After each row, carry the thread back to the left side and work from left to right, slipping the needle under both the loop of the stitch above and the thread that was carried across.

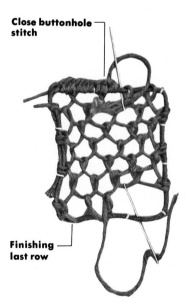

Close buttonhole stitch

Finishing last row

Buttonhole stitch
Tie the working thread to the outline thread at the upper left corner. With a blunt needle, bring the thread down under the top outline thread, forming a loop under and to the right of the needle. Keep the loops fairly loose and alternate the direction of each succeeding row.

Darning
This is a simple over-and-under weaving of the working thread between the opposite sides of the outline thread. If there are other threads parallel to the outline thread, weave in an over-one, under-one pattern.

Finishing (bottom)
On the last row of any stitch, loop the thread around the bottom outline thread after each stitch.

Close buttonhole stitch (top)
Cover the outline thread with a row of buttonhole stitches very close together after the filling stitches are completed.

Double buttonhole stitch
This is a variation of the buttonhole stitch above. Instead of a single stitch formed on the horizontal thread, two stitches are worked close together. The loops should be less rounded than those of the buttonhole stitch. Notice, too, how the rows of stitches are staggered.

Spider motif
Attach the outline thread in a circle, then stretch the working thread across the center of the circle several times. Carry the working thread to the center and weave over and under the radius threads in ever-bigger circles.

The Village Church in Lace

Enlarge the pattern (Figure E) and transfer onto construction paper. Outline the shapes with the outline thread, then fill the spaces with the indicated stitches. (The key to the stitches is at upper right; see also the color photograph on page 147.) Hide all the ends of thread in the final outline of close buttonhole stitch. Do not outline the darned sections with close buttonhole stitch. For the hanging as shown, use one 2-ounce spool of white linen thread, No. 10/2. If you wish to make the hanging smaller or larger, use a thickness of thread that is in proportion. After removing the lace from the paper, mount it between two squares of clear glass or acrylic plastic and suspend it with nylon monofilament or fishing line.

Key to stitches
D = Darning
1 = Buttonhole stitch
2 = Double buttonhole stitch
3 = Twisted buttonhole stitch
4 = Filet knot

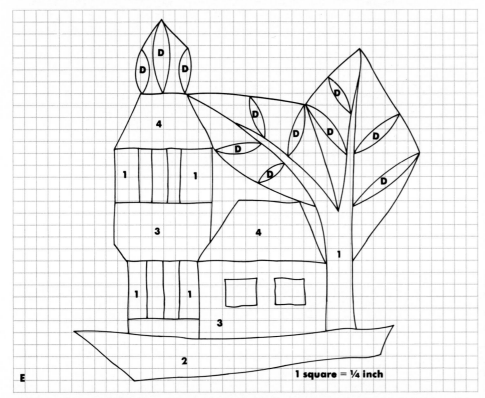

1 square = ¼ inch

Figure E: This is the pattern for the village church hanging shown in the color photograph on page 147. The stitch key is at the upper right; directions for enlarging the pattern are on page 117.

Modern art necklace ¢●🧍🐀

This necklace is a combination of needle lace and bobbin lace (Figure F, page 158). The center circle of the pendant is needle lace and should be worked first. As shown in the photograph at right, none of the shapes (other than the edge of the circle) are outlined in close buttonhole stitch but you can outline them if you wish. Use three 2-ounce spools of No. 10/2 linen thread, one each in red, mauve and beige; follow the photograph for placement of colors. The key to the stitches is on page 158.

The rest of the necklace is bobbin lace tape, which is worked according to the directions for the collar and cuffs (page 153). Pin the needle lace circle into the empty space on the draft for the bobbin lace, and work the bobbin lace tape around it. As you work, join the bobbin lace to the needle lace with sewings.

Start the bobbin lace at the back opening and work around to the opposite end where the ends of the thread will form a button loop. Work close buttonhole stitch over this loop and sew a small button on the other end. When the tape is finished, the two parts will be completely connected.

The modern art necklace is a combination of two lace techniques: the inner circle of the pendant is needle lace and the curved outer tape is a continuous length of bobbin lace.

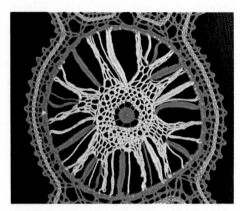

The needle lace circle above is the center of the pendant in the combination lace necklace.

Key to stitches

S = Spider
1 = Buttonhole stitch
2 = Twisted buttonhole stitch

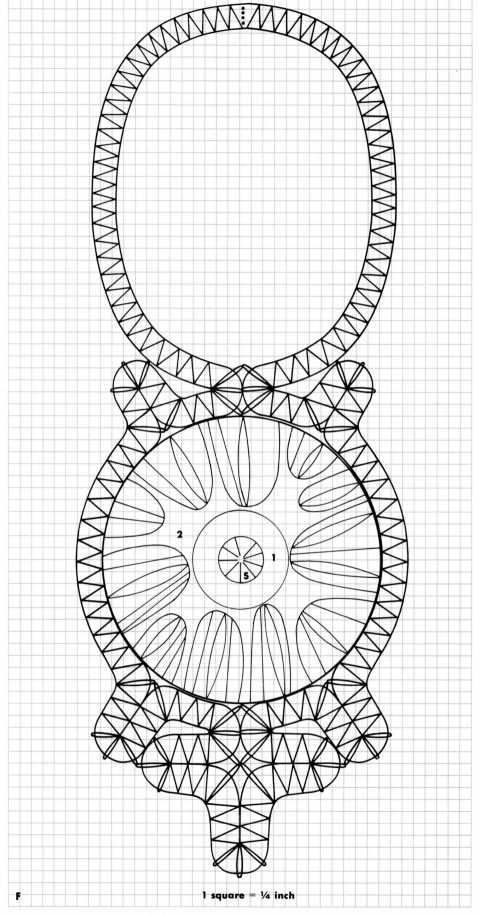

Figure F. At right is the pattern for the combination lace necklace. See the stitch key above and instructions for enlarging patterns on page 117.

F

1 square = ¼ inch

INDEX